THE WELLSPRINGS OF MUSIC

CURT SACHS

CURT SACHS

THE WELLSPRINGS
OF MUSIC

Edited by

JAAP KUNST

A DA CAPO PAPERBACK

Library of Congress Cataloging in Publication Data

Sachs, Curt, 1881-1959.
   The wellsprings of music.

   (A Da Capo paperback)
   Reprint of the 1962 ed. published by M. Nijhoff, The
Hague.
   Bibliography: p.
   Includes index.
   1. Ethnomusicology. 2. Melody. 3. Musical meter
and rhythm. I. Kunst, Jaap, 1891-1960. II. Title.
[ML3547.S2W4 1977]   781.7   77-23410
ISBN 0-306-80073-X

This Da Capo Press paperback edition of *The Wellsprings of Music*
is an unabridged republication of the first edition
published in The Hague, Netherlands in 1962.
It is reprinted by arrangement with Martinus Nijhoff.

Copyright © 1962 by Martinus Nijhoff

Published by Da Capo Press, Inc.
A Subsidiary of Plenum Publishing Corporation
227 West 17th Street
New York, New York 10011

To
IRENE
after fifty years
of married life
and collaboration

EDITOR'S PREFACE

When Irene Sachs asked me to take charge of the practically completed manuscript left by her late husband, and to prepare it for the press, I felt moved and honored to have been entrusted with the task to bring Curt's last work safely into the harbour. In favoring me with the editing of the book, Irene may have thought of the long discussions we had together, Curt Sachs and I, during two successive years. It was in his study when, with the little gramophone on the piano, the manuscript sheets piled up before us, we listened intently to the records, merging our opinions or deviating, and thus consolidating a bond of common interest and warm personal friendship.

Be it as it may and although at the moment I am still recuperating from a serious operation, I have tried to carry out this task in the shortest possible time and to the best of my knowledge and ability.

I have avoided making important changes in the text, though I have been tempted occasionally to put a question mark in the margin, when our views differed somewhat in degree or emphasis. But in Sachs' reasoning one thing follows from the other in such a way as to make it unfeasable to attempt revisions without compromising the logic of the whole. Only once – in the field of Indonesian music, where I feel particularly at home – have I omitted some facts I knew to be interpreted less correctly. Further, insofar as possible I have supplemented the bibliographical data in the footnotes.

The sum and substance of the book is a truly monumental discussion of the development of the melodic element in all its aspects (including rhythm). This development has been traced and analysed step by step, silhouetted against a general cultural historical backdrop, in a calm, clear manner, seasoned with typical mild "Sachsonian" humor and illustrated with a wealth of examples and evidence. I doubt whether any other of us ethnomusicologists would have been capable of writing such a comprehensive study: Sachs had at his fingertips a phenomenal amount of factual information. Sometimes, under his wise guidance, complicated propositions become surprisingly simple. The reader will be as fascinated as I was by the originality of some of his conclusions, captivated by his penetrating comparisons, and charmed by his rich and expressive language.

After having lived with this book for a period of some months, I realize all the more what the death of Curt Sachs means to the musicological world.

"The Wellsprings of Music" forms a worthy close to that long series of publications his boundless energy and unsurpassed knowledge have given us.

I feel greatly indebted to Dr. Eric Werner, New York, for his decisive encouragement towards the publication of this work and for the active interest he took in it. I want also to express my gratitude to the musicologist Miss Marijke Charbon, The Hague, for having made an Index of Names and for some useful suggestions.

Amsterdam, 15th February 1960   JAAP KUNST

ℛ❦ℛ

My dear friend Jaap Kunst did not live to see this book in print. I wish to express my deep gratitude to him, whose dedicated help and unfailing and devoted interest made its publication possible.

After Jaap Kunst's death, his assistants, Messrs. Ernst Heins and Felix van Lamsweerde, took over with selfless loyalty. They read the proofs and saw the manuscript through its final stages. They were aided by Miss M. van Walraven. The Royal Tropical Institute, Amsterdam, kindly granted time for their work.

IRENE SACHS

NOTE – The letter group *EFw* in the *footnotes* stands for "Ethnic Folkways Library," a vast collection of primitive, oriental and folk music from every part of the world on L.P. recordings, published in New York under Moses Asch as producer and Harold Courlander as editor-in-chief.

TABLE OF CONTENTS

ONE

THOUGHTS AND METHODS

I. PRELIMINARIES

Western music, the pride of our culture, is no longer what it should be and was: the highlight of our day, edifying and blissful. Our modern lives are *ad nauseam* saturated with music and wouldbe music. I do not speak of the dizzying quantity of concerts and recitals – we attend them or stay away as we please. But we cannot have our coffee break without the blaring interference of a non-stop loudspeaker on the wall or a jukebox in the corner; the savings-bank pours music over our head while we pass a check across the counter; railroad cars and buses feed us catchy or sentimental tunes instead of improving the service; and the neighbors force us to share in their radio and television orgies.

Men of high civilization have become voracious hearers but do hardly listen. Using organized sound as a kind of opiate, we have forgotten to ask for sense and value in what we hear.

In primitive music, on the contrary, sense and value are paramount qualities. Not only is singing indispensable for special events, like wedding and childbirth, puberty rites and death, and whenever luck must be forced on adverse powers in hunting, harvest, and sickness. It also acts when regular work, as rowing a boat, or rocking a child, or grinding edible roots, demands and gives a rhythmical impulse. In this interweaving with motions and emotions, music is not a reflex, remote and pale, but an integral part of life. As Fürer-Haimendorf puts it exquisitely in words, this music "resounds in the darkness, gripping the singers and blending them one and all, till they finally merge in the unity of the dance. This rhythm is more than art, it is the voice of man's primeval instinct, the revelation of the all-embracing rhythm of growth and decay, of love, battle and death." [1]

[1] Christoph von Fürer-Haimendorf, *The naked Nagas*, London, 1939, p. 208.

These words could not have been written half a century earlier. Older travelogues – up to 1900 – present us with queer and often foolish descriptions of primitive music and often ridicule what to the natives is their most sacred expression. One of the oldest comprehensive books in our field, Wallaschek's *Primitive Music*,[2] teems with quotations of this kind.

Matters have changed, luckily. In modern works by educated anthropologists one may read about the extraordinary charm of haunting tunes or of "the delightful transitions from one musical phrase to the other which retain an element of surprise however often one may hear them." [3] R. F. Fortune tells us that "most truly Dobuan mourning is as fine as finest bird song," [4] and Marius Barbeau says of the mountain songs of the Tsimshian Indians in the Northwest that they are "swaying and ethereal. The voices of the singers, especially the women, are beautifully lofty and lyrical in character. Like the songs of Mongolia and Siberia, they are imbued with color; color and expressiveness of the voice are an essential feature of the native singing on both sides of the Pacific Ocean." [5]

Many a modern composer has been fascinated by the charm of some primitive or oriental melody or a special feature like the Javanese isotonic scale. But when they borrow a native theme – of course in western dressing – such contact belongs in the history of western music and does not justify our endeavors to find, understand, and interpret the musical idioms of non-western peoples. Such mistake would amount to seeing in the awkward Romanesque-Gothic stew of Harvard's Memorial Hall a justification for studying the history of medieval architecture.

Rather should our search bring home to everybody the inimitable uniqueness of all art and discourage artificial exotism and pseudo-archaism, unless the spirit of modern art makes legitimate an opening of the gates. Debussy, Bartók, and Stravinsky are cases in point.

[2] Richard Wallaschek, *Primitive music*, London, 1893; German translation as *Anfänge der Tonkunst*, Leipzig, 1903.
[3] Von Fürer-Haimendorf, *The Raj Gonds of Adilabad*, London, 1948, vol. 1, pp. 406 ff.
[4] R. F. Fortune, *Sorcerers of Dobu*, London, 1932, p. 255.
[5] Víola E. Garfield, Paul S. Wingert and Marius Barbeau, *The Tsimshian: their arts and music*, New York, 1952, p. 98.

Such music cannot be bought in stores, but comes from faithful tradition or from personal contributions of tribesmen. It is never soulless or thoughtless, never passive, but always vital, organic, and functional; indeed, it is always dignified. This is more than we can say of music in the West. As an indispensable and precious part of culture, it commands respect. And respect implies the duty to help in preserving it.

In pursuing our goal, we are particularly rushed, as the venerable heritage of archaic cultures is threatened with imminent extermination. The melodies of primitive man, an organic, essential part of his spiritual life, fall victim to Christian missionaries, Soviet agents, European colonizers, and American oil drillers. And primitive as well as folk melodies are hopelessly succumbing to a technical age with military service and factory work, with rapid buses, planes, and cars, with phonographs, radios, and television sets. "One of the most tragic things about contact of the aboriginal with civilization is the destruction of art and culture that so frequently follows." [6]

A moving instance of such extermination is the fate of music in the steppes of Central Asia. Not long ago, the autobiography of the great Kazakhian rhapsodist Dzhambul called it "a mighty power ... irresistible as the tempest." [7] Today, we read in Haslund-Christensen's report "On the Trail of Ancient Mongol Tunes":[8]

"When in 1923 I arrived in Central Asia for the first time I found the whole of this isolated world, with its sparse nomad population, like a living reminder of a remote past ... On my return to Central Asia in 1936 I found that the few years during which I had been absent in the civilized world had brought about greater and more radical changes than the whole of the previous five hundred years put together ... The occupying powers had begun to enrol Mongol youth in their respective schools and armies, and the whole population was now being exposed to the effective batteries of modern propagandistic

[6] Verrier Elwin & Shamrao Hivale, *Folk-songs of the Maikal Hills*, London etc., 1944, p. xv.
[7] E. Emsheimer, *Singing contests in Central Asia*, in *Journal of the International Folk Music Council*, vol. 8 (1956), p. 28.
[8] *Reports from the scientific expedition to the Northwestern provinces of China*, VIII, Ethnography 4, Stockholm, 1943, pp. 20 ff.

technique ... Troubadours who had themselves spent their youth at the feet of the old masters to learn the chants and folk-songs of the past were now without a single disciple to whom they could pass on their precious inheritance ... Singers and musicians ... were incarcerated in the prison of the town for having been too deeply rooted in the past ...."

Sad, too, is what we hear from Assam, on the Gulf of Bengal: [9]

"A bell rang, feebly and 'tinnily,' and the sound of singing rose in our ears. Were these Naga voices? It sounded like a hymn or a chapel-chant – or perhaps not quite like either. This singing was entirely different from Naga music, the melodies were not in harmony with Naga expression – as discordant as the ugly tin-roofed chapel amidst the palm thatches of the village houses. People with sullen faces came out of the chapel; they seemed to me mere shadows of Nagas, or, even worse, caricatures of Europeans ...."

In 1949, a former army doctor in the service of China described to me how "recruits from inner China ... where there are neither radios nor movies" were forced to learn "the modern – and fully western – national anthem of China. Some officer sang it once to them, without accompaniment, and after that the men, somewhere between one and three hundred, were forced to sing it every morning on hoisting the flag ..." [10]

Thus indigenous music is killed in the interest of poor and second-hand western trash.

The loss is greater than most of us might realize. It means irresponsible annihilation of an organically grown and vital part of culture and a substitution of 'popular,' rootless, inane, and often commercial hits. It means the increasing vulgarization of our globe.

---

[9] Von Fürer-Haimendorf, *l.c.*, p. 55.

[10] W. Lurje, in a letter to, and translated and communicated by, Curt Sachs, in *Journal of the American Musicological Society*, vol. 3 (1950), pp. 292 ff.

II. THE ADVENT OF THE ETHNOMUSICOLOGIST*

The two pillars of European education during the Middle Ages and the Renaissance were theology and the classics. Constantly dealing with the Holy Scriptures and the books of Antiquity, the musical writers could not eschew at least a literary contact with the musical worlds of the Bible and of the Greeks. Much as they were engrossed in the musical problems of their days, in tuning, intervals, and counterpoint rules, they kept a loose connection with the half primitive half oriental sphere of either one. Even early treatises on music opened with a reverent if noncommittal bow to the Hebrews and Hellenes, to Miriam and David, to Pythagoras and the Roman Boethius. True, the music of the Bible was irretrievably lost, and the dozen relics of Greek composition that we own today had not yet been rediscovered. Although the scholars had not the slightest conception of the music itself, they had been trained in the intricate art of interpreting, however questionably, the many passages on music in the Holy Scriptures and in the writings of ancient Greece.

So powerful was this education even in later times that the earliest of the great musical histories, Padre Martini's three-volume *Storia della musica* (1757–1781) covered nothing but Antiquity. But far from being exclusively Graeco-Roman, it included chapters on the Hebrews from "the creation of Adam," indeed, on the Egyptians, the Chaldeans, "and other oriental peoples."

Martini's British successors were less generous. Charles Burney's *General history of music* (1776) did not bother with "Chaldeans and other oriental peoples"; but at least it opened its discussions with a good-sized chapter on Egyptian music. Sir John Hawkins, in his *General history of the science and practice of music* of the same year, went not even that far. In true cavalier fashion he did away with all the "barbarians."

---

* Much of this section has been printed in the author's contribution to *Some aspects of musicology*, New York, The Liberal Arts Press, 1957. Reprinted by permission of the American Council of Learned Societies and of the publishers. Cf. also: the author's *The Orient and western music*, in *The Asian Legacy and American Life*, New York, John Day, 1942, pp. 56–69.

Their best music – as he wrote in the Preface – "is said to be hideous and astonishing sounds. Of what importance then can it be to enquire into a practice that has not its foundation in science or system, or to know what are the sounds that most delight a Hottentot, a wild American, or even a more refined Chinese?"

This is, no doubt, a challenging statement. After all, the "more refined Chinese" based his music very definitely on science, and all the ancient world from Egypt eastward to the coast of the Pacific had its musical "foundation in science or system." This, of course, Sir John could hardly have known. But as a student of Hellenic sources he should at least have realized that the *chroai* or shades in tuning Grecian scales with their manifold and often very unfamiliar, irrational steps from note to note were thoroughly oriental and hence no less inferior and "hideous" than all the music éxcluded from his gigantic work. Worse: he scorned oriental music not because it *was* hideous, but because it was *said* to be hideous. He did not even take pains to know that music himself and felt no urge to test the hearsay. As to the Greek and Hebrew chapters, on the contrary, there was no danger of unfavorable reports: conceivably, no earwitness was at hand. The two sections of the book were easily filled with learned quotations from literary sources well known to all the erudite contemporaries. The music itself was absent, to be sure; but being Biblical or Greek, it must have been perfect by definition.

Four years after Burney and Hawkins, Laborde stressed the universalistic viewpoint of the French. His *Essai sur la Musique* of 1780 discusses again, as Martini's *Storia* had done, "Chaldean and other oriental peoples," Hebrews, Egyptians, and Greeks. But he also included Chinese and Japanese, Siamese, Arabs, Persians and Turks, Negroes, and many others.

The Germans kept out of the picture. Johann Nicolaus Forkel's *Allgemeine Geschichte der Musik* of 1788, in two volumes, limited Antiquity once more to Egypt, the Bible, Greece, and Rome; and after him, the recent theory of evolution gave an even sharper edge to the concept of history. The Orient and the Primitives were mentioned, although in a negative light, since any claim to our own perfection required the production of humbler predecessors. In K. C. F. Krause's certainly not top-ranking *Darstellungen aus der Geschichte der Musik* (1827), we read with astonishment: "In Antiquity, which was the childhood of music (!), only simple, unadorned melody was known, as is the case today with such peoples as the Hindus, Chinese, Persians, and Arabs, who have not yet progressed beyond the childhood age (!)." This is a truly Hegelian progressivism: how far have we come in our mature age (or is it senility, if not worse?)! Not to mention the profound ignorance behind the notions of Hindus, Persians, and Arabs singing in "simple, unadorned melody" – they who are unrivalled masters in the art of highly adorned singing and leave simplicity to the lower forms of children's songs – and to the West.

It means modulation to a different key to open the *Histoire générale de la musique* of 1869 by the Franco-Belgian François-Joseph Fétis. He offers sections, not only on India, China, and Japan, but also on Kalmucks, Kirghizes, Kamtchadals, and others. For to Fétis' imaginative insight, *l'histoire de la musique embrasse celle du genre humain* – the history of music is the history of mankind.

These words we should write upon the posts of our house.

John F. Hullah's *History of modern music*, written only two years after Fétis, was not exactly a landmark and could be passed over in tactful silence, were it not for opinions that still haunt quite a number of musicological minds. "Much as the Orientals have or have had" a "music of their own," this music "as at present practised ... has no charm, nor indeed meaning, for us ... The European system, though the exigencies of practice prevent its being absolutely true, is nearer the truth than any other." Oriental music, then, has no charm, no meaning, and is more remote from truth – this is indeed an unmistakable answer to the appropriative question: 'What does that music mean to me? Can I enjoy it?'

The opposite urge, to widen the field, was not always successful either. Theological and classic ideals were too strong and blinded the greatest authors. The reader who reaches for the monumental *Geschichte der Musik* by August Wilhelm Ambros (1861) finds a whole *Buch* on the *Kulturvölker des Orients*, indeed on the Primitives. But on these pages he also finds the most bewildering pronunciamentos such as: "Assyrian music seems (!) never to have risen above the level of a mere sensual stimulus"; or: the music of Babylon "was quite certainly (!) voluptuous, noisy, and far from simple beauty and noble form"; and Phoenician music was mainly meant to drown "the cries of the victims who burned in the glowing arms of Moloch." What horrible brutes! Even the hope that they may have mended their ways before old Ambros was reprinted in 1887 is futile: the third, "*gänzlich umgearbeitete*" edition has left these monstrous lines intact.[11] If the re-editor, engrossed in Westphal's then recent theories on music in Greece, knew nothing of the fabulous excavations between the Two Rivers, nothing of the impressive art of Sumer, Babylonia, Assyria, should he not have known from the books of Kings and Chronicles that the Phoenician King Hiram helped his friend Solomon with skilled artists and workmen to build the Temple in Jerusalem? And did not this very Temple import a number of musical instruments from Phoenicia, among which the soft-sounding harps and zithers (*nvalim* and *asorot*) were quite unable to drown the desperate screams of Phoenicia's burning victims?

THE GENERAL FAILURE of universal music histories is the more surprising as an interest for non-western music had unmistakably appeared even before Sir John's and Burney's time. Travel diaries of the eighteenth century had begun to add a specimen or two of native songs in modern notation. These, it is true, were rather doubtful sources, since untrained, unsuited men had squeezed what they heard into familiar scales and rhythms of Europe – by hook or by crook. Did not in the same volumes the illustrations, too, falsify and 'idealize' the characteristic types of foreign races in the likeness of ancient statues and render their garb in the drapery of ancient gods [12] that art schools were teaching?

---

[11] Prof. Sachs could have added one more appalling quotation from Ambros, occurring, however, in the first edition only, as being apparently no longer palatable when the later editions were prepared: "Auf Java geht die Tonkunst in barbarische Trübung über, so dass sich hier ihre letzte Spur verliert" – i.e. "In Java music is degenerating into such a barbaric mess that there its last vestiges are being lost." (J.K.).

[12] Cf. also Richard Thurnwald, *Die menschliche Gesellschaft*, vol. 2 of *Repräsentative Lebensbilder von Naturvölkern*, Berlin, 1931, pp. 6 ff.

After these early attempts, it was an epochal moment when Jean-Jacques Rousseau printed quite a few exotic melodies in his *Dictionaire de Musique* (1768) – from Finland, from *les sauvages du Canada,* and from China. The Chinese example later found a place of honor in providing local color for Weber's *Turandot* overture.

Oriental musicology was born eleven years after Rousseau's work, when in 1779 Father Joseph Amiot's painstaking *Mémoire sur la musique des Chinois, tant anciens que modernes* was posthumously printed. We still consult this work with respect and profit.

It might be permissible to link the advent of ethnomusicological interest with Romanticism, which in all the arts consisted "in a high development of poetic sensibility towards the remote, as such ... In the middle of the eighteenth century, that romantic attitude (heralded by Jean-Jacques Rousseau) can already be recognized ... in a tendency to take interest in remote kinds of art." Indeed, Romanticism "allows the poetic interest of distant civilization to supplant the aesthetic interest of form ... Under the influence of this poetry, Nature's unconsidered variety became the very type and criterion of beauty, and men were led by an inevitable consequence to value what is various, irregular, or wild, and to value it wherever it might be found." [13]

Less than twenty years after Amiot, in 1798, Napoleon invaded Egypt and caused an impressive number of French scholars in various fields of knowledge to study the country in all its aspects, past and present. After years of additional research in the *Bibliothèque Nationale,* the various works were gathered together in a gigantic *Description de l'Egypte,* with almost three of the twenty-five volumes being devoted to music: (1) *Mémoire sur la musique de l'antique Egypte,* (2) *De l'état actuel de l'art musical en Egypte,* and (3) *Description historique, technique et littéraire, des instruments de musique des orientaux.* The author of these three musical essays was Guillaume-André Villoteau.

One cannot easily exaggerate their merits.

Based on keen observation during three and a half years of intensive field work, they are uncompromisingly correct and

[13] Geoffrey Scott, *The architecture of humanism,* Garden City, 1954, pp. 41, 43, 60.

free of the preconceived ideas of a European. Villoteau, it must be said, had his prejudice when he first set foot on Egypt's shore. But, while studying with a native music teacher, he soon realized that correct intonation was not a monopoly of western man. Indeed, the European system was by no means, as I just quoted from Hullah, "nearer the truth than any other." After all, western man had changed his ideas about tuning in a long evolution and was in Villoteau's time replacing the artificial mean tone temperament by the no less 'untrue' equal temperament. In Egypt, Villoteau came to understand that oriental music, though basically different from ours, was neither less near to truth nor inferior; it had its own scientific foundation and must therefore be judged according to laws of its own.

Meanwhile, an English High Court judge in Calcutta, William Jones, had in 1784 written *On the musical modes of the Hindoos*, of which a German translation by F. H. v. Dalberg came out in 1802 under the more general title *Ueber die Musik der Indier*. Dalberg added to the original text and appended a number of music examples beyond the one melody that Jones had given. But when he quotes his main collector, an English musician in India, as saying that he had had no small trouble in setting the native tunes in a regular (!) "tempo" (he means rhythm), we cannot accept them without reserve and distrust. How the 'regularization' was done can indeed be seen from the neat notation of a children's prayer heard in Malabar in the Southwest of the subcontinent. The same piece, or at least a close variant, was later recorded on an Edison cylinder, found its way to the Phonographic Archives of Berlin, and was published in 1904.[14] The recorded original is sung, as many children's songs of India, in the typical, charming *triputa* rhythm of seven beats or 4 + 3 in the measure.

Ex. 1

But this was too strong a medicine for the good musician from England.

[14] Cf. Otto Abraham und Erich M. von Hornbostel, *Phonographierte indische Melodien*, in *Sammelbände der Internationalen Musikgesellschaft*, vol. 5 (1904), p. 361, reprinted in *Sammelbände für vergleichende Musikwissenschaft*, vol. 1 (1922), p. 261.

And so it came to pass that his "regularized" version proceeded in the most insipid, hobbling, and banal six-eight.

Ex. 2

WE NEED NOT follow up the subsequent attempts of the nineteenth century; this book is no bibliography. Suffice it to say that exotic musicology in its earlier stage covered almost all oriental high civilizations, and that a good many of the studies published in those decades have become classics.

Excellent or poor, the character in all of these studies was quite similar: the elusive pitches of China or Japan, the melodic and rhythmical patterns of India or the Muhammedan lands, the musical philosophies and musico-cosmological systems of the East in general, in short, everything theoretical that could be gathered from native writings was presented to western readers as a proof that oriental music was a very serious and scientifically founded art worth our careful study. The musical instruments as well were described, depicted, and interpreted in numberless papers and books.

Music, the subject proper, was conspicuously absent.

The decisive turn came in the eighteen eighties. Baker's doctoral thesis on the music of the North American Indians (1882) [15] made the lore of primitive music an academic subject; and two years later, in an important survey of the musical sciences, Guido Adler in Vienna already acknowledged *Musikologie* – our modern ethnomusicology – as a new and "very meritorious" sideline.[16] In the following year, Carl Stumpf, then in Leipzig, published an excellent study of the songs of Bellacoola Indians.[17] Early in the nineties, Hagen wrote another doctoral thesis, this time on Pacific natives;[18] and in the follow-

[15] Theodor Baker, *Ueber die Musik der nordamerikanischen Wilden*, Leipzig, 1882.

[16] Guido Adler, *Umfang, Methode und Ziel der Musikwissenschaft*, in *Vierteljahrsschrift für Musikwissenschaft*, vol. 1 (1885), p. 14.

[17] Carl Stumpf, *Lieder der Bellakula-Indianer*, *ib.*, vol. 2 (1886) pp. 405–426. Reprinted in *Sammelbände für vergleichende Musikwissenschaft*, vol. 1 (1922) pp. 87–104.

[18] Karl Hagen, *Ueber die Musik einiger Naturvölker (Australier, Melanesier, Polynesier)*, Hamburg, 1892.

ing year, Richard Wallaschek brought out the first comprehensive book on primitive music as a whole.[19]

WHILE GERMANS raised the new branch of musicology to an
academic level, men in England and the States gave it a degree
of exactness still unknown on the Continent.

The first in time was an Englishman, Alexander John Ellis
(1814–1890). This prolific, versatile scholar, far from being
a musician, focused his attention mainly on phonetics and
spelling reform. In the course of his research, he made himself
familiar with acoustics and the psychology of hearing, and, in
doing so, met face to face the thrilling problems of exotic scales
and their unusual steps. Fortunately, we might say, he had no
musical ear and thus avoided the naive reliance on so unreliable
a sense. Instead, he took refuge in mathematics and devised an
ingenious computing system of *cents* or hundredths of an equal-
tempered semitone. The details of this system will be expounded
in the following section; its gist is this: the clumsy ratios, so far
in almost exclusive use to express the interval between two
notes, are logarithmically transformed into handy, clear, and
graphic single numbers. The autosuggestive mishearing of the
western musician was hereby eliminated; our arbitrary evaluation of intervals yielded to mathematical exactness.

Ellis published this epoch-making method in his *Tonometrical
observations on some existing non-harmonic scales*, a paper first
printed in the *Proceedings of the Royal Society* (1884) and reprinted in the following year in the *Journal of the Society of Arts*
under the simplified title *On the musical scales of various nations.*[20]
"The final conclusion is," in his own words, „that the Musical Scale
is not one, not 'natural,' nor even founded necessarily on the laws of
the constitution of musical sound so beautifully worked out by
Helmholtz, but very diverse, very artificial, and very capricious."

This was a new realization and the decisive step away from the
standards that the West takes for granted.

[19] Richard Wallaschek, *Primitive music*, London, 1893; in German: *Anfänge der
Tonkunst*, Leipzig, 1903.
[20] E. von Hornbostel published a German translation, *Ueber Tonleitern verschiede-
ner Völker*, in *Sammelbände für vergleichende Musikwissenschaft*, vol. 1, München,
1922, pp. 1–76. – Cf. also Jaap Kunst, *Alexander John Ellis*, in *Die Musik in Geschichte
und Gegenwart*, vol. 3 (1954) col. 1284 ff.

While Ellis was giving musicology a mathematical foundation and a theoretical tool of highest precision, another man, though unwittingly, presented us with a practical tool, whose boundless value is too well known to require renewed emphasis. Thomas Edison had begun, at the age of thirty (in 1877), to transform the vibrations of human voices into curves engraved in the wax coating of rotating cylinders. At first, the sounds were blurred, harsh, and creaking. But the revolutionary invention had been made. Sound, with its characteristic inflections and individual timbres, could be recorded, reproduced, and preserved for future generations; the aural counterpart of photography had become a reality.

The paths of Edison's phonograph and the lore of exotic music converged in 1889 when Dr. Jesse Walter Fewkes (1850–1930) – eminent anthropologist and, eventually, Chief of the U.S. Bureau of Ethnology – took such a machine along while studying the Passamaquoddy in their Maine reservations and, one year later, the Zuñi in New Mexico. His output was delivered to Benjamin Ives Gilman (1852–1933), of Harvard and shortly afterwards secretary of the Museum of Fine Art in Boston, who transcribed the Zuñi cylinders and printed the melodies in western notation in the first volume of the *Journal of American Archaeology and Ethnology* (1891). Two years later, the German philosopher and psychologist Carl Stumpf reported on Gilman's paper in the *Vierteljahrsschrift für Musikwissenschaft* and reproduced his transcriptions.[21] The new branch of learning was thus established both in the U.S.A. and in Europe, in the ethnological as well as the musicological literature.

Incidentally, Gilman's transcriptions bypassed the subtleties of Ellis' cents, which had indeed been devised for the scale-conscious music of oriental high civilizations, but not for the inconsistent intonations of primitive melodies. All that he did to show deviations from the western system was to add a dash above or below when a note was sensibly higher or lower than on his test harmonium. And Stumpf agreed with a quotation from Helmholtz's *Sensations of Tone:* "Who would split firewood with a razor?"

---

[21] Carl Stumpf, *Phonographierte Indianermelodien*, in *Vierteljahrsschrift für Musikwissenschaft*, vol. 8 (1892), pp. 127–144; reprinted in *Sammelbände für vergleichende Musikwissenschaft*, vol. 1 (1922), pp. 113–126.

IT TOOK LESS than half a generation after these events to establish phonographic archives in a number of cities on either side of the Atlantic. (The chronological order of these archives is not safe, since some sources indicate the date when an actual archive with a curator, an assistent, a technician, and a budget was organized, while others are satisfied to mark the year in which the earliest recording found its way into some science museum, only to mildew and disappear in the basement).

These archives were meant to collect and conserve exotic cylinders (and, later, discs and tapes), to have them ready for serious studies, and to encourage the use of recording machines on scientific expeditions. I myself witnessed for many years how, with the Berlin *Phonogramm-Archiv* as their headquarters, Carl Stumpf and his disciple Erich M. von Hornbostel persuaded explorers to take an Edison along, to record songs they might hear in native villages, and to bring them back for conserving treatment, dubbing, storage, transcription, and analysis. The result was beyond all expectation. Ethnologists became eager, able phonographers and delivered an ample harvest to be taken care of in the *Archiv*. Dozens of German ethnological works of that time include special chapters on music, based on this harvest and unselfishly contributed by Von Hornbostel.

Similar activities and similar archives can be found today in many countries, and first of all in the United States.[22]

THE NEW BRANCH of learning – what was its name to be?

The Germans called it originally *Vergleichende Musikwissenschaft* in analogy to *Vergleichende Sprachwissenschaft;* the Americans and English followed with *Comparative musicology,* and the French with *Musicologie comparée.*

These names were acceptable fifty or sixty years ago when haphazard bits of information trickled in: a box of Edison

[22] Erich M. von Hornbostel, *Geschichte des Phonogramm-Archivs der Staatlichen Hochschule für Musik in Berlin*, Berlin, 1927, p. 4 ff. – id., *Das Berliner Phonogramm-archiv*, in *Zeitschrift für vergleichende Musikwissenschaft*, vol. 1 (1933), pp. 40 ff.

George Herzog, *The collections of phonographic records in North America and Hawaii*, in *Zeitschrift für vergleichende Musikwissenschaft*, vol. 1 (1933) pp. 58 ff. – id., *Research in primitive and folk music in the United States*, Bulletin 24 of the American Council of Learned Societies, Washington, 1936.

Frances Densmore, *The study of Indian music*, in *Smithsonian Report for 1941*, Washington, 1942, pp. 527–550.

Jaap Kunst, *Ethnomusicology*, The Hague, 1959, pp. 16 ff.

cylinders from some North American tribe, a few doubtfully rendered melodies from Mongolia, or the music of a touring theatrical company from Siam. With this handful of unrelated samples out of an enormous stock still unknown, and unable to draw connecting lines at so early a date, the scholars could not but compare their findings, weighing likeness against difference.

But today 'comparative musicology' has lost its usefulness. For at the bottom every branch of knowledge is comparative; all our descriptions, in the humanities no less than in the sciences, state similarities and divergences. Even in the history of music we cannot discuss Palestrina's Masses without comparing them with Lasso's or Victoria's or with his own motets. Indeed, all our thinking is a form of comparison: to speak of a blue sky is comparing it with a grey or a purple one. Walter Wiora is certainly right when he emphasizes that comparison can denote only a method, not a branch of learning.[23]

After the name of Comparative Musicology had fallen into disrepute, leading men in the field began to speak of Ethno-musicology or, in German, of *musikalische Völkerkunde*, and, in French, of *ethnologie musicale*.[24] The term seems to have been used for the first time in 1950.[25] According to a resolution of the American Society for Ethnomusicology during the International Congress of Anthropological and Ethnological Sciences in Philadelphia, September 1956, the title Ethnomusicology is to be written without a hyphen. With or without the hyphen, this word is somewhat unwieldy and its meaning obscure to people who have not even a clear idea of musicology without a prefix. The *musikalische Völkerkunde* of the Germans and the *ethnographie musicale* of the French seem to put an exaggerated stress on the ethnological part of the aggregate.

For an aggregate it is, not only in name. The man who works in this field sits on the fence between musicology and ethnology. This must not be held against him – one needs only run over the bulletin of some modern university to find quite similar

[23] Walter Wiora, *On the method of comparative melodic research*, in: *Journal of the International Folk Music Council*, vol. 9 (1958) pp. 55 ff.
[24] Cf. also: Willard Rhodes, *Toward a definition of ethnomusicology*, in *American Anthropologist*, vol. 58 (1956) pp. 457–463.
[25] In Jaap Kunst, *Musicologica* (Amsterdam, 1950).

aggregates: astrophysics, psycho-physiology, palaeo-botany, and dozens of similar fusions. Connecting ethnology and music, the ethnomusicologist, like the astrophysicist and other composites tries to break the ties of departmental seclusion and aims at a merger on a higher level.

III. THE ETHNOMUSICOLOGIST'S WORKSHOP

Activities of the ethnomusicologist are divided into two successive stages: field work and desk work.

Fieldwork is done while the explorer stays in a native village. And the word 'stays' must be stressed. A tourist can never hope to achieve what the scientific explorer accomplishes in weeks, in months, or even in years.

Inversely, it will not do bringing the 'natives' to our cities and record their music in commercial studios or academic laboratories. They are as a rule very ill at ease in an alien environment and rarely yield the qualities available at home in familiar surroundings in the midst of their fellow tribesmen and on the very occasions for which their songs are intended. They often refuse, quite rightly, to sing a wedding song without an actual marriage or a funeral dirge when there is no death.[26] To them it would be the same kind of frivolous profanation as it would be in the West (excepting the stage) to simulate nuptials, a deathbed, or a funeral for the benefit of press photographers. Even a civilization as literate as that of India shows this deep-rooted oneness of music and life: certain melody patterns are assigned to certain definite hours of the day and cannot easily be transferred to other hours in the interest of some concert or recording session. *L'art pour l'art*, or music for the sake of music, does not exist in the primitive world; nor is it imaginable in a considerable part of the highly civilized East. A song is an essential, inseparable element in primitive life and cannot be isolated from the conditions that are its cause, its sense, and its reason of being.

---

[26] Cf. also Bishop Redly in Carl Stumpf, *Lieder der Bellakula-Indianer*, in *Vierteljahrsschrift für Musikwissenschaft*, vol. 2 (1886), p. 411, reprinted in *Sammelbände für vergleichende Musikwissenschaft*, vol. 1 (1922), p. 93.

It is hardly necessary to emphasize that the singer who has been, euphemistically speaking, 'acculturated' through military service, trade with white hawkers, or employment in port towns, mines, and factories is of little value unless the researcher takes greater interest in the dynamic change and decay of native music than in the most traditional forms available.

Reception, adventures, and success in the village are impossible to anticipate, and much depends on the knowledge and good will of the guide and interpreter. Generally speaking, the difficulties are the same in musicology and in anthropology, on which the interested reader may consult the report of a seasoned explorer: Chapter 20 on The Ethnographers Laboratory in M. J. Herskovits' *Cultural Anthropology* (New York, 1955, 4/1960).[27]

I also recommend to look into Frances Densmore's musical experiences with American Indians.[28] But in all admiration for her incessant, diligent work, I must take exception to one of her principles, which I deem rather dangerous and inadmissible: she told her singers that they "must sing in a steady tone and not introduce the yells and other sounds that are customary to Indian singers. The recording," she said, "is not intended to be realistic, but to preserve the actual melody." The sentence is a challenge. What is an "actual melody?" Certainly not an abstract sequence of notes shorn of all its characteristic traits. Everyone versed in European folksong as well as in primitive music knows the importance, the indispensable role, the expressive and sometimes eerie power of those interrupting shouts, be they magic incantations addressed to a demon or simply discharges of excess vitality. What is the sense of improving the techniques of recording and at the same time neglecting a faithful, realistic, unpolished, and undistorted rendition?

The musicological explorer might find any shade of behavior between the extremes of an unlimited willingness to show

---

[27] Also in Hoebel, Jennings, Smith, *Readings in anthropology*, New York, 1955; Cornelius Osgood, *The selection of a community for anthropological study* and *Ethnological field techniques* (pp. 6–17); Philip Phillips, James A. Ford, James B. Griffin, *Archaeological field work* (pp. 17–21). – Cf. also: Hugh Tracey, *Recording African music in the field*, in *African Music*, vol. 1 (1955) no. 2, pp. 6–11; J. Manchip White, *Anthropology*, New York, 1955, pp. 170 ff.; Jaap Kunst, *Ethnomusicology* (The Hague, 1959), 3rd. ed. pp. 14–16.

[28] Frances Densmore, *The study of Indian music*, in *Smithsonian Report for 1941*, Washington, 1942, p. 536.

musical prowess with gusto and pride, and an invincible shyness to exhibit sacred songs or a deadly fear to lose one's self, as with that Eskimo who in honest simplicity said: "My songs are part of my soul, and if the demon in the white man's magic box steals my soul, why, I must die." [29]

The explorer might find one village familiar with the phonograph from preceding visits, and another one to which the phonograph is novel and the incomprehensible intention of the white man and his whole complicated procedure utterly intimidating. When Mrs. M. Selenka visited the Vedda in inner Ceylon in 1907, she had to tell them that "the box hid a little birdie eager to hear the Vedda sing. But he could hear them only if they came quite near. With long intermissions and the gentle persuasion on the part of the interpreter, I succeeded to seat three of them close enough to the horn." [30]

Things are essentially easier today, not only because phonography is more widely known and needs no longer a tale of inquisitive birdies, but also because the phonograph itself has basically changed. Modern phonography facilitates the process both in technique and in its psychological possibilities [31] in a similar way as the photographer snaps you unawares when you are relaxed instead of demanding rigid, unnatural poses in front of a slow-working black-clothed camera.

The old forbidding horn or receiving funnel from which you were not allowed to swerve by a handbreath has disappeared. The easily portable Edison phonograph of 1877 with its crank and spring action and with wax cylinders fragile and hard to preserve yielded to Emil Berliner's heavier 'gramophone' with shellac disks, patended in 1887; to electric manipulation with a tiny, often freely movable microphone that we can carry about to any vantage point and even hide from the singer (1925); to Peter C. Goldmark's long-playing micro-groove machines (1948); and ultimately, so far, to magnetic tape recorders. Created by the Danish inventor Valdemar Poulsen as early as 1898, tape

---

[29] Christian Leden, *Ueber die Musik der Smith Sund Eskimos*, in *Meddelelser om Grønland*, vol. 152 (1952), p. 22.

[30] Max Wertheimer, *Musik der Wedda*, in *Sammelbände der Internationalen Musikgesellschaft*, vol. 11 (1909/10), p. 300.

[31] Latest monograph: Roland Gelatt, *The fabulous phonograph*, Philadelphia & New York, 1955.

has after a rather erratic career come into its own and offers to workers in the field the advantages of easy transportation and handling, excellent rendition, a capacity of practically indefinite recording without interruption, and an equally indefinite number of playbacks without a measurable deterioration.[32] In 1955, a New York distributor presented a "Grooved Tape-Disk," developed in Cologne and said to play eight hours of uninterrupted music on three miles of a sound track one-thousandth of an inch in diameter.[33]

Whether on cylinders, disks, tapes, or tape-disks – phonography has grown indispensable in musical field work. The times when musicians (and non-musicians, too) proudly referred to their more or less well trained ears are gone. We know from bitter experience how unreliable and deadly prejudiced man's senses are, how easily we project into a totally foreign style of music the tempered melody steps and even-stressed rhythms of western tradition, and, hence, how small the documentary value of such unverified impressions is. As a leading anthropologist has expressed it: "We hear music, no less than we produce it, in terms of very subtle conditionings that make up our musical enculturation."[34]

Still, even under such favorable conditions the ear is not always up to expectation. Much as a listener may be trained in analyzing unfamiliar types of music, he has at times desperate difficulties with melody steps others than the ones of our habitual well-tempered system or with confusing rhythms and counterrhythms.

The first fact that I touched upon – "steps others than the ones of our habitual well-tempered system" – confronts the ethnomusicologist with two essential problems: how to measure and how to express them more correctly than by an embarrassed "a bit larger (or shorter, smaller) than a wholetone." Of necessity, we look around for mechanical help. But, at least for the purpose of field work, the helping device should, in Jaap Kunst's words, be "easily transportable, of a simple manipulated construction, and able to stand a certain amount of knocking about. It should further," he adds, "not be too ex-

---

[32] S. J. Begun, *Magnetic recording*, New York, 1949.
[33] New York Times, 1955, April 13.
[34] Melville J. Herskovits, *Cultural anthropology*, New York, 1955, p. 282.

pensive to buy and maintain; musicologists do not, as a rule, excel as possessors of earthly riches, and only a very few are privileged to receive adequate financial assistance from scientific institutions or interested private persons." [35]

TONE-MEASUREMENTS can be obtained either acoustically or visually.

The older acoustical methods might in general suffice for the less subtle needs of primitive music, while they are hardly fine enough for the purposes of oriental music. They compare the pitches heard with a sounding standard of satisfactory pitch persistence and measuring gradation. Helmholtz used a set of spherical brass resonators; Ellis availed himself of quite a battery of tuning forks. Stumpf and Von Hornbostel followed Appun's *Tonmesser*, a kind of harmonium with many reeds at short tonal distances but without actual keys; and Von Hornbostel also devised a tiny *Reise-Tonometer* for field work: a single reed with a tuning wire manipulated by a dial, which indicated the frequency when the spinning hand, in shifting the wire up and down along the reed, had tuned it to the pitch of the note to be measured. Jaap Kunst sticks to his monastic monochord, a narrow soundbox with graded surface and a movable bridge under a metal string. After adjusting the open string to the pitch of a tuning fork or pipe, any tone heard in the phonograph (or its octave) can be reproduced on the monochord by moving the bridge to a position where the ear is reasonably certain that the two pitches, on the shortened string and in the phonograph, are identical. The grading on the surface allows for an approximate and in most cases sufficient measurement (except when the bridge draws too close to the motionless end of the string). The plucked sound, breaking off at once, is another drawback.

All these acoustical methods suffer from multiple approximation. (1) It is the ear that decides on the equality of the pitch to be measured and the pitch to be the standard. (2) The distances from standard to standard are as a rule so wide on the test instrument that the pitch to be tested lies between two of them

[35] Jaap Kunst, *Musicologica*, Amsterdam, 1950; 3rd edition (as *Ethnomusicology*), The Hague, 1959, p. 10.

at a point left to our estimate. (3) In many cases the acoustical method provides only one octave of standards and hardly ever the whole range of men's and women's voices and of instruments that we might want to test. The solution is transposition by an octave or even two, once more incumbent on our unreliable ears.

The visual methods are essentially more exact, notably those based on modern electronics. As the principal apparatuses, we use the oscilloscope, the stroboscope, and the electronic counter.

The oscilloscope, ignoring sound as an audible phenomenon, makes the sound waves or oscillations visible and measurable and allows for a photographic reproduction of single notes as well as of melodies. In the case of such a photographic recording, we speak of photophonography.[36]

Oscilloscopic writing has of late been greatly improved, above all by Olav Gurvin at the University of Oslo.[37] In the U.S.A., Charles Seeger of Santa Barbara (California), in collaboration with V. C. Anderson of San Diego, is developing an oscillograph which needs neither processing nor mathematical calculations. A heated stylus traces the waves by melting the coat of a special plastic graph paper 63.5 mm wide. The design that the stylus leaves permits the instantaneous reading of all the pitches of an unaccompanied melody, including exact rhythm, the subtle changes that a vibrato entails, and, additionally, the finest shades of speed.[38]

The stroboscope, unlike the oscilloscope, centers around a disk of alternately black and white sectors. Under the control of a dial, the disk reacts to a light fed from the sound source. When the sectors or 'spokes' appear to stand still, the dial is indicating exactly the frequency of the outside sound. When the spokes seem to move clockwise, the outside pitch is higher than the standard inside; when counter-clockwise, the pitch is lower.[39]

---

[36] Milton E. Metfessel, *Phonophotography in folk music*, Chapel Hill, 1928. – M. Grützmacher und W. Lottermoser, *Ueber ein Verfahren zur trägheitsfreien Aufzeichnung von Melodiekurven*, in *Akustische Zeitschrift*, vol. 2 (1937).

[37] Olav Gurvin, *Photography as an aid in folkmusic research*, in *Norveg*, vol. 3 (1955). – Karl Dahlback, *New methods in vocal folkmusic research*, Oslo, 1958.

[38] Charles Seeger, *Toward a universal music sound-writing for musicology*, in *Journal of the International Folk Music Council*, vol. 9 (1957), pp. 63–66.

[39] Milton E. Metfessel, *The strobophotography*, in *Journal of General Psychology*, vol. 2 (1929), pp. 135 ff. – R. W. Young and A. Loomis, in *Journal of the Acoustic Society of America*, vol. 10 (1938), pp. 112 ff. – Fritz A. Kuttner, *Der stroboskopische Frequenzmesser*, in *Die Musikforschung*, vol. 6 (1953), pp. 235–248.

Electronic counters are probably handiest for measuring single pitches. They convert acoustical into electrical phenomena and answer a tone by the appearance of the exact frequency number in current figures – way beyond the range of audibility, from one cycle per second up to 120,000 cycles.[40]

A RELIABLE EAR is indispensable during the second phase: when the ethnomusicologist sits down at home, studies the yield of his field work, and makes it accessible to readers who have not heard the originals. While the machine plays back the recorded pieces, he eagerly tries to catch the tonal picture. This time, the ear is not engaged in the weird and hopeless multi-activity of the non-phonographer: to follow in an impossible haste lest a note should get lost, to evaluate the passage just heard, to write it spasmodically down longhand while the singer is already far ahead, and in all this to fail inevitably. We find it a tremendous help to turn back the pick-up as often as necessary and repeat the piece or an elusive phrase until we are ready to transcribe it into our western notation and thus enjoy the benefit of leisurely study as well as of careful control. But also he who studies a piece after the transcriber has a new and badly needed control. For transcriptions are too subjective to be trusted uncritically and should, wherever possible, be compared with the phonographic original.

A BIG HOWEVER stands behind these gadgets. Much as they are perfected, welcome, and indispensable, they serve one purpose only: the faithful measurement of the constituents in the melodies we hear from the phonograph. But the most precise of pitches and metrical values have only a limited merit. Even the unsophisticated songs of the earliest among the primitives are much more than lifeless sequences of incoherent pitches and lengths. Indeed, the less sophisticated a song is, the less we can rely on individual pitches and lengths, which, when consciously handled, belong to systematic music. Our own 'blue' notes in jazz and similar types of music are a case in point.

The editor's essential task is organization, analysis, interpre-

40 *Hewlett-Packard Journal*, vol. 6, no. 11 (July 1955).

tation of the raw materials that the phonograph provides; it demands grouping, phrasing, and punctuating. This is, beyond the gadget's power of precision, a musician's chore – though not a musician who arrogantly relies on a purely western education or, much worse, on his "unfailing instinct" (which is the prerogative of animals, not an asset of men). Only he who knows the pitfalls of western habits and has learned to escape them is up to such intricate, delicate work and can hope to do justice to eastern and primitive music.

And even such a man is far from being infallible. When we compare an original phonogram with a transcription made by another person, we will more often than not disagree. This is not necessarily a question of keener ears, but rather of the analytical apparatus in the brain – just as two painters of equal ability (and even photographers) might be at variance in seizing the likeness of a model. Indeed, our own transcriptions will often be unsatisfactory when we resume and revise the work of yesterday. One cannot too earnestly warn the student against accepting printed transcriptions as gospel truth.[41]

THE SECOND PROBLEM – how to express steps other than the ones of our well-tempered system – pivots around numbers, fractions, divisions, and logarithms. The pitches that we hear differ in only one factual, physical quality: the frequency of vibrations or, in other words (as we understand it today) the number of to's *plus* fro's in which a string (or any other sounding object) moves during a second. Thus, our tuning forks, in rendering the standard a', vibrate 440 times in a second – 440 times back and 440 times forth. This so-called frequency is in all cases the unique, unavoidable measure of a single note.

It is more complicated to describe a step or distance between, or interval of, two notes (step or distance and interval are psychologically not identical; but we may here be allowed to neglect the difference). To express this interval in numbers, we do not subtract, but must divide the two frequencies. When one of the two notes vibrates 440 times per second, and the other one 330 times, their interval is 440 : 330, or 4 : 3.

But ratios are not always that simple. Let the two notes have

41 See also: Jaap Kunst, *Ethnomusicology* (3rd. edition, The Hague, 1959), pp. 37 ff.

435 and 391½ vibrations, and we get a fraction ungraphic, unwieldy, irreducible. If we compare this fraction with another one that the nearest neighboring step provides – 391½ : 348 – we would not, in fact we could not, from the forbidding looks of these two ratios become aware that eitherone expresses exactly the selfsame distance of a wholetone. They differ in their constituent numbers, because, quite individualistically, they tell us about the accidental relations of a', g', and f', but fail to indicate the general sizes of two wholetones, which after all are the same whatever note in the whole range of hearing you take as the starting point. The situation is as abnormal as if we would express the distances from Boston to New York and from New York to Washington in different, complicated ratios instead of reading simply the mileage from road maps and time-tables.

In order to attain such a musical mileage, two needs are obvious: (1) to express similar distances by identical numbers, regardless of pitches and frequencies; (2) to express them so that the numbers, firmly lodged within a frame-work of fixed standards (as on graph paper) give instantly a clear picture of the size in question.

The only way to meet these needs is to transform frequency numbers into logarithms. This transformation implies automatically a transformation of the original awkward division into an easy subtraction: $\log (x : y) = \log x - \log y$. By the simplest of operations this subtraction can be expressed by a single number which, answering the first of our needs – "to express similar distances by identical numbers, regardless of pitches and frequencies" – is the log of the interval in question, or log i.

Need (2) – "to express distances so that the numbers, firmly lodged within a frame-work of fixed standards, give instantly a clear picture of the size in question" – was met by the Frenchman Félix Savart (1791–1841) and his system of logarithmic *savarts*. Outside France, the *savarts* have been supplanted by Alexander J. Ellis' system of *cents* (1884). One *savart* equals 3.99 or, rounded off, 4 *cents*, and the semitone is expressed by 25 *savarts* and 100 *cents*.

The following is Ellis' principle. All possible shades of pitch are contained in one octave, which has the frequency ratio of

2 : 1 or, short, of 2. An octave contains in our 'well-tempered' system twelve equal semitones, each of which, mathematically speaking, amounts to $\sqrt[12]{2}$. In Ellis' system, each semitone is divided into 100 *cents*, and the whole octave, consequently, into 1200 *cents*. Thus,

a semitone has	100 cents,
a wholetone,	200 cents,
a minor third,	300 cents,
a major third,	400 cents,
a fourth,	500 cents,
a tritone,	600 cents,
a fifth,	700 cents,
a minor sixth,	800 cents,
a major sixth,	900 cents,
a minor seventh,	1000 cents,
a major seventh,	1100 cents,
an octave,	1200 cents,

To abbreviate our excursion into the dreaded mathematical field, let us leave the theoretical aspects and try the practical application. To find the cents of a distance or interval, you take the following steps.

(1) Find the frequencies of your two notes by one of the methods already mentioned in this section – monochord, tonometry, stroboscopy, phonophotography, oscillography, electronic counting.

(2) Find the two logarithms and their difference, or log i.

(3) This log i can easily be transformed into cents with the help of the following table.

cents	log	cents	log	cents	log
1.	.00025	10	.0025	100	.025
2.	.00050	20	.0050	200	.050
3.	.00075	30	.0075	300	.075
4.	.00100	40	.0100	400	.100
5.	.00125	50	.0125	500	.125
6.	.00151	60	.0151	600	.151
7.	.00176	70	.0176	700	.176

cents	log	cents	log	cents	log
8.	.00201	80	.0201	800	.201
9.	.00226	90	.0226	900	.226
				1000	.251
				1100	.276
				1200	.301

To give an example: suppose your log i is .12461, you find yourself close to .125 and hence to 500 *cents*, which are the equivalent of an equal-tempered fourth. If you are interested in absolute correctness, you add the two columns of logs and cents:

$$
\begin{array}{ll}
.100 & 400 \\
.0226 & 90 \\
.00201 & 8
\end{array}
$$

which reproduces the .12461 of log i and the resulting cent number 498, numerical symbol of the perfect fourth.

Other shortcuts were made by Erich M. von Hornbostel,[42] R. W. Young,[43] and Heinrich Husmann.[44]

When no table of logs is at hand, a detour can be made with the help of an auxiliary number and four arithmetic operations, as subtraction, multiplication, addition, and division. These cumbersome procedures have been described in earlier books [45] and need no resumption – the less so as they have in the meantime been superseded by the mechanical device of the *music rule*.

The music rule, devised in 1949 by Marcus Reiner, professor at the Technion of Haifa, Israel, with the musical collaboration of Edith Gerson-Kiwi in Jerusalem, is constructed like an ordinary slide rule, which shifts two twelve-centimeter scales along one another. The left scale pictures the equal-tempered octave *c'–c''* from 264 to 528 cycles (double vibrations or frequencies); full dividing lines mark every ten cycles, and four broken lines in between, every two cycles. The distances up from line

---

[42] Erich M. v. Hornbostel, *Eine Tafel zur logarithmischen Darstellung von Zahlenverhältnissen*, in *Zeitschrift für Physik*, vol. 6 (1921), pp. 29 ff.

[43] R. W. Young, *A table relating frequency to cents*, Elkhart, Indiana, 1939.

[44] Heinrich Husmann, *Fünf- und siebenstellige Centstafeln zur Berechnung musikalischer Intervalle*, Leyden, 1951.

[45] Curt Sachs, *The rise of music in the ancient world*, New York, 1943, p. 28.

to line, however, are not equal as on our thermometers, but become steadily shorter. The reason is obvious. The differences between the two frequency numbers of any interval transposed upwards grow steadily larger; if you compare the wholetone distances c'–d' and, an octave above, c''–d'', the result will be:

d' has 297 vibr.	d'' has 594 vibr.
c' has 264 vibr.	c'' has 528 vibr.
diff.: 33 vibr.	diff.: 66 vibr.

In frequency numbers, the distance is in the upper octave twice as wide; but to the musical ear and to the cent system it is exactly the same. The only way out is to shrink the spaces from line to line in the same ratio in which the vibration numbers grow wider apart; in our example: the space between c'' and d'' is on the music rule just half as wide as the space between c' and d'. (The d'' is actually not on the rule). All the spaces narrow on their way up.

The right-hand scale matches the left one in its length of twelve centimeters. But since it represents the unchangeable octave of 1200 cents (or *ellis*, as the two Israeli scholars call them), this length is divided by full lines into centimeters, each of which comprises the one hundred cents of a semitone, and, by broken lines, each centimeter is divided into ten degrees of ten cents. All that the measuring person has to do in order to transform a distance into cents is: (1) shift the cent scale so far that its base line stops exactly opposite the frequency number of the lower note; and (2) find the cents opposite the frequency number of the upper note. In case one or both notes exceed the range of the c'–c'' octave, there is an additional move: (3) for the octave above, the cycles on the left side must be multiplied by 2, and the number of cents increased by 1200; for the octave below, the cycles must be divided by two, and the cents diminished by 1200.

For practical purposes this approximation will suffice. For theoretical preciseness it is easy to give the music rule a larger size, maybe 24 centimeters, and augment the number of Reiner's subdivisions on either scale.

Three years after Reiner, Fritz Bose came out with an almost identical '*nomogramm.*' [46] Instead of a slide rule, it necessitates a separate rule in millimeter division to be laid against the logarithmic vibration scale (which amounts to the same). Moreover, its vibrations are marked from five to five cycles, as against the more accurate division from two to two cycles on Reiner's model.

IN SPITE of all these refinements, we are still very far from a faithful transcription of the fleeting impression on our ear into a lasting impression on our eye. The reasons are evident. At first, there is in primitive or oriental music no silent composing with paper and pencil. Dreamily humming and strumming, composers create their melodies, and even after polishing rugged passages do they not pen a definite version. On playing in public, they are not bound to an authentic printed form, to an *Urtext*. There is none. Producing and reproducing fuse into a delightful unit; the well-wrought, mentally definite form and the indefinite, momentary impulse reach a perfect balance. Any notation would spoil this equilibrium in the undue interest of finality; it would destroy the potentialities of a free-flowing melody in favor of stagnant impersonality. Although there are a few native notations in countries of high civilization – in India as well as the Far East and the Muhammedan world, – they are poor and vague and assist recollection rather than performance or study. Be their symbols borrowed from the alphabet or from descriptive gestures like the 'neumes' of the Middle Ages, be they fingering guides like the instrumental 'tablatures,' or conventional signs for certain groups of notes, they render at best a lifeless skeleton.

What makes it worse is that our notes on four or five staff lines and in the spaces between them are intended to serve a diatonic gender with its alternation of steps and halfsteps. More accurately: the original concept was meant for ancient Europe's tertial chains with infixes, such as C ^{d} E ^{f} G ^{a} B or D ^{e} F ^{g} A ^{b} C, to be discussed later in this book.

Reading oriental music from western staff lines is just as deceptive as reading oriental poetry in a twenty-six letter

[46] Fritz Bose, *Ein Hilfsmittel zur Bestimmung der Schrittgrösse beliebiger Intervalle*, in *Die Musikforschung*, vol. 5 (1952), pp. 205–208.

transliteration without array of 'diacritical' dashes, tildes, dots, and hooks. The staff lines and spaces entice the reader into a fatal misconception. The notes, let us say, of a Siamese melody, which has neither whole nor semitones, have no proper place anywhere on the staff. Forced upon and between the five lines, they deceive the reader with perfect fourths, thirds major and minor, and seconds major and minor where there are no such steps at all. They also deceive the reader by suggesting, in the conflict between the familiar lines we see and the unfamiliar steps we hear, that the exotic melodies in question are out of tune, in other words, that the West is right and the East is wrong. Additionally, our script is not prepared to show the nasaling, yodeling, vibrating, gliding, falsetto shades, which, almost more than structure, are characteristic traits of the various musical idioms outside the West. The unexperienced reader deciphers such notations as a student would decipher a Koran text after studying Arabic from a grammar: the Arab would not be able to identify the *sura*, nor would the Westerner recognize the same text when read by a native.

Out of this want, Otto Abraham and Erich M. von Hornbostel published in 1909 "Suggestions for the transcription of exotic melodies." [47]

Most of their suggestions adapt the well-known symbols, like notes, flags, keys, ties, slurs, dots, to the special needs of non-western music. Among the newly invented signs I want to mention only the inverted fermata which occurs quite often in transcriptions:

   ⌣ means the shortening of a note, and
   (⌣) means a lesser shortening of a note.

These symbols are objectionable. The dotted arc is a familiar symbol of lengthening, both in our current notation and in that of the ethnomusicologist. It is again used in ethnomusicological transliteration when we want to indicate in a symbolic scale at the end of a melody what relative degrees of weight and frequency its individual pitches have. In such symbolic scale, we write

---

[47] Otto Abraham und Erich M. von Hornbostel, *Vorschläge für die Transkription exotischer Melodien*, in *Sammelbände der Internationalen Musikgesellschaft*, vol. 11 (1909), pp. 1–25.

the most important pitch (according to its frequency, stress, or end position) as a wholenote, the next important one as a half-note, and so forth; and we introduce the fermata sign to mark an intermediate shade of rank. Inverting the unmistakable symbol of lengthening to indicate the opposite meaning would be just as artificially rationalistic as turning the Cross upside down to symbolize non-Christian faiths: the form of a symbol impresses our eyes much more than does its position. Incidentally, our current notation inverts the fermata anyhow when its place is below the note to be lengthened, without changing therewith or even inverting its purport. Are we allowed to use a symbol now for one meaning now for its opposite?

Parentheses, on the other hand, are generally accepted as symbols of an aside, but not of a diminution. Both signs are ungraphic.

Although the Abraham-Hornbostel suggestions are as a whole still valid, we follow today the recommendations of a number of experts convened at Geneva in July 1949 by the *Archives Internationales de Musique populaire*, which were resumed in *C.I.A.P.* (*Commission Internationale des Arts populaires*) *Information*, nov.–déc. 1949 (nos. 15–16) and in *Document du Conseil International de la Musique* (Unesco), 1950. Among the symbols suggested at that time, there are little arrows, aimed up or downward to raise or lower the note by a microtone; an arc opening downward ('convex') marks a slight lengthening of a note, and an arc opening upward ('concave'), a slight shortening.

Renouncing the current staff notation, a number of scholars have replaced the symbols on lines by round or angular curves, where the ordinate stands for pitch, and the abscissa for duration.[48] This form of writing is meant to depict the general trend and flow of a melody and has as such advantages in certain cases. But it is neither accurate nor graphic enough to be exclusively accepted.

Weighing the merits and defects against each other, we find that even the most painstaking method will not give us ultimate

---

[48] Examples: B. I. Gilman, *Hopi songs*, in *Journal of American Ethnology and Archaeology*, vol. 5 (1908). – E. Lineff, *The peasant songs of Great Russia*, London, 1905; *id.*, *Velikorusskiia piesni*, vol. 2, St. Petersburg, 1911.

satisfaction. No musical script can ever be a faithful mirror of music, just as no spelling, phonetic or otherwise, can give an adequate idea of the sound of English, French, or any one language to those who do not master it. Even for western music our western notation is quite unsatisfactory from many viewpoints. Leaving this latter problem to the many untiring reformers around us, we might, for our present concern, take heart in the rapid growth of phonography, which makes a good deal of our writing symbols superfluous by restoring music to the ear – where it belongs.

But as long as we still are forced to notate what we hear, three details should be observed.

(1) It is often confusing and perfectly useless to transcribe a piece exactly in the original key when this tessitura requires many sharps and flats. Native singing does not follow tuning forks, nor does it depend on the 'ethical' character of a certain tonality. Another singer would very probably perform the same piece in a different key. Why must we impose on the reader the fortuitous pitch of a primitive melody when a simple transposition by a semitone rids him of the dead ballast of superfluous accidentals? How much more readable would the six-sharp songs in B. I. Gilman's Zuñi collection be if a shift by a semitone up or down gave them instead a single sharp or one flat! Our duty to scholarly accuracy can be amply fulfilled by adding the short remark: "original a semitone higher (lower)."

Such transposition, however, should never exceed one semitone. Otherwise, characteristic tessituras might get lost in a fictional range. He who knows the eerie, solemn prayers of Tibetan lamas, which so often dwell down by (great) C,[49] or even the songs of North American Indians, which easily descend to E or, in women's parts, to e, will realize that a transposition by more than a semitone would distort the very character of that dark-colored music.[50] And just as notation must keep the lower ranges intact, it should in other cases preserve the opposite impact of extreme height – as in East Transcaucasia, where an Azerbaijani tenor freely and without falsetto enters on c'' and ascends to a

---

[49] *EFw* FE 4504 (P 504) IV 13.
[50] Cf. Frances Densmore, *The study of Indian music* in *Annual Report*, Smithsonian Inst. for 1941, Washington, 1942, p. 542.

woman's e'',[51] while, next door, Uzbekistani women go quite naturally up to b''.[52]

An exception must certainly be made when a number of melodies are written below one another and transposed to the same pitch for easier comparison.

(2) Avoid all key signatures reminiscent of those which we write in western music. Created for tonality in our harmonical sense – such as A major or B minor – they are nonsensical and dangerously misleading in the transcriptions of early melodies which have no such tonality. Give a transcription just the signature of the few sharps or flats that you do not like to repeat all the time within your notation, but not more. Do not argue that, while you have only a sharpened C in your piece, you should liberally add an F sharp in the signature since in our western music no C sharp occurs without an F sharp. All that you achieve with this illogical, illicit addition is to suggest one of our major or minor tonalities, from which primitive melodies are aeons away. In a similar way, it is inadmissible to print an F sharp signature at the beginning of each staff, thus implying a G major or an E minor, although F sharp does nowhere occur in the melody at all.[53] Such procedure becomes suicidal when the sharp not only is completely absent from the piece but must be re-naturalized wherever there is an F: for all that the melody is not G major but, if the transcriber thinks he cannot do without an accepted scale name, at best Mixolydian.[54]

The worst examples that come to my mind are a couple of Pawnee songs, each of a one-step pattern. One of them, just a zigzag of d and e, appears in the masquerade of D major, with two sharps as the signature which raise the two non-existent notes f and c.[55] If the author thinks he cannot do without the make-believe of a western scale, why not just as well D minor?

[51] *EFw* FE 4505 (P 505) IV 16; FE 4416 (P 416) I 3, II 1. Also: FE 4501 (P 501) I 1 (from Syria).

[52] Other examples of high tessitura in: Richard Wallaschek, *Primitive music*, London, 1893, pp. 75 ff., and *Anfänge der Tonkunst*, Leipzig, 1903, pp. 77 ff.

[53] Cf. No. 43 in Frances Densmore, *Teton Sioux music*, Washington, 1918, with an F sharp in the signature without a a single F in the pentachordal melody. How does the author know that, if there were one, the singer would sharp it?

[54] Cf. the example transcribed by D. Arakchiev, in *Proceedings of the Musico-Ethnographical Commission*, vol. I, p. 293, Music Supplement.

[55] Transcribed by Edwin S. Tracy in Alice C. Fletcher. *The Hako, a Pawnee ceremony*, Washington, 1904, p. 70.

The other one, a *skiriki* or coyote warrior song,[56] boasts of three sharps, but consists in the second part only of the two unsharpened notes *a* and *e*. The transcriber, unable to think of any two notes outside the twenty-four tonalities that the tidy equal temperament of Europe provides, decided for *A* major. Why did he not choose *A* minor, which would have allowed him to dispense with all the three ghost accidentals? There is no answer. The obsession of tonality where there is no tonality, with all its high-handed decisions, is beyond reason and justification.

Even the method of Mieczyslaw Kolinski, otherwise an excellent, leading ethnomusicologist, fails. He squeezes the primitive melodies into a system of church modes and imaginary cycles of fifths and succumbs, in my opinion, to an ill-fated attempt at over-classification.[57]

(3) Take good care to write the necessary accidentals in the front signature on the line or in the space exactly where they belong. An *F* sharp that occurs exclusively in the one-lined octave must appear in the first space and not, as in modern notations, on the fifth line. A wider melody range might easily leave this two-lined *F* unsharpened.

I also suggest that the bass clef so often used in transcriptions of men's songs should be replaced by the modern *G* or violin clef over an 8 as a transposing symbol in the interest of a unified script (although I do not doubt in the least that the readers of ethnomusicological books and papers are perfectly able to decipher the *F* clef).

IV. THE QUESTION OF ORIGIN

Questions of origin fascinate the laymen no less than historians. To see the Mississippi, the Nile, or the Danube in all their quiet majesty is an unforgettable experience; but it is still more exiting to find their sources and watch the new-born streamlets trickle from under the rocks.

---

[56] Natalie Curtis, *The Indians' book*, New York, 1906.

[57] M. Kolinski, *Suriname music*, Part III of Melville J. and Frances S. Herskovits, *Suriname folk-lore*, New York, 1936. – Kolinski's system has been adopted, for example, by Alan P. Merriam; cf. his *Songs of a Rada Community in Trinidad*, in *Anthropos*, vol. 51 (1956).

The currents of history, alas, delude our curiosity: while the age of man spans millions of years, historical evidences hardly cover five thousand of them or a tiny fraction of one percent. All that which precedes these evidences is wide open to guess and conjecture.

The origin of music has likewise been a favorite object of guess and conjecture. Primitives trace it occasionally to animals of their world: the Luiseño in southern California relate that music was invented in the earliest times, and Lion, Eagle, Raven, Frog, Deer and others were the first musicians.[58] The ancient high civilizations appointed one of their gods to be the inventor or at least a patron of music – Thot in Egypt, Narada in India, Apollo in Greece. An exception is Judaism, which as a monotheistic religion had no special divinity available; Genesis 4 : 21 just mentions Jubal as "the father of all such as handle the harp and the pipe," without taking trouble to trace the roots of so innate an expression as singing. The ancient Chinese, quite modern in this assumption, already believed that music had had a slow development.[59]

The later West draped its guesswork with the flowing gown of the scholar. It pretended to find the origins of music, now in the imitation of singing birds, now in shouts to signal "over the hills and far away," or in the natural rhythmic alleviation of organized toil,[60] indeed, in human speech.[61]

Not one of all the allegedly scientific theories is borne out by facts. At best, some of their connections are in the realm of possibility; and even the possibilities are depressingly weak. A shout or a bit of regular work may doubtless have led to a melodic strain or a rhythmic pattern; but can they have begotten music as a whole in all its ramifications?

Lately, the derivation from speech has been modified via the so-called tone languages.[62]

[58] Constance Goddard DuBois, *The religion of the Luiseño Indians*, in *University of California Publications* in *American Archaeology and Ethnology*, vol. 8 (1908), p. 166.

[59] Lü Pu-We, *Shi Ch'un Ts'iu* [3rd. century B. C.], ed. Richard Wilhelm, p. 66.

[60] Karl Bücher, *Arbeit und Rhythmus*, Leipzig, 1896 (3rd ed. 1903, 5th ed. 1918). – Erich M. von Hornbostel, *Arbeit und Musik*, in *Zeitschrift der Internationalen Musikgesellschaft*, vol. 13 (1912), pp. 341–350.

[61] Latest résumés: Robert Lach, in *Handbuch der Musikgeschichte*, ed. Guido Adler, 2nd ed., Berlin, 1930, vol. 1, pp. 3 ff. – Géza Révész, *Der Ursprung der Musik*, in *Internationales Archiv für Ethnographie*, vol. 11 (1941), pp. 65 ff.

[62] Fritz A. Kuttner, *Die verborgenen Beziehungen zwischen Sprache und Musik*, in *Musica*, vol. 5 (1951), pp. 13 ff. – Marius Schneider, *Primitive Music* in *The New Oxford History of Music*, 3rd ed. (1957), vol. 1, pp. 6–7.

In a number of languages past and present, sounds are not only long and short or stressed and unaccented, but also, in a musical sense, ascending, level, descending, or medium, high, and low. Tone languages, as they are called, may appear in two forms. Only one of them justifies the name.

We do not speak of tone languages when inflections follow local traditions and habit rather than need, as the dropping off at the end of a word in northern Germany and, instead, the rise in southern Germany. Such inflections do not change the meaning of words, but are at the very best, oratorical shades, beyond any regional idiom: even in languages as unmelodic as English and German, words like *no* and *nein* express as a rule a question as they glide upwards; descending, they stand for a statement or an interdiction. No language proceeds in an absolute monotone.

But in other languages, say Chinese or Siamese, the tone is absolutely essential to identify the meaning of a syllable which might have a quite different sense according to whether it is high or low in pitch, or rising or descending.[63] The same can be said of languages around the Gulf of Guinea. In Yoruba, the word *oko*, when middle-pitched, means 'husband,' when low-pitched, 'spear,' when ascending, 'hoe,' when descending, 'canoe.' "Tones are more significant in Yoruba than vowels and consonants."[64] The language of the Jabo in eastern Liberia assigns to the syllable *ba* four totally unrelated meanings, depending on its pitch: spoken on high pitch, it means 'to be broad,' in the middle register, 'namesake,' on a somewhat lower one, 'tail,' and spoken quite low, it is a particle expressing command.[65] The language of Uganda has, like ancient Greek, three 'accents': a lift of the voice or 'acute,' a half-lift to a medium pitch, and a lift and following drop below the unaccented level or 'circumflex.'In speaking, these inflections are carefully observed, since, for example, a word like *musala* has seven meanings unless the inflection serves as a determinative. But they also must be observed in melody.[66]

[63] On tone languages in general, see Kenneth L. Pike, *Tone languages* (Ann Arbor, 1948).

[64] Ulli Beier, *The talking drums of the Yoruba*, in *African Music*, vol. 1 (1954) No. 1, p. 29.

[65] George Herzog, *Speech-melody and primitive music*, in *The Musical Quarterly*, vol. 20 (1934), p. 453. – Also A. M. Jones, *African music*, Livingstone, 1949, pp. 11 ff.

[66] Joseph Kyagambiddwa, *African music from the source of the Nile*, New York, 1955, pp. 22 ff.

Speech, as a consequence, can often be understood without words. In northern Transvaal, the Venda, who are not allowed to speak during initiation ceremonies, communicate satisfactorily by whistling; and a similar expedient is reported from the Isle of Gomera in the Canaries.[67] There is an almost exact analogy on European ground. Scandinavian herdspeople substitute voices for horns and horns for voices, and even the vocal melody "did not need a text to be quite understood by people and cattle as a signal of command and of recognition.[68]

An inverse substitution is the so-called mouth music on the Hebrides.[69] Bagpipes, as a symbol and stimulant of Scotch nationalism, were prohibited for some time after the Scots had risen in 1745 to throw off the English yoke. Their lilts and dances, however, were imitated vocally and are sung to this day on the Hebrides alongside with the redeemed pipes.

With all these substitutions we are in the midst of the important horn-, drum-, whistle-, and slit-drum languages in Melanesia, Africa, and South America, all based on the realistic imitation of speech-pitches and rhythms, not on conventional Morse codes with symbols long and short. Of greatest consequence are the slit-drum languages. Their renditions are particularly faithful as the drum lips alongside the slit are bevelled off at changing angles to render different pitches – up to six [70] – so that the striking sticks can easily reproduce all the intricacies of speech melodies. George Herzog has given us a detailed analysis of a four-note horn-language in Liberia and asserts that on the whole it renders actual speech tones; [71] and so does Herbert

[67] Percival R. Kirby, *Primitive music*, in George Grove, *Dictionary of music and musicians*, New York, 1955, vol. 6, pp. 921 ff. – Cf., as an older source, Richard Wallaschek, *Primitive music*, London 1893, and in German, as *Anfänge der Musik*, Leipzig 1903, p. 33 in either ed. – For Gomera see: A. Classe, *The Silbo Gomero*, in *Scientific American*, 1956, and *id.*, *Phonetics of the Silbo Gomero* in *Archivum Linguisticum*, vol. 9 (Glasgow, 1957), pp. 44 ff.

[68] Carl-Allan Moberg, *Om vallåtar*, in *Svensk Tidskrift för Musikforskning*, vol. 37 (1955), pp. 28 ff., 94. – *EFw* FM 4008 (P 1008) II 6 (Norway). – Liv Greni, *Ueber Vokaltradition in norwegischer Volksmusik*, in *Les Colloques de Wégimont*, vol. 1 (1954-5) pp. 154 ff.

[69] *EFw* FE 4430 (P 430) I 3.

[70] Dorothy R. Gilbert, *The lukumbi, a six-toned slit drum of the Batetela*, in *African Music*, vol. 1 (1955) no. 2 pp. 21-23.

[71] George Herzog, *Speech melody and primitive music*, in *The Musical Quarterly*, vol. 20 (1934), pp. 454 ff.

Pepper for Central Africa.[72] Only Henri Labouret, who studied the whistle languages of tribes to the north of the Gulf of Guinea, tells us how one of them comprised merely two pitches; the signals, he thinks, are purely conventional.[73]

This is in a way confirmed when André Schaeffner reports from the same region that its drum language consists in *formules rhythmo-mélodiques* equivalent of words without any phonetic connection with spoken language.[74] This would bring at least one kind of drum language into the neighborhood of the vocabulary of our military bugle languages.

The exchange between words and instrumental sounds can even assume three phases: vocal – instrumental – vocal. In Africa, it would occur that at first the words of a message are translated into slit-drum beats, that, however, in the momentary absence of such an instrument its message is shouted – not in the original, pre-instrumental words, but in syllables, like *ke, ki, le,* or *li,* which render the beats of the translation into the drum message.[75]

The Gulf of Guinea extends language imitation even to the so-called musical bow – a simple bow like that of an archer, whose string can be stopped at various places with a tiny stick and struck with another stick, while an end of the wood is held in the player's mouth to get audibility, resonance, and changing pitches. One such bow piece, from the Bassa in Liberia, has been recorded; [76] the story that the seemingly so barren single string relates is no less than eighteen lines long.

A bow language existed in Hawaii as well.[77]

To the mutual assimilations of vocal and instrumental melodies, of speech and of music, we could easily add the case of Vedic cantillation in the liturgy of India, where "the transition from speaking to singing, and back to language is so continuous

---

[72] Herbert Pepper, *Musique Centre-africaine*, in *Encyclopédie Coloniale et Maritime*, vol. *Afrique Equatoriale Française* (1950).

[73] Henri Labouret, *Les tribus du Rameau Lobi*, Paris, 1931, pp. 195 ff.

[74] André Schaeffner, *Les Kissi*, Paris, 1951, pp. 26–47.

[75] For a fairly exhaustive bibliography of drum languages (up to Aug. 31st. 1958) see Jaap Kunst, *Ethnomusicology* 3rd. ed., The Hague 1959, and its *Supplement*, ibid. 1960, s.v. talking drums.

[76] *EFw* FE 4465 (P 465) I 4. – Cf. also Schaeffner, *l.c.*, p. 64.

[77] Helen H. Roberts, *Ancient Hawaiian music*, no. 29 of the *Bernice P. Bishop Museum Bulletin*, Honolulu, 1926, pp. 18 ff. – Edwin G. Burrows, *Polynesian music and dancing*, in *The Journal of the Polynesian Society*, vol. 49 (1940), pp. 334 ff.

that a definite line of demarcation cannot be drawn." The quoted authority goes on: "The Hindu [*Inder*] have in their speech enunciation a distinct trend toward musical intonation, indeed a rudimentary recitative [*Sprechgesang*] – an impression confirmed in personal dealings with Indians." [78]

There are counterexamples, to be sure. In Amerindian melodies, the accents "do not always correspond to the accents in the words of a song when spoken." [79] And modern Chinese music can be so diametrically opposed to spoken language and so little concerned with the tones of speech that theaters distribute the texts of their operas which otherwise would be incomprehensible in their melodic disguise.

But even if there were no deviations from speech, what do these speech inflections prove or, for that matter, Monteverdi's *stile recitativo e rappresentativo* and Wagner's *Sprechgesang*? Is there a proof that speech inflections preceded singing? And if they did? *Post hoc, ergo propter hoc*, 'after this and hence on account of it,' is the worst of arguing fallacies. Musical imitation of language at any time does not evince a linguistic origin of music.

Even an original identity of music and language cannot be accepted. Had it existed, the separation of the two could only have happened in order to build up two very different forms of utterance: an emotional idiom (singing) as distinct from a communicative idiom (speaking). But, as far as we can judge, a good deal of primitive music remains totally unemotional, while language is often emotional, excited, and passionate. Furthermore: birds sing, too, and therewith testify to the existence of melody in the realm of animals; but no animal has an articulate language of vowels and consonants or words and sentences beyond impetuous sounds like grunting, barking, or roaring. The sounds of mamals are quite unmelodious; and the calls and twitters of birds have in their well-patterned uniformity hardly a linguistic quality: "language proper is culture, and out of the reach of the birds." [80] In the world antedating the age

[78] Erwin Felber, *Die indische Musik der vedischen und der klassischen Zeit*, in *Sitzungsberichte der Kais. Akademie der Wissenschaften in Wien*, Phil.-Hist. Kl., vol. 152 (1912), pp. 9, 10.
[79] Frances Densmore, *The study of Indian music*, in *Smithsonian Report* for 1941, Washington, 1942, p. 544.
[80] William Howells, *Back of history*, Garden City, 1954, p. 56.

of man, the precursors of language and the precursors of music are distinctly separate. Why should man have unified the two, only to sever them anew?

In the face of so many chance opinions without any proven facts we are resigned to leave the puzzling question alone, instead of presenting mere suggestions with the air of authority – just as the linguists, too, have shelved the once so urgent question of the origin of languages and abandoned the speculative reconstruction of presumptive ancestors, like Ur-Indoeuropean or aboriginal Semitic.

A chapter on origins must not overlook that early travel literature occasionally reports the total absence of singing and dancing from the lives of certain tribes.[81] Such statements might all too readily be accepted as a proof, or at least as an indication, that music and the dance developed only in later stages of culture. Such accounts must however be read with a good amount of scepticism. They are nowhere supported by facts, just as "early reports of peoples lacking language or fire, morals or religion, marriage or government, have been proved erroneous in every instance." [82] At best, such statements could be due to cultural shrinkage under adverse circumstances; but it is more probable that they derive from the explorer's failure to hear any music or see any dance while visiting the tribes. For unless the white man from abroad has been accepted as a reliable friend, the primitives often shy from exhibiting their sacred songs and dances; rather they pretend that they have none.

THE QUESTION OF ORIGIN cannot be solved. The beginnings of music are lost in the days of yore, as are the rudiments of speech, religion, and the dance. All we can achieve is to follow these manifestations back to the time when the curtain slowly rose over the earliest act of mankind's history.

Even here, the difficulties of arriving at an answer are obvious and insurmountable. Music, fleeting and evanescent, has left

[81] e.g. the Charrúa in Uruguay and the Guaraní in Argentina. Cf. Don Felix de Azara, *Reisen in dem südlichen Amerika, 1781–1801*, in *Journal für die neuesten Land und Seereisen*, vol. 6 (1813), pp. 77 ff., 111. – Also two Brazilian tribes, recently discovered by Hans Becher (New York Times Aug. 7, 1958).

[82] George P. Murdock, *Universals of culture*, 1946, reprinted in, and quoted from, Hoebel, Jennings, Smith, *Readings in anthropology*, New York, 1955, p. 4.

no trace but those surviving in the tenacious traditions of living people. To detect these traces and to exploit the hints they might give, we must of necessity join the non-musical scholars who wrestle with the thorny problems of culture in times that ante-date history proper: the prehistorians and the anthropologists or ethnologists.

THE PREHISTORIAN works in a vertical way: he excavates the tombs and fireplaces of ages long past – the deeper they lie the older they are. By and large they divide the older parts of pre-history into three Stone Ages. The Older Stone Age or Palaeolithic Era and the Newer Stone Age or Neolithic Era, with a connecting Middle Stone Age or Mesolithic Era. The Older Stone Age may have begun more than half a million years ago; the Mesolithic, tentatively, twenty thousand years ago; and the Neolithic about seventy-five hundred years before the present. But the dates differ from region to region, and the whole stratification applies in the first place to western Europe and not necessarily to other countries and continents.[83] Thus the prehistorian's chronology, connecting the excavated strata in terms of time, is more or less relative: he operates with the concepts 'before' and 'after' without providing accurate years or centuries.

Recently, it is true, the so-called radio-carbon or C[14] method, developed in the United States by Willard F. Libby, Hans Suess, Meyer Rubin, and others, in the Netherlands by Hessel de Vries, has begun to provide absolute dates if the fossils are organic matter and not older than 30,000 years.[84] Since half of the radioactive carbon 14 in a fossil decays at a rate of about 5,570 years, the amount still found provide the age of the fossil. The unqualified reliability of the method has just been challenged by Frederick E. Zeuner at the University of London: alkali might wash out some of the carbon 14 and therewith cause the illusion of greater age.[85]

Another modern method of approximate dating consists in

[83] This chronology follows Garrod, Zeuner, and Braidwood, as quoted in Melville J. Herskovits, *Cultural anthropology*, New York, 1955, p. 38.
[84] Willard F. Libby, *Radiocarbon dating*, Chicago, 1952. – Also: Robert F. Heizer, in A. L. Kroeber, *Anthropology today*, Chicago, 1953, pp. 14–17, and in Hoebel, Jennings, Smith, *Readings in Anthropology*, New York, 1955, pp. 54–58, with bibliography.
[85] The New York Times, Sunday, February 3, 1957, p. 15.

testing the amount of fluorine, a non-metallic element that bones absorb during their underground stay.

The enormous spans before the use of metal are called the Stone Age, as man, still ignorant of melting and molding metals or else residing in regions without ores, used stone to shape his weapons, tools and implements. In the Palaeolithic and Mesolithic, such stones were simply though carefully chipped; in the Neolithic, they were elaborately polished. But this distinction in which we once believed is no longer quite valid. Often, techniques overlapped; polished stone might still belong to an age otherwise palaeolithic, and chipped stone survived in the Neolithic. Nor must it be forgotten that a stone age pattern of culture could easily exist without much stone in evidence: in tropical countries, other substances, like gourds, bamboo, and coconut shells and, generally, bones and wood permitted to live without the cumbersome chipping of stones. Bones excepted, excavators will hardly find their traces; for objects so perishable do not resist the rot of thousands and ten-thousands of years. For this reason, archery, with its wood-and-fiber bows and slight and slender shafts, had completely disappeared from palaeolithic layers and was attributed to neolithic cultures exclusively, until prehistorians found Old Stone Age arrowheads and saw the bows unmistakably depicted on cave murals of the Upper Palaeolithic and the Mesolithic.

The Neolithic revolution added houses, probably basketry, agriculture, and the domestication of animals other than the dog, who had already been tamed in the Palaeolithic.[86] Pottery, at least in Africa, can no longer be credited to the Neolithic Age; it is common in the Mesolithic times of that continent and seems to have been invented in the Upper Palaeolithic.[87]

In due time, the potentialities of ore were discovered, and such metals as copper, copper-tin bronze (about 3500 years ago), and iron (about 2500 years ago) superseded primeval stone, bamboo, and wood, and material civilization assumed historical forms. But even in metal times, two classes often continued using stone: the humbler layers of society, for reason of cheapness, and the performers of religious rituals, for reasons of tradition.

[86] But cf. Richard Thurnwald, *Repräsentative Lebensbilder von Naturvölkern*, vol. 1 of *Die menschliche Gesellschaft*, Berlin, 1931, p. 25.

[87] Sonia Cole, *The prehistory of East Africa*, New York, 1954, pp. 26, 191.

ANTHROPOLOGY ENTERS THE PICTURE at this point. For in the coexistence of Stone and Metal Age in the same society, we face the principal topic of cultural anthropology: the cultural lag, which even in our present time has caused essential parts of humanity to live in conditions and forms that high civilizations have left innumerably long ago. Thus the anthropologist gains a synopsis of the various successive civilizations living alongside on the present surface of the earth. What to the prehistorian is a dim progression in hundred-thousands of years, is to the anthropologist a lucid, live existence side by side.

Indeed, in defiance of our gigantic advance to the Iron, the Electric, and the Atomic Ages, tribal groups, retired to refuge areas in impenetrable virgin forests, have to this day persisted in the Stone Age existence that their ancestors might have lived some ten or a hundred thousands years ago.

Thus we find palaeolithic survivals all over the world, in single traits as well as in almost the whole of culture. Asian and African pygmies, the Botocudos in eastern Brazil, most Fuegians, and many other peoples can be termed palaeolithic. They all are food gatherers and nomadic hunters with blowguns or arrows; they use chipped stone implements and, instead of huts, protective roofs or wind-screens; they go stark naked or nearly so and do not practice farming or pottery.

Mesolithic and neolithic survivals are by far more frequent than palaeolithic remainders.

It might be wise to make the present tense in all these statements tentative. Many of the authoritative monographs from which we derive our knowledge of these peoples were written half a century ago. In the meantime, much of the seclusion and cultural retard found on the threshold of this century may have come to a partial or total end. This handy present tense is after all nothing else but what Chapple and C. S. Coon once called the "ethnographic present." Indeed, "it is unlikely that a tribe will behave in 1953 in the way in which an observer described it in 1883 or even 1923." [88]

While writing these lines, I received a letter from Georges Condominas, discoverer of the sounding stones in the *Musée de l'Homme* in Paris. As to Madagascar, he says, I would be

[88] J. Manchip White, *Anthropology*, New York, 1955, p. 171.

disappointed – "I have seen only few instruments you have described; acculturation on the High Plateaux is very strong." [89]

Rigid, immutable cultures do not exist; all civilizations have been open to change and renovation, in the past as well as today. Intertribal contact was unavoidable; palaeolithic men were nomads who under the pressure of changing climates or depleted stocks of game would cover enormous territories and encroach on grounds that other people claimed; many tribes demanded exogamy or marriage outside of the group; interpenetration, neighborly barter, warfare did the rest. Weapons, tools, and implements as well as habits, thoughts, and melodies [90] were freely exchanged, and most civilizations are so thoroughly and differently mixed that every human group and even every single man represents an individual mixture.

CULTURES HAVE CHANGED in the last half century, and with the cultures, the two sciences in charge of them, anthropology and prehistory. Much of the rigid dogmatism·in their beginnings is no longer valid, and the whole picture of development and coëxistence has grown more flexible. It is the normal trend that a new generation of scholars oppose the views of their predecessors. For "in science as in life, it is a good practice to attach from time to time a question mark to the facts one takes most for granted, to question the fundamental postulates or facts which require no demonstration; for a fact as a postulate is largely the opinion of those who should know – and those who should know are but human, and therefore liable to err." [91]

This reaction seems to climax in the apodictic statement that contemporary primitive societies "were preceded by other forms of society of which we can learn nothing, even indirectly ... we can know only certain aspects of a vanished civilization." [92] This ultra-sceptical attitude betrays an assumption that the elements of a civilization are unrelated and therefore not indicative of the whole; and such an assumption makes of culture

---

[89] Paris, Dec. 21, 1956.
[90] Cf., e.g. Jaap Kunst, *A Study on Papuan Music* (Weltevreden, 1931), pp. 37–38; A. M. Jones, *African music*, Livingstone, 1949, p. 16.
[91] M. F. Ashley Montagu, *Man's most dangerous myth*, 3rd ed., New York, 1952, p. 33.
[92] Claude Lévi-Strauss. *Race and history*, Paris, 1952, pp. 8, 17.

history a mere kaleidoscope in which a number of colored bits of glass unite in ever new, entirely haphazard combinations. This would be regrettable. Less sceptical scholars will rest satisfied with the conviction that certain forms of civilization – like the lack of clothing, of huts, and of planting – are coherent elements of a well defined cultural pattern and exclude potential components of a contradictory quality. We do not need the total number of bones to reconstruct the skeleton of an extinct mammal or, for that matter, of a culture.

And we should be builders, not wreckers.

In a wiser, up-to-date discussion of these problems, Melville J. Herskovits makes the concession, so valuable from the pen of a critical master: "Inference is a workable and useful tool if held within its limitations." [93] And beyond the Atlantic, Richard Thurnwald has concluded in complete agreement that, though the facts at the bottom of comparisons are only similar and never entirely identical, careful conclusions are possible and advisable.[94]

ARCHAIC CULTURE AND MAN HIMSELF, the man whom prehistory and anthropology tried to portray, have changed their valuation. The naive and arrogant underestimation and misunderstanding of these cultures and men created in the sixteenth century the beginning colonial exploitation, which needed an alibi for its bestial crimes by proving that the "natives" were at best subhuman. It made me feel ashamed for our time when I found that as early as 1758 a French colonial officer who saw and described the impressive burial customs of the Natchez Indians in Louisiana protested against the brutal word savage.[95]

'Primitive' men – as we usually call them today – live infinitely closer to unharnessed nature than do we;[96] and they live without the help of organized, scientific thinking. Though firmly guided by experience and oral tradition, they have no insight

[93] Melville J. Herskovits, *Cultural anthropology*, New York, 1955, chapter 3 and p. 32.
[94] Richard Thurnwald, *o.c.*, vol. 1, *Repräsentative Lebensbilder von Naturvölkern*, Berlin, 1931, p. 88.
[95] Le Page du Pratz, *Histoire de la Louisiane*, Paris, 1758, in John R. Swanton's English translation reprinted in Hoebel, Jennings, Smith, *Readings in Anthropology*, New York, 1955, p. 254.
[96] Cf. the significant title of Richard Thurnwald's book *Der Mensch geringer Naturbeherrschung*, Berlin, 1950.

into the complex connection of cause and effect. Still, no human being can lead the life of a beast. No human being is devoid of civilization; for it is just civilization that separates men from animals. Even on his lowest perceptible level man speaks rich, involved languages, devises elaborate weapons, tools, and implements, has proto-religious ideas, organizes tightly knit societies, and follows ethical rules. For lack of a better name, we may best call aboriginal man a primitive, and his civilization, low. But the epithet low is definitely an undesirable discrimination. Even 'primitive' implies too much of an order of precedence to be to the taste of modern anthropology, and many writers prefix it with an embarrassed, face-saving 'so-called.' The term archaic might be preferable.

Some recent scholars have taken refuge in the appellations scriptless and non-literate (as distinct from illiterates within a literate society). But the prefix non- and the suffix -less, of themselves correct, give even to these qualities a negative and hence disparaging tint. A glance at the Middle Ages confirms our hesitation. Charlemagne, resplendent king of the Franks and emperor of the Holy Roman Empire, tried in vain to learn the difficult art of writing. Indeed, all through the earlier Middle Ages hardly anyone except a few monks and cleric-scribes was able to read or to write: as late as the thirteenth century, the knightly *minnesinger* Walter von der Vogelweide was expressly praised for writing his verses in his own hand. Not to speak of the appalling majorities of illiterates in allegedly literate civilizations both in the East and the West.[97]

With all these reservations, the importance of script as a criterion of culture cannot easily be overrated. Originally devised to carry the memory of kings and their feats beyond the lifespans of men and dynasties, although to a certain degree also to keep account ledgers in trade, it has more and more become a surrogate of memory. We write, not only what we want to communicate to other people for lack of oral contact, but also that which we ourselves fear will be forgotten. Ancient nations chiseled monumental inscriptions in stone; we moderns have notebooks and calendars, as the complex character of modern civilization has

[97] Cf. the terminology in Mieczyslaw Kolinski, *The determinants of tonal construction in tribal music*, in *The Musical Quarterly*, vol. 43 (1957), pp. 50 ff.

forced us to disburden our memories. Writing has allowed us to remember as well as to forget.

It is evident that the growing transfer from memory to reading means objectivation, indeed, mechanization. As long as no written records interfere, the reproduction of something remembered involves production: the Homeric bard precedes the prose reports of Herodotos; history is still a poet's epos, and Clio, its Muse, stands on the Parnassos next to Erato, the patron of lyrics. Reproduction from memory is rarely mechanical; it has the prerogative of poetical license, reflects the personality of the relator, is often imaginative, and sometimes presents us with pieces of immortal creation.

If we justly replace 'relator' by 'singer,' we carry the contrast of scriptless and literate into the musical field.

Scriptless societies have, as a matter of course, no way of notating music; the oldest notations of which we have knowledge – Babylonian, early Jewish, Vedic, Greek, and others – draw their signs from the symbols of current alphabets. But the sentence cannot be inverted: music without notation is not limited to scriptless societies. Many ancient notations were merely devised by priests for priests and cantors, and some were even kept secret: "The initiated may show it to the uninitiated." [98] While in religious music notation had a definite place in order to prevent the present and future generations from breaking sacred traditions, secular music relied on free invention and memory, in the high civilization of the West as well as in those of the East. Notation became indispensable only under the pressure of worked-out polyphony. Still, in and outside the polyphonic style the script was sketchy even in Europe; the chord-improvising 'realizers' of figured basses during the Baroque Age were just given a fundamental bass-part to build upon to the best of their skill and imagination; and the melody singers and players of the same era performed from a skeletal script which left to everyone the right and the duty to embellish and vary the script at his discretion or, in the words of the Flemish musician Adriaen Petit Coclicus (1552), to spice the meat with salt and mustard. Improvisation on the spur of the moment

[98] Curt Sachs, *The mystery of the Babylonian notation*, in *The Musical Quarterly*, vol. 27 (1941), pp. 62–9.

reached into the nineteenth century, and even today a scriptless performance is, at least in principle, expected in the cadenza of a concerto. But the sparse survivals of improvisation practice do not change the vital fact that western art music is literate: extant originals bind the performer and force him into obedience.

An actually scriptless tradition lives only in folkmusic. No composer writes it down to have it played; but, inversely, a notation that we may find, is taken from live performance; the melodies follow oral tradition and are at the same time open to wide individual and regional changes.

Beyond its musical scriptlessness, folk music on the whole cannot be easily reconciled with general literacy. With exceptions, it is most authentic, best, and richest in times and regions where illiteracy prevails. Evidence are the South of the States and the South and the East of Europe. This is easy enough to explain: the backbone of a scriptless culture are tradition and memory; both vanish under the impact of general literacy, and with them fade the imagination and creativeness of uneducated performers. Literacy and folk art bloom in inverse ratio.

THE FUNDAMENTAL PROBLEMS of human early history, it appears, are equally less in the foreground of our thinking and hence less rigidly answered. The basic alternative of monogenism and polygenism, that is, the opposite theories that all mankind has descended from one single ancestral type or else from several of them, has for the moment not the importance it was given in the nineteenth century. The question in how far cultural elements spread in 'diffusion' from one people to other through marriage, war, and trade, or developed by 'evolution' or innate disposition, finds individual answers rather than dogmatic decisions and sweeping generalizations. And a worldwide organization of culture patterns, as in the German *Kulturkreis-Lehre*, is met with admiration, but also with scepticism. Most suspicious are we of the slippery and often criminally exploited concept of 'race,' in which biologically transmitted genes are all the time confused with environmental culture.[99] "The word 'race' has been so

---

[99] The venerable sire of a none too brilliant family of musical racists is François-Joseph Fétis, *Sur un nouveau mode de classification des races humaines d'après leurs systèmes musicaux*, in *Bulletins de la Société d'Anthropologie*, n.s., vol. 2, Paris, 1867.

abused that it has become at once meaningless and too full of meaning." [100]

All these concepts will be rarely found in this book – not from want of daring on the author's part, but from a hardwon insight into the unbelievably complicated and treacherous web of ever-changing cultures, tribal nomadism, and unidentifiable mergers of patterns. Besides, musicologists, as spokesmen of a small, however significant component of culture, can at best be expert witnesses in this lingering lawsuit but hardly judges or jurors.

---

[100] J. E. Manchip White, *Anthropology*, New York, 1955, p. 73.

TWO

EARLY MUSIC

V. THE OLDEST MUSIC: TUMBLING STRAINS

Turning to music proper, we face the old trouble of all musical writing: descriptions of musical works and styles are hard to put in words, even harder to read and absorb, and almost impossible to translate into actual images. Yet, the issue cannot be avoided and the attempt must be made. But the reader should recur to good recordings as often as possible.

In describing non-western music, be it oriental or primitive, one must strictly refrain from misusing incongruous concepts of western music. The terminology that has been learned in music school applies to a harmonic structure of music and is inappropriate, indeed misleading and distorting in descriptions of non-harmonic, non-western music.

Most unjustifiable is placing the current labels 'major' and 'minor' on non-western melodies, according to whether the note the describer thinks more or less rightfully to be the third is at a major or minor distance from the alleged 'tonic.'[1] How does he act when the third, as so often, is larger than the minor third of our pianos or else sensibly shorter than the major third, or, as a so-called neutral third, just in the middle between them? Is that Dirge of the Eagles in northern British Columbia [2] 'major' or 'minor'? The note *c*, in this case the third without a doubt, is in Marius Barbeau's transcription now natural, now slightly heightened by a little + sign, now even more sharped by a bracketed sharp over a plus, now fully sharped. In other words, the third is disconcertingly vague. And this is not the only example of thirds that refuse to be crammed into our major-

---

[1] As a shocking example, I recommend the reading of the Minor and Major chapter in Richard Wallaschek, *Primitive music* (London 1893) and *Anfänge der Musik* (Leipzig 1903).

[2] Marius Barbeau, *Asiatic survivals in Indian song*, in *The Musical Quarterly*, vol. 20 (1934), p. 111.

minor dualism. Our 'blue' notes pose a similar problem. Moreover, major and minor are almost inseparable from a harmonic
system foreign to the primitives and apt to misrepresent their
musical language. To understand this idiom, follow the advice
of Wagner's Hans Sachs:

> *Der eignen Spur vergessend,*
> *Such davon erst die Regeln auf.*
> (Away from course and custom,
> Do find the standards of its own).

Still worse than simply dubbing primitive melodies 'major'
or 'minor' is the amateurish habit of conferring ready-made
moods upon them in line with the unfounded belief of the West
that major must be gay and minor sad. Small wonder that on
reading such abuses of *Affektenlehre*, pseudo-aesthetics, and
Music Appreciation, one is under the impression that nine tenths
or more of all the world's humanity are deeply melancholy.
As a rule, such lamentable sadness is ascribed to a depressing
environment. But I am afraid that this environmental depression
applies to the visitor from Europe much more than to the well-
acclimatized natives of the endless steppes and *llanos*. Religion,
too, is not entirely absent from the causes of sadness. Many
decades ago, I read in the dictionary of some East African language, compiled by a French missionary – the author's name and
book unfortunately long forgotten – that all the native tunes
were in minor because the joyousness of major is denied to everybody who does not believe in the Christian God. I refrain from
commenting and leave the answer to those familiar with the
Gregorian chant.

Incidentally, not even in the West is minor a compulsory
mode of mourning, and vice-versa. Many definitely mournful
pieces are written in the major mode – at random: Lasso's
Tragico tecti syrmate and *Tristis est anima mea*, Hans Leo
Hassler's later hymnalized *Innsbruck ich muss dich lassen*, Marin
Marais' beautiful *Tombeau pour Lully* for viol and harpsichord,
a *Plainte* by François Couperin le Grand, the dead march in
Handel's oratorio *Saul*, and, in the nineteenth century, Silcher's
popular melody for Heinrich Heine's *Lorelei*.

THE OLDEST PIECES of music, it must be emphasized, are purely vocal and, hence, pure melodies.

Since the concept of melody is far from being unambiguous, it might here be defined as the audible movement of a singing voice (or, much later, of an instrument) from the beginning of a piece through all successive steps to its end. But beyond the lifeless sum total of its individual steps, we take for granted that such a movement be an organic, living whole with breath and flow, with tension and relaxation. It is not necessarily 'melodious' or sweet-sounding, as the opera fans demand and the dictionaries set forth. (Whether or not the metrical values of the notes in a melody should enter the definition is irrelevant as long as we limit our discussion to primitive music).

But even on the earliest level, a melody is never anarchic or arbitrary. It follows certain, almost unbreakable rules.

As a consequence of this lawfulness, the surviving tribes of palaeolithic culture use two clear-cut styles side by side; and they do it without geographic divide, in whatever part of the world they might have settled.

The most fascinating of the oldest melody patterns may be described as a 'tumbling strain.' Its character is wild and violent: after a leap up to the highest available note in screaming fortissimo, the voice rattles down by jumps or steps or glides to a pianissimo respite on a couple of the lowest, almost inaudible notes; then, in a mighty leap, it resumes the highest note to repeat this cascade as often as necessary. In their most emotional and least 'melodious' form, such strains recall nearly inhuman, savage shouts of joy or wails of rage and may derive from such unbridled outbursts.

The crudest style of this kind of melody seems to be preserved in Australia. Midway between howling and singing, it is described by an ear witness as performed with "frenzy" and "spasm" in a "steadily growing excitement" and with a "good deal of passion." [3]

Today, we possess an easily accessible North Australian

[3] E. Harold Davies, *Aboriginal songs of Central and Southern Austrialia*, in *Oceania*, vol. 2 (1932), pp. 454–467. – Cf. also Trevor A. Jones, *Arnhem Land music* in *Oceania*, vol. 26 (1956), p. 336, republished in A. P. Elkin and Trevor A. Jones, *Arnhemland Music* (Oceania Monograph No. 9), Sydney, 1957.

recording,[4] in which the soloist starts his cascade in a fortissimo falsetto on *e″* while several voices throw in the lower third *c″*. After a long *sostenuto*, he reaches up for *g″* and tumbles in an audacious curve to a final *c′*, as shown in the following illustration:

Ex. 3*

This music carries meaningless syllables, but no words; it is purely emotional and keeps completely independent of the definiteness of words.

While such fierce haphazard cascades can hardly be transcribed in the neat notation of the West, others, in almost every part of the globe, are less turbulent and at a pinch accessible to our five-line staffs. Nowhere are these tamer 'stair melodies' more impressive than among the North American Indians – in the Northwest as well as in the Southwest.[5] The most beautiful of them, full of noble pathos and powerful passion and yet restrained and solemn, is of particular historical interest, as it belongs to the earliest set of melodies ever recorded by a phonograph.[6] It was sung by the Zuñi in New Mexico and spans the amazing range of more than two octaves in an essentially tertial organization.

Ex. 4

It also was very probably a tumbling strain when in the eighteenth century women of the now extinct Abipón in Argen-

* Transcr. C. S.

4 *EFw* FE 4439 (P 439) II 3.

5 Cf. e.g. Garfield, Wingert, Barbeau, *The Tsimshian*, New York, 1952, example no. 64. – Also David P. McAllester, *Enemy Way Music*, Cambridge (Mass.), 1954, no. 14.

6 Benjamin Ives Gilman, *Zuñi melodies*, in *Journal of American Archaeology and Ethnology*, vol. 1 (1891). – Carl Stumpf, *Phonographi(e)rte Indianermelodien*, in *Vierteljahrsschrift für Musikwissenschaft*, vol. 8 (1892), pp. 134 ff., and in *Sammelbände für vergleichende Musikwissenschaft*, vol. 1 (1922), p. 120.

tina, they too lamenting their dead, toppled down from the highest to the lowest note and did it with whistling hisses (*ein pfeifendes Gezische*).[7]

The Indians may have obtained their tumbling strains from Asia via the Bering Strait: Marius Barbeau found a Japanese tune closely resembling some of the Yukon and of northern British Columbia. At the beginning, he says, it "scaled a high curve, touched a top note, then dropped over wide intervals to the bottom, where it droned leisurely just as do the tunes of a number of typical Indian songs." Unfortunately, Barbeau gives no notation of the Japanese melody;[8] but his description is unmistakable and would be fully convincing if it were supported by more and better evidences.

A similar example, from a Japanese *no* play,[9] looks more convincing. Anyway, the closely related folksong of Korea has definitely tumbling strains.[10]

The instrumental music of Japan as we know it today has occasionally a remarkable kinship to vocal tumbling strains. The following piece of theatrical music, played on the popular three-stringed lute or *samisen*,[11] descends in all its phrases and from the depth leaps back to the upper octave or even the double octave *e″*.

Ex. 5

Altogether, the majestic strains of the Indians remind us of the melodies we hear when Polynesians wail for their dead. Excitedly, the voice would leap up no less than two octaves and reach the three-lined *c* sharp.[12]

[7] Martin Dobrizhoffer, *Geschichte der Abiponer*, vol. 2, Wien, 1783, p. 367.

[8] Marius Barbeau, *Asiatic survivals in Indian song*, in *The Musical Quarterly*, vol. 20 (1934), p. 108.

[9] Constantin Brailoiu, *Sur une mélodie russe* in Pierre Souvtchinsky (ed.), *Musique Russe*, II, Paris, 1953, p. 380, no. 176.

[10] *EFw* FE 4424 (P 424) I 6.

[11] From: O. Abraham and E. von Hornbostel, *Tonsystem und Musik der Japaner*, in *Sammelbände der Internationalen Musikgesellschaft*, vol. 4 (1903), p. 349 no. 2, and in *Sammelbände für vergleichende Musikwissenschaft*, vol. 1 (1922), p. 222 no. 2.

[12] E. G. Burrows, *Songs of Uvea and Futuna*, in *Bernice P. Bishop Museum Bulletin*, vol. 183, Honolulu, 1945, *passim*.

Edwin G. Burrows heard quite similar songs in 1947 on
Ifaluk Atoll in the Caroline Islands. Mourners were sitting by
a dying man. The wailing, while not regular, followed a general
pattern. "Starting on a high note (how high varies from a shrill
shriek to a medium tone), the voice descends in a whine, *portamento*, to a low pitch, repeated with slow, equal time value. Then
up a minor third for one tone, down again for one or more. This
rise and fall of a minor third sometimes repeated. Sometimes
all sang in unison. Again one group sang low, another
higher.
Several times, when I tested the interval between them, it was a
perfect fourth, or nearly enough to sound so to me. The interval
from the first high note to the low monotone varied, but was
often an octave or very near it. The last tone often broke into a
shuddering sob. At the end of some phrases, a short wail, one or
a few notes." [13]

On another occasion (January 15, 1948): "Each line of the
song – they are known songs, not improvisations, for all the
people sang the same words – was sung mainly on a monotone,
with the occasional rise of a minor third noted earlier. Sometimes
the rise amounted to a major third. Between each two lines was
a long cry, without definite pitch. There was great variation in
these. Some could be called shouts, other howls, still other
shrieks. Then the voice would drag down, *portamento*, to
the pitch on which the lines were being intoned. There
was some singing in parallel parts. Noted major third and
fourth."[14]

A PERIODIC, AUDACIOUS RECAPTURE of the higher octave is
the essential, identifying trait of tumbling strains, even on a
level as primitive as that of Australia and Torres Straits, not to
enumerate later habitats.[15] This is the more remarkable, as
outside the tumbling strains the octave is by no means a self-
evident interval in primitive music.

---

[13] *id.*, *Music on Ifaluk Atoll in the Caroline Islands*, in *Ethnomusicology*, vol. 2, (1958),
p. 10.

[14] *ib.*, p. 13.

[15] Samples in *EFw* FE 4428 (P 428) I 3, 6 (Watutsi); FE 4500 (P 500) I 1 (Zulu);
FE 4500 (P 500) B I 15, II 2, FE 4432 (P 432) I 6 (Haiti and Trinidad); FE 4401
(P 401) I 1, 3 b (Sioux); FE 4401 (P 401) II 2 (Navaho); FE 4445 (P 445) I 2, 7
(Flathead).

Ex. 6*

From the octave as the primary concept, tumbling strains developed by inner consolidation and not by accretion and expansion, as did the horizontal melodies to be discussed in the following section. The beginnings of this process were fierce and unruly, with the stepping stones inside the octave left to chance without an idea of scales and steps. Little by little the picturesque wildness yielded to a solid organization in recurrent distances, with a preference to either fifths or fourths or thirds.

TUMBLING STRAINS, with the forceful intonation of the highest notes and the subsequent flagging on a melodic descent, give an impressive example of physiologically conditioned changes in intensity. Indeed, everyone of our own singers and wind players knows the difficulties of intoning a high note softly and a low note with force.

It is tempting to attribute to such correlation of pitch and intensity the double meaning of the words high and low in quite a number of languages. Whoever learns French is told to read *à haute voix*, that is, aloud; and in a similar way our Italian teacher might recite his Dante *a voce alta*.[16] In late medieval France, *les instruments hauts*, as trumpets, drums, and shawms, were penetrating and served outdoors; *les instruments bas*, as strings and flutes, were soft enough for indoor use. And to find our way back to the archaic level: the Bellacoola Indians in British Columbia have likewise one word for strong and high, and one for soft and low.[17] In the Pacific, the Hawaiians have

* Watutsi, after Rose Brandel.

[16] High and low seem to be concepts of the West. The Bantu speak of small and great (Hugh Tracey, *The state of music in Bantu Africa*, in *African Music*, vol. 1 (1954), p. 9), as well as the Javanese (Jaap Kunst, *Music in Java*, The Hague 1949, vol. I p. 101). On the inversion of high and low in ancient Greece and the Semitic languages, cf. Curt Sachs, *The rise of music in the ancient world*, New York, 1943, pp. 69 ff.

[17] C. Stumpf, *Lieder der Bellakula-Indianer*, in *Vierteljahrsschrift für Musikwissenschaft*, vol. 2 (1886), p. 410, reprinted in *Sammelbände für vergleichende Musikwissenschaft*, vol. 1 (1922), p. 92.

exactly the same ambiguity. But when their voices "go high and low," they sing crescendo and diminuendo without any change of pitch within their one-note cantillation (cf. example 23 on p. 70).[18] Their shade of intensity is emotionally conditioned, not physiologically.

Otherwise, changes in intensity do not often occur in primitive music.

THE EVIDENTLY RAPID DOMESTICATION of tumbling strains has forced us to discuss in the same part on Early Music types of greater and of lesser age. In the interest of coherence, even more recent forms of tumbling strains should be outlined in this chapter, though they no longer are part of the lowest observable level of music.

As a rule, they cling to the old characteristics: that the octave stands out as the backbone of the skeleton; that again and again the melody leaps up to recapture the higher octave; and that within the octave certain descending intervals become established landings.

This establishment developed in two directions: a triadic or tertial and a tetrachordic or quartal pattern. The triadic pattern shall be our first topic.

A chronology of triadic octaves in the primitive world is not yet possible. Such melodies occur in every possible shade. Some appear in root and some in six-four position (to borrow terms from harmony). This amounts, in the terminology of scale structures, to 'authentic' and 'plagal' or, as I suggested in an earlier book, to fourth-over-fifth and to fifth-over-fourth melodies.[19] In either case we meet, now empty skeletons, now fully or partly heptatonic and diatonic structures.

Neat examples of tumbling strains organically transformed into triadic octaves are found in a recorded song of the Mandingo in Liberia. [20] and the following song of the Vogul, a Finnish people on the northern end of the divide between Europe and Asia.

Ex. 7*

---

* After Väisänen.

18 Helen H. Roberts, *Ancient Hawaiian music*, Honolulu, 1925.

19 Curt Sachs, *The rise of music in the ancient world*, New York, 1943, p. 65.

20 *EFw* FE 4465 (P 465) I 1.

The skeleton is empty but for an occasional 'infix' or filler [21] in the thirds. One would hardly suspect this 'civilized,' western melody to descend from tumbling strains – as it stands on paper, it could easily introduce some symphonic movement of Brahms. And yet it reminds us remotely of wild and passionate wails. For it has the unmistakable leap up to the top of the range, the cascade down to the lowest note and, again and again, the recapture of the upper octave and a repetition of the whole pattern.

The same traits occur, among many others, in melodies of the Navaho [22] and also of the Teton Sioux [23] which however have infixes and plagal structures, with the triad above and the tetrachord below.

It seems that tumbling strains developed even into formations of a mere sixth instead of the habitual octave, as in the following example from Ruanda in East Africa: [24]

Ex. 8

Indeed, on seeing Junod's old notation of a Baronga tune as he heard it, we are irresistibly tempted to call it a tumbling strain, although it has only four descending notes in the narrow ambitus of a fifth.[25] Beagle Bay Australians [26] and the Wanyamwezi in Central East Africa,[27] on the other hand, leap to the upper ninth or tenth:

Ex. 9

[21] Cf. Sachs, *l.c.*, p. 37.

[22] Musical examples in David P. McAllester, *Enemy Way music*, Cambridge (Mass.), 1954.

[23] Frances Densmore, *Teton Sioux music*, in *Bureau of American Ethnology Bulletin* 61. Washington 1918 no. 43.

[24] Erich M. von Hornbostel, *Gesänge aus Ruanda*, in *Wissenschaftliche Ergebnisse der deutschen Zentral-Afrika-Expedition 1907–08*, vol. 6 I (1917), ex. 8.

[25] Henri-A. Junod, *Les Ba-Ronga*, Neuchâtel, 1898, p. 146.

[26] Carl Stumpf, *Die Anfänge der Musik*, Leipzig, 1911, p. 122.

[27] Erich M. von Hornbostel, *Wanyamwezi-Gesänge*, in *Anthropos*, vol. 4 (1909), ex. 5.

At the end of this long migration, we meet a familiar melody
from ancient Greece, the *skolion* or drinking song of the Graeco-
Sicilian composer known as Seikilos: [28]

Ex. 10

The charming piece has the well-stressed range of an octave
in fifth-over-fourth arrangement. In Greek terminology, its mode
is Phrygian; counterpoint nomenclature would call it Hypo-
mixolydian. The lower fourth is pentatonic, the upper fifth,
heptatonic. Like a genuine tumbling strain, the melody leaps from
the *mesè* or tonal center up to the highest note and cascades
down to the final note an octave below. Eleven of the twelve
measures move within the upper fifth; and only the last measure
descends to the lower tetrachord. Strophic repetition, very
probable in so short a melody though, as a matter of course, not
carved in the tomb *stèlè* that has preserved the tune, would provide the recapture of the highest note by way of the *mesè*.

Around and behind this delightful song stand the untold
thousands of fifth-over-fourth melodies created between India
and Europe.

OPPOSED TO TRIADIC OCTAVES are the octaves formed by two
conjunct or disjunct tetrachords. These terms as well as a conjunct example of the Iroquois Indians with an appended octave
at the bottom will be discussed in the second-part section on
The Fate of Quartal and Quintal Patterns. Similar melodies are
sung by the Pawnee Indians.[29]

The following, disjunct example from Croatia betrays the
derivation from pristine tumbling strains in its definite descent
and its recapture of the higher octave:

[28] Printed in Curt Sachs, *The rise of music in the ancient world*, 1943, p. 245.
[29] Tracy's transcription in Alice Fletcher, *The Hako ceremony*, Washington,
1904, p. 103.

Ex. 11*

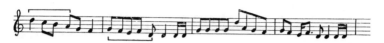

For once, we meet with the rare case of a development from the most aboriginal types to modern forms through a steadily growing organization from within and through interpenetration with other structural patterns.

VI. THE OLDEST MUSIC: ONE-STEP MELODIES

Side by side with tumbling strains, we meet on the lowest cultural level an apparently less emotional type of melody, which in its most rudimentary form consists of only two pitches sung in alternation. The voice moves up and down and more or less describes a horizontal zigzag line.[30]

The words alternation and zigzag might easily suggest a regular pendulum progression to and fro. Such shuttle motion does not exist, unless we think of a trill at moderate speed. Sometimes the upper and sometimes the lower note is struck more often and assumes the role of a principal, starter or final. This makes the melody either 'hanging' or 'standing':

Ex. 12**

Ex. 13***

* After Wiora.
** East Flores, after Jaap Kunst.
*** Eskimo, after Zygmunt Estreicher.
[30] Cf. Zygmunt Estreicher, *Teoria dwytonowych melodii*, in *Kwartalnik Muzycky* VI (Warschau, 1948). – General on form: Mieczyslaw Kolinski, *The structure of melodic movement, a new method of analysis*, in *Miscelánea de Estudios dedicados al Dr. Fernando Ortiz*, La Habana, 1956, pp. 881–918.

Ex. 14*

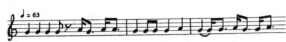

One note – as in example 14 – might be so predominant in importance and frequency, and the other note so subordinate, that we are tempted to speak of an appogiattura in the modern sense. Alternation, after all, demands a certain balance of the two notes, both in weight and in quantity.

A simple zigzag – up and down or down and up – might readily be labeled monotonous. In doing so, we use 'monotonous' in its current figurative sense but risk having it understood in the literal sense as a composite of *monos*, 'one' and *tonos*, 'tone.' With this ambiguity, the reader is caught in the cobweb of terminology and cannot be spared a few minutes of semantics for the sake of clarity and consistency.

SOME RECENT ETHNOMUSICOLOGICAL WRITINGS name the to and fro of two notes, not monotonic, but ditonic, which, de-Grecized, means 'of two tones.' Accordingly, they call the aggregates of three and more notes tritonic, tetratonic, and pentatonic. This is inadmissible or at least impractical and dangerously misleading.

The word ditonic is illicit for two reasons. Phonetically, ditonic differs from the everyday term diatonic merely by the absence of an *a*, which is in English pronunciation almost inaudible after *i*. Moreover, not many readers might realize that the first word derives from *di*, 'two,' and the second, from *dia*, 'through.'

The component 'tonic' is even worse, since, instead of one, it has no less than six different and even contradictory meanings. (1) In the form tonic, an adjective used as a noun, it stands for the main, gravitational pole of a harmonized or harmonizable melody. The original Greek noun, *tonos* (and hence, via Latin and Old French, our 'tone') is related to 'tension' and means (2) acoustically speaking, any regular sound as opposed to

* A women's dance from Ifaluk, Carolines, after George Herzog.

irregular noises; (3) the pitch, vibration number, or frequency of such a sound, say *C* or *C* sharp; (4) its color or timbre, warm or cool; (5) a melody pattern (like 'psalm-tone'); and (6) the distance or interval of a major second. There is a degree of danger in handling a word with six different meanings. In composition with *di*, it may become outright destructive; for in its Grecian homeland, as well as in the western Middle Ages, *ditonos* meant logically twice the distance of a major second and was the accepted term for the major third. Thus nobody should confuse the issue by re-introducing a well established term for something entirely different and even contradictory.

'Tritonic,' again, must not be used for a melody of three notes. In musical terminology, it has a place of long standing as the uncontested name for a succession of three wholetone steps, such as *F G A B* or, without the intermediaries, the stretch *F–B*, both in succession or as a dissonance.

The word pentatonic, on the contrary, is universally accepted to denote a scale (or melody) of only five steps *in the octave* – mostly, though by no means always, three seconds and two thirds, as in the Far East or in the Celtic countries.

We will studiously avoid such 'ambiguous' words, to make an understatement. Terminology is meant to clarify, not to confuse.

The concept that we need is 'step.' Its meaning is quite unequivocal; and, strictly speaking, no melody has 'tones' or 'notes'; as a form of musical *movement*, it is a series of steps (or even of leaps) while the notes are simply stations and terminals. All considered, we had much better call the primitive patterns one-step, two-step, three-step melodies, even if such terms, not being Greek, are somewhat less impressive.

To use at least a Latin-derived word, we could hardly denote the approximate size of the step as a secondal one-step melody, when the two alternating notes are a major or minor second apart; in a tertial one-step melody, a major, neutral, or minor third; in a quartal melody, a, usually descending, fourth; in a quintal melody, a fifth. Later on, after having met more complicated melodies, it will be easier to speak of single seconds, thirds, fourths, and fifths, as opposed to double, triple, quadruple, or quintuple such intervals.

WE DO NOT KNOW what factor determines the size of a tribal group's characteristic step. It is certainly not the degree of narrow-mindedness that early scholars ascribed to primitives: the narrower the mind, the narrower the step. This was an illicit equation. People do not stick to shallow secondal patterns because they stand on the lowest rung of the cultural ladder. Nor are the fourths and fifths reserved for bolder climbers. Often, a person's sex appears to be the shaping power; women seem to prefer a smaller step, just as they do in dancing, while men proceed in larger strides and leaps. Here and there, the customary motor habits of a tribe, so often conditioned by its way of life, might play a decisive role; or it might be the geologic formation of the habitat, as flat or mountainous, wide-open or enclosed; and, occasionally, even its climate. But whenever a satisfactory quantity of evidence seems to speak for one of these possibilities, there are always discrediting counterexamples which cannot be identified as justifiable exceptions. Thus, if little Eskimo girls sing empty fourths in unison,[31] this very archaic, female, and, in fact, infantile music proves that wide steps are not necessarily dependent on advanced mentality or on sex:

Ex. 15*

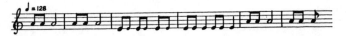

Indeed, adult Eskimo women might sing in fifths and at times overdo them to form a kind of minor sixth.[32]

The opposite pole of the globe presents another disconcerting example of empty fourths: Fuegian medicinemen sing them in their rituals: [33]

Ex. 16**

* Transcr, C. S.
** After von Hornbostel.
[31] *EFw* FE 4444 (P 444) II 1.
[32] Z. Estreicher, *Cinq chants des Esquimaux Ahearmiut*, in Geert van den Steenhoven, *Research-report on Caribou Eskimo law*, La Haye, 1956.
[33] Erich M. von Hornbostel, *The music of the Fuegians*, in *Ethnos* (1948, posth.), p. 102, first staff.

while the most characteristic and most frequent pattern of the
Patagonians is strait and secondal. Add western Polynesia to
these antipodes.[34] Here, too, we have no convincing explanation
to offer.

A strict *non liquet* applies to the realm of secondal melodies.
Their distribution is truly universal, and special conditions
– as sex, climate, and others – are not apparent. At best, the
seconds are so frequent in the very lowest civilizations that we
must assign them to the earliest known societies of mankind,
without siding in the dispute of the monogeneticists and the
polygeneticists for or against a one-home origin of man.

The situation is not much clearer in the realm of the third.
Tertial patterns, too, are most universal; but the map of distribution shows a particular denseness in Negro Africa, which in
turn is nearly devoid of fourths. Indeed, the third appears to
have almost the monopoly in Black Africa. Is this a case of
racial condition? I doubt it. The fourth is equally absent from
Europe, excepting much of the East and the Southeast, while
the third is all dominating. Again, as far as our knowledge goes,
the Asiatic world has a tertial North and a preponderantly quartal
South, from Tibet all the way down to Indonesia. Thus we must
face the possibility that an originally tertial region, the whole
Old World of Asia, Europe, and Africa, was in a remote past cut
into two by an East-born wedge of quartal melody.[35]

In Indian America, tertial and quartal melodies live alongside
without betraying any clue to a convincing chronology or
stratification.

This section deals with single steps only, leaving multiple
steps to the Second Part.

SINGLE STEPS from note to note remain very often unchanged
within a melody or even in all the melodies of a tribe. But, as a
matter of course, the listener should not expect that the steps
we call seconds, thirds or fourths be identical with those of our
pianos. They have a considerable latitude[36] and might even run

[34] E. G. Burrows, *Native music of the Tuamotus*, in *Bernice P. Bishop Museum Bulletin* 109, Honolulu, 1933, p. 74.

[35] Curt Sachs, *The road to major*, in *The Musical Quarterly*, vol. 29 (1943), pp. 381–404. – Also *id.*, *Towards a prehistory of music*, in *The Musical Quarterly*, vol. 24 (1938), p. 147 ff.

[36] Cf. e.g. Hugh Tracey, *The state of folk music in Bantu Africa*, in *African Music*, vol. 1 (1954) p. 9.

into one another so that the transcriber is uncertain whether to rate some step as a second or as a third, as a third or a fourth.[37] A good transcription will indicate the cent number of the distance and herewith remove any doubt.

The situation worsens when for the sake of expressiveness good singers (much more than poor ones) expand or shrink the steps on purpose. This is particularly true of the Amerindians, who have no scale-wise tuned instruments and hence no standardized interval. At times, they rise up to a major third above the original pitch; and they also would, in 'vertical augmentation,' increase the step as such.[38] We know similar techniques from Japan, where a flutist is expected to drive the pitch up after attacking correctly. Yemenite Jews as well as Persian Jews sharpen the notes the more their frenzy increases.[39]

EMPTY STRUCTURES might be the right term for the one-step patterns discussed so far. There are just the two structural notes a second, a third, a fourth, or a fifth apart. But the emptiness of these patterns can be, and often is, disturbed by additional, auxiliary notes that some richer imagination or a different motor habit impose.

As long as the nucleus is clearly recognizable as such, any additional note in the melody is an *affix* if it joins the nucleus outside [40] and, when the specification is necessary, more distinctly a *suprafix* added above or an *infrafix* added below. Secondal melodies can be adorned with *affixes* only. Tertial, quartal, and quintal patterns, on the contrary, have had a growing tendency towards resolution into smaller steps. The filling notes within a third, a fourth, or a fifth are called *infixes*.

Ex. 17*

* Lithuanian daina, after Wiora.

37 Cf. *EFw* FE 4446 (P 446) (Mato Grosso) II 1.

38 Cf. David McAllester in *Journal of the American Musicological Society*, vol. 10 (1957), p. 45.

39 Curt Sachs, *The rise of music in the ancient world*, New York, 1943, p. 81, after Idelsohn.

40 Cf. the characteristic *f*, *g*, and *b♭* in a dream song of the Temiar in inner Malaya (rec. in *EFw* FE 4460 (P 460) I 1).

Such fillings must not be mistaken for melodies of several consecutive seconds, which might look rather similar – *C D E*. The third, fourth, fifth would still act as the structural frame, and the fillers are merely non-structural stepping stones. Of thirds, usually only the major ones are cleft. Minor thirds, too close to the size of a wholetone, do not need a stepping stone and use it rarely. A fine example is the archaic melody from Lithuania on *EFw* FM 4009 (P 1009) I e, whose seventeen double verses use exclusively the notes *FE♭ D*.

A structural fourth or 'tetrachord' with or without infixes often keeps the minor third intact, so that one infix suffices to divide the quartal frame into a minor third and a wholetone, usually with the third above and the second below. This is the kernel of the so-called pentatonic gender, which will be discussed in the second part of this book. When tetrachords are cleft into three steps (as a rule two wholetones and one semitone) we speak of two infixes, an upper and a lower one, and call the fourth diatonic or heptatonic. Three basic arrangements are possible (here taken in the usual descending order): the semitone at the lower end, tone, tone, semitone or T T s (Greek Dorian); the semitone in the center, T s T (Greek Phrygian); and the semitone above, s T T (Greek Lydian) All these arrangements can be traced to primitive civilizations.

The two infixes within a tetrachord are rarely of equal weight and importance. In the following Rumanian lullaby the tetrachord reads *d c b a;* but far from being peers, the note *b* occupies only 3 time units, where *d* takes 15, and *c* and *a*, either one 14. There is only one possible interpretation: the infix *c* has almost become skeletal, while *b* is still a passing note. The melody as such is nearly pentatonic in the form second-above-third:

Ex. 18*

It happens in folksongs – Rumanian and others – that towards the end the structural fourth, by addition of an inferior note, becomes a fifth. When such is the case,[41] the added note must

---

* After Riegler-Dinu.
[41] As on *EFw* FE 4419 (P 419) II 7 from Rumania.

not be called a tonic (as has indeed been done); it is simply an infrafix. The title tonic – misleading as it is in a tetrachordal melody – can only apply to one of the tetrachordal terminals.

Almost an oddity – when seen from a modern western viewpoint – are pentatonic tetrachords with the infix so close to one end of the skeleton that the five-semitone span of the fourth appears in the forms $4 + 1$ or $1 + 4$ and not, as usually, in the form $2 + 3$ or $3 + 2$. Yet this strangely unbalanced tetrachord is neither artificial nor unnatural; it must be very old as it can be found in many places all over the world.[42] To all these evidences we ought to add the famous *Kol nidrei* sung on the eve of the day of Atonement:

Ex. 20

In all these cases the semitone is situated above the third. In reverse, with the major third above the semitone, this tetrachord is a characteristic trait of Tunisian Berber music,[43]

---

[42] Examples:

America: Uitoto, Colombia (Fritz Bose, *Die Musik der Uitoto*, in *Zeitschrift für Vergleichende Musikwissenschaft*, vol. 2 (1934), musical supplement, pp. 10, 12, 13, 15, 16, 19); Pawnee, U.S. (Alice C. Fletcher, *The Hako: a Pawnee ceremony*, Washington, 1904).

Europe: Faeroer, due north of Scotland (Walter Wiora, *Europäischer Volksgesang*, Heemstede, 1952, p. 19).

Africa: Ethiopia (*EFw* FE 4405 (P 405) II 2), ex. 19:

Ex. 19

(transcr. C.S.)

Asia: *Korean folksongs* (*EFw* FE 4424 (P 424 I 2)); Buriat Mongols (Carl Stumpf, *Mongolische Gesänge*, in *Vierteljahrsschrift für Musikwissenschaft*, vol. 3 (1887), p. 303); India, rāgas *bihāg* and *tilanga.*

Pacific: West Carolinas (George Herzog, *Die Musik der Karolinen-Inseln*, Hamburg, 1936, pp. 315, 349 ff.); Marind-anim, New Guinea (Jaap Kunst, *De inheemse muziek in westelijk Nieuw-Guinea*, Koninklijke Vereniging Indisch Instituut, Mededeling 93 (1950), pp. 51 ff.).

[43] Erich M. von Hornbostel, *Phonographierte tunesische Melodien*, in *Sammelbände der Internationalen Musikgesellschaft*, vol. 8 (1906/07), p. 31, reprinted in *Sammelbände für vergleichende Musikwissenschaft*, vol. 1, (1922) p. 311 ff. – *Id.*, and Robert Lachmann, *Asiatische Parallelen zur Berbermusik*, in *Zeitschrift für vergleichende Musikwissenschaft*, vol. 1 (1933) p. 4.

but also occurs in the archaic Javanese two-step orchestras *munggang* and *kodok ngorèk*.[44]

We shall meet such major-third pentatonics again in a later examination of double and triple fourths.

ALL TETRACHORDAL ORGANIZATIONS must be treated with the greatest care. To be more explicit, the reader is referred to a well recorded folksong from Anatolia (Asia Minor).[45] The listener faces a confusing fact: the two infixes are uncertain and variable enough to make the tetrachord $d'-a$ now Lydian (in the Greek sense of the word), now Phrygian, now Dorian, now even 'gypsy' with one of the wholetones augmented at the cost of the other wholetone, as in our so-called harmonic minor scale. In fact, here as elsewhere, such terms express mere approximations; infixes, free from rule or consistency, are mobile and subject to the singer's discretion. In this context I well remember Von Hornbostel's bewilderment when, in 1932, the two of us attended a Coptic service in Cairo: all the tetrachords so neatly engraved in an edition of Coptic chant he had studied were due to the transcriber's imagination and, to say the very least, deba-table.

Even in a system as thoroughly established as that of ancient Greece the infixes were officially granted an incredible liberty. The *chroai* or 'shades' within the otherwise normal scales, of which we read in Archytas, Aristoxenos, Ptolemy, and other theorists, were hardly more than futile attempts to mathematize, legalize, and codify what in fact was entirely left to the player's taste and whim. Hence Ptolemy's tolerance when, instead of insisting on lawful correctness, he openly admitted that "players of the lyra favored (!) two normal forms of intonation ... Those who performed on the kithara preferred (!) ..." [46] The border-notes of the tetrachord were *hestotes* or 'immovably' fixed; the infixes were freely movable.

BARE FIFTHS are frequent in the music of Bushmen and Patagonians, Lapps and Eskimo:

[44] Curt Sachs, *The rise of music in the ancient world*, New York, 1943, p. 129.
[45] *EFw* FE 4404 (P 404) I 7 (Asia Minor).
[46] Curt Sachs, *l.c.*, pp. 211–215.

Ex. 21*

Such quintal patterns occur in songs of the Menominee Indians[47] with two infixes but without a semitone:

Ex. 22

These melodies cannot possibly be mistaken for double thirds as not one of the infixes forms a third.

Sixths, transcribed now as minor now as major, have been found in Polynesia.[48]

FOR TUMBLING STRAINS I once coined the term 'pathogenic' or 'passion-born.' The name is still to the point and has generally been understood. But I hesitate to continue calling the usual horizontal melody 'logogenic' or 'word-born.' Experience has shown that the term suggests something close to the *stile recitativo* of the early seventeenth century or to Richard Wagner's more or less faithful rendition of natural speech inflection rather than a neutral, indifferent vehicle of words. Like the tunes of our hymnals, primitive melodies are often used for entirely different texts and hence cannot be considered text-born. At best, they are insignificantly adapted to deviations in the number of syllables.[49]

Indeed, the words themselves are often immaterial and little apt to shape a melody in their own image. California Indians, says a Spanish mission report from 1811, do not make any statement in their songs, "but only use fluent words, naming birds, places of their country, and so on." [50] Among many

* After Lucy Lloyd and A. Weisbecker.

47 Frances Densmore, *Menominee music*, Washington, 1932, p. 71, ex. 39.

48 E. G. Burrows, *Native music of the Tuamotus*, in *Bernice P. Bishop Museum Bulletin* 109, Honolulu, 1933.

49 Example: Walter Kaufmann, *Folk-songs of the Gond and Baiga*, in *The Musical Quarterly*, vol. 27 (1941), p. 280.

50 A. L. Kroeber, *A mission report on the Californian Indians* in *University of California Publications in American Archaeology and Ethnology*, vol. 8 (1908), p. 19.

parallels, the Sakai of Malacca recite long series of river and mountain names. A song of the South Californian Luiseño ends: "I have mentioned all the names of the seasons and stars ..." [51]; and Polynesians carry these lists of incoherent items so far that E. G. Burrows dedicates a whole section of his Tuamotu book to "Enumeration Songs." [52]

Emancipation from meaningful words also are the nonsense burdens of our kindergarten ditties, the numberless *jiggety jigs* and *tootle tootle toots*. Their time-honored predecessor is the omnipresent *fa la la* at the stanza end of Italian *balletto* songs around 1600. Actually, such refrains can be traced to archaic music. The Caucasus Georgians have their *delivodelivodeli;* [53] the almost untouched Caribou Eskimo sing their *ja-ja-ha-ja-ja* refrains,[54] the Copper Eskimo their *i ya i ya*,[55] and the Smith Sund Eskimo their *nalegak-nalegaksoak*.[56] Beyond the matter of refrains, John Ross, who discovered this last tribe in 1818, mentions that the tribesmen sang for ten minutes merely on the syllables *amnaj sjah* and *hejaw heja*.[57] Indeed, in the music of the Flathead Indians, "very few of the songs have texts; rather the majority employ nonsense syllables usually beginning with the consonants *h* and *y*." [58]

Textless are also the rapt *nigunim* of Chassidic Jews on *ay* or *bay*, on *oi* or *doi* [59] – syllables probably no more "non-sensical" than the *glossolalia* of religious ecstasy which the English Bible calls the "speaking with tongues" (Corinthians I 14). In a similar way the Cheremisses in east central Russia sing their sacred songs without texts.[60] Indeed, the East African Watutsi sometimes

[51] Constance Goddard DuBois, *The religion of the Luiseño Indians*, in *University of California Publications in American Archaeology and Ethnology*, vol. 8 (1908), p. 19.

[52] E. G. Burrows, *Native music of the Tuamotus*, in *Bernice P. Bishop Museum Bulletin* 109, Honolulu, 1933, pp. 42–45.

[53] Victor Belaiev, *The folk-music of Georgia*, in *The Musical Quarterly*, vol. 19 (1933), p. 422.

[54] Zygmunt Estreicher, *La musique des Esquimaux-Caribous*, in *Bulletin de la Société Neuchâteloise de Géographie*, vol. 54 (1948), p. 4.

[55] Helen H. Roberts and D. Jenness, *Eskimo songs*, Ottawa, 1925, p. 23.

[56] Christian Leden, *Ueber die Musik der Smith Sund Eskimos*, in *Meddelelser om Grønland*, vol. 152, no. 3 (1952), p. 9.

[57] *ibid*. p. 9.

[58] Alan P. Merriam introducing *EFw* FE 4445 (P 445).

[59] Good examples in Chemjo Vinaver, *Anthology of Jewish music*, New York, 1955, pp. 259–281. – Cf. also Frances Densmore, *The use of meaningless syllables in Indian music*, in *American Anthropologist*, vol. 45 (1943), pp. 160 ff.

[60] Communication by Dr. Yury Arbatsky (New York, 1956).

sing whole sections of their songs without any words or even
syllables.[61]

In the face of all this evidence, we must realize that many
melodies in this group are not word-born at all. Thus it might
be better to drop the term 'logogenic' and to speak of horizontal
and of tumbling melodies.

QUITE TO THE CONTRARY, words that matter might arrest the
melodic flow and find a musically unassuming expression without
the help of interesting rhythms or melody proper. Such is the
case in the liturgic recitations on one unchanging pitch, as in
Gregorian psalms, prayers, and lessons. There is, as a rule, a
flexa or lower cadential note as a mark and remainder of lessening
voice force, and there might be initial and final melody formulas.
But the steps that they form are not essential; whether the voice,
after a score of even-spaced eighthnotes, sinks with the *flexa* by
a semitone or a wholetone or even a third is irrelevant except
from the viewpoint of modal correctness (cf. ex. 68 on p. 172).

All that counts (in principle) is the monotonous seriation of
a single note, which in humility avoids drawing the hearer's
attention from the sacred words to a melodic cloak.

One-tone recitation is not limited to any particular Church.
A classic example of this repetitive or stationary style are in the
archaic world the solemn ancient songs of Hawaii, in which
often dozens of measures repeat the upper note before the singer
gives way to the needs of structure and vocal effort and marks
the end of a phrase by touching the lower note.[62]

Ex. 23

Also the Maori of New Zealand delight in one-note recitations,
from which they swerve only seldom to some auxiliary note a
second or a minor third apart.[63] The islands in between perform

---

[61] *EFw* FE 4428 (P 428) I 5.

[62] Helen H. Roberts, *Ancient Hawaiian music,* in *Bernice P. Bishop Museum
Bulletin* 29, Honolulu, 1926.

[63] *EFw* FE 4433 (P 433).

their stationary recitations without dropping to auxiliary pitches; after a shout, the second part might follow a semitone higher and end on a still higher final note from which a cadential glissando trails down.[64]

The Polynesian picture would not be complete without the graceful dances of sitting women, to whose quiet, sleepily moving arm and torso movements the stationary litany style appears particularly adequate.[65]

The distribution chart of one-note melodies records furthermore the (musically primitive) Caroline Islands;[66] dark-skinned Jahai Semang pygmies, who live in Malaccan jungles on the lowest cultural level;[67] Buddhist priests[68] and South Arabian warsingers;[69] the *mestwirebi* bards of Caucasian Georgia;[70] and Serbs in magic incantations whose occasional auxiliary notes are sigh-like and often microtonic.[71] But in most examples the one-note recitations are nothing but episodes or repetitions within an otherwise alternating style. As an example of a intermediary position, I quote a Pawnee song of eleven measures with only two and a half measure adding *b* and *a* to the otherwise exclusive *e*,[72] and a Cheyenne melody, where the whole second part consists in nineteen measures on *d* and *e*.[73]

Because in the current of culture and time – as later sections will show – alternation patterns grew often from one step to two steps, from two to three steps, and so forth, the conclusion would seem logical that litany-like melodies on one note (or nearly so) must be older even than two-note melodies. But counting is a poor help in cultural history, the more so as repetition and alternation seem to differ beyond comparison, one

[64] E. G. Burrows, *Songs of Uvea and Futuna*, in *Bernice P. Bishop Museum Bulletin* 183, Honolulu, 1945, p. 64. – Cf. also: *id.*, *Native music of the Tuamotus*, in *Bulletin* 109 (1933).

[65] Cf. Curt Sachs, *World history of the dance*, New York, 1937, pp. 37, 175, 188.

[66] George Herzog, *Die Musik der Karolinen-Inseln*, in *Ergebnisse der Südsee-Expedition 1908–1910*, II B, *Band* 9, II. *Halbband*, Hamburg, 1936.

[67] Mieczyslaw Kolinski, *Die Musik der Primitivstämme auf Malacca*, in *Anthropos*, vol. 25 (1930), pp. 588 ff.

[68] *EFw* FE 4449 (P 449) I 2.

[69] *EFw* FE 4421 (P 421) I 4.

[70] Robert Lach, *Gesänge russischer Kriegsgefangener*, in *Akademie der Wissenschaften in Wien, Phil.-Hist. Klasse, Sitzungsber.*, vol. 205, Vienna, 1931.

[71] *EFw* FE 4434 (P 434) I 2.

[72] Transcibed by Edwin S. Tracy in Alice C. Fletcher, *The Hako: a Pawnee ceremony*, Washington, 1904, p. 116.

[73] Natalie Curtis, *The Indian's book*, New York, 1907, no page.

exhibiting the need for either rest or for tension, and the other, for leisurely motion. The only statement that we dare propose is: one-note, as well as two-note formations belong in the earliest age of man.

Those who believe in a parallel evolution of the human individual and the human kind will be satisfied to find both the one-note and the two-note formations among the very first babble songs of small children. The psychologist Heinz Werner recorded such songs a few decades ago.[74]

BOTH HORIZONTAL AND TUMBLING STRAINS are often found within the same tribe [75] and indeed within the same piece. This peaceful coexistence in so many cases forbids a separate attribution of either style to certain races or minor groups. Nor does it allow us to think of different layers of the Palaeolithic. The way in which the two species mingle rather bares two different roots of singing, one derived from the violent howl, and the other, from recitation. There are at least two roots of mere melodical urge, not even counting the motor impulse of rhythm – how can one possibly search for "the" origin of music?

A CONSPECTUS OF A MORE general, stylistic nature may end this rather technical section.

All art is dual in its concept and trend; it satisfies opposite urges, and often at the same time and in the same civilization. It might be imitative to the border of illusion and suggest the reality of an object, a situation, or an experience of the senses. Or, on the contrary, it can be designedly abstract, non-imitative, totally unconcerned with objective reality. In between, we have all shades of transition from one extreme to another; harsh reality idealized or weakened to mere abstraction and, in the other direction, ornamental, playful, meaningless patterns enlivened and transformed to a suggestion of well-known objects or symbols. This happens in painting, engraving, and sculp-

---

[74] Heinz Werner, *Die melodische Erfindung im frühen Kindesalter*, in *K.K. Akademie der Wissenschaften zu Wien, Phil. -Hist. Klasse, Sitzungsber.*, vol. 182 (1907), no. 4. – See also Bruno Nettl, *Infant musical development and primitive music*, in *Southwestern Journal of Anthropology*, vol. 12 (1956), pp. 87–91.

[75] Cf., e.g., Hall and Nettl, *Musical style of the Modoc*, in *Southwestern Journal of Anthropology*, vol. 11 (1955), no. 1 and 2.

ture; and it also happens in poetry, music, and the dance. The two basic forms of early melody discussed so far seem to fit very well in this general picture. Tumbling strains, I said, "recall savage shouts of joy or wails of rage." They are not passionate but highly naturalistic; they first repeat, then merely imitate, and at last only suggest the unbridled outbursts of strong emotions familiar both to the singers and to the listeners. Horizontal melodies, on the other hand, being sometimes a steady repetition of the same note, sometimes a ceaseless repetition of two notes at different pitches, remind us much of those unassuming, primitive ornaments which iterate the same little dot or dash around the rim of a bamboo quiver or zigzag across the osiers of a basket, without any intention of imitating or expressing the inner and outer experiences of man. Either type develops away from its own to the opposite type: tumbling strains move from natural, genuine wails to tame and neat stylizations; horizontal tunes adjust themselves to the correct inflection, meter, and meaning of the words they carry and become realistic speech melodies, i.e., imitations, as in the following "Harken Israel" of the Babylonian liturgy:

Ex. 24*

She-ma Is-ra-el A-do nai E-lo-he-nu A-do-nai e-had.

Occasionally, the profiles of melodies, partly taken from pre-phonographic publications,[76] have been interpreted as actual images, say, of longing and gentleness, of mountains and rivers, of the sun, the wind, and the earth. It is not only possible but quite probable that here and there the text creates automatically a melodic symbol. But unless the tribesmen themselves point out and explain this symbolism, it is utterly dangerous to read it into a foreign, primitive melody which one has never heard. It is even more dangerous than the notorious abuses of the 'hermeneutic' method applied to the music of Europe.[77]

* After A. Z. Idelsohn, *Hebräisch-orientalischer Melodienschatz*, vol. 2, Wien, 1922.
[76] Cf., e.g. Werner Danckert, *Tonmalerei und Tonsymbolik in der Musik der Lappen*, in *Die Musikforschung*, vol. 9 (1956), pp. 286–296.
[77] The latest publication on the subject: Nils-Eric Ringbom, *Ueber die Deutbarkeit der Tonkunst*, Helsinki, 1955.

While we must be wary where the symbol is meant to be an automatic, almost unconscious part of the creative act, we are safer in the face of a conscious, intentional art of illustration. Most of the latter belongs in post-primitive times. The dramatizations of scenes of war and quarrel in southern Arabia [78] are, no doubt, on a post-primitive level; and this is also true when the Iru in Uganda describe their hunting parties in long cantatas from the first alarm on the trumpets to the kill and the noisy distribution of the meat in a dialogue, climaxing in a final chorus of all the hunter's horns.[79] The semi-dramatic, gesticulating recitations of professional and almost professional minstrels also belong in a later stratum and will be touched upon in the penultimate section.

On a lower level, certain musical imitations are reminiscent of the realistic cave paintings in southern France, the north of Spain, and Bushmansland with their striking movements of men and beasts.[80] One of the most characteristic examples is provided by Bushmen, who skilfully render the typical gaits of their many animals by softly beating their bows in adequate rhythms. With just as much gusto, the Kayabi in the Mato Grosso imitate the voices of birds, otters, monkeys, and jaguars;[81] and with exquisite art the Eskimo render the cries of geese, swans, and walruses – not for entertainment, not for magical purposes, but simply to bring these animals within the hunter's shooting range.[82] In mythical accounts, the Apache act the songs of smaller birds "in falsetto, while that of the slowwitted lumbering giant is intoned in a gruff voice." [83] New Guinean Papua weave into their songs and flute melodies the voices of birds and other animals, which perhaps "play a certain part in the(ir) religious ideas." [84] Finally, North Australians, famous also for rock paintings and naturalistic wood carving, imitate on awkward wooden trumpets the dancelike movements of the 'Native

[78] *EFw* FE 4421 (P 421) I 6, 7.

[79] K. P. Wachsmann, *Folk musicians in Uganda*, Kampala, 1956, p. 7.

[80] Cf., e.g., Herbert Kühn, *Primitive Kunst*, in Max Ebert, *Reallexikon der Vorgeschichte*, vol. 10, Berlin, 1927–1928, pp. 264–292.

[81] *EFw* FE 4446 (P 446) I 10.

[82] *EFw* FE 4444 (P 444) II 2, 3. Also FE 4446 (P 446) II 7.

[83] Morris Edward Opler, *An Apache life-way*, Chicago, 1941, p. 455.

[84] Van der Sande in Jaap Kunst, *A study on Papuan music*, Weltevreden, 1931, pp. 7 ff.

Companion,' a graceful blue-gray bird with long thin legs, and of other birds.[85]

We also have an Australian recording of a singer describing, and perhaps with humor, the drilling of soldiers, commands, marking time, marching, halting, and marching again.[86] A. P. Elkin gives a good idea of descriptive melodies in Australia, with the song of the anvil imitating "vividly the darting of sparks and the 'cry' of resounding noise when the heated iron is struck with the hammer. The 'boat song' pictures a boat with mast and sail and an auxiliary engine and the singer travelling in it. And the 'washing song' portrays the clothes, washed, hanging on the line, blowing in the breeze, and then being ironed." [87]

The strange doings of the white man are suggestive indeed: the Temiar in inner Malaya celebrate *Bah motoh*, the spirit of the motor boat, in an overwhelming blend of naturalism and stylization.[88]

But in general, expression outside of what we somewhat embarrassedly call by the undefined name of 'art,' avoid naturalism and even realism – much the same as small children do not copy nature. They draw with their eyes on the paper, not on objects, and merely from a composite of memory and imagination; their simplified, suggestive pencil strokes are not realistic. And this is true of all folk art.

The songs in animal stories, an archaic part of Amerindian music, are imitations of animal cries, "although not necessarily very naturalistic." [89] Our folksongs are so neutral and uncharacteristic that the same, unchanged melody can be sung for all the stanzas, indeed, for texts in different, contrasting moods, and even for unrelated poems. Only by exception does the true folksinger abandon his noncommittal melody to become a dramatic actor. There is an easily accessible instance in the Sicilian tragi-comic eloge for a departed donkey with the marvelous rendition of his bray.[90] But this might be a survival of

[85] *EFw* FE 4439 (P 439) I 7; cf. also A. P. Elkin, *Arnhemland music*, in *Oceania*, vol. 25 (1956), reprinted 1957 (*Oceania Monograph* no. 9).

[86] *EFw* FE 4439 (P 439) I 2.

[87] Elkin, l.c. vol. 24 (1953), p. 91; reprinted 1957 (*Oceania Monograph* no. 9).

[88] *EFw* FE 4469 (P 460) II 2.

[89] George Herzog, *Special song types in North American Indian music*, in *Zeitschrift für vergleichende Musikwissenschaft*, vol. 3 (1935), p. 9.

[90] *EFw* FE 4520 (P 520) II 2.

the ancient semi-parodical dirges or *epikedia* for animals, to be
expected on the classical soil of Magna Graecia.[91] More to the
point is that Mississippi folksong of the Old Woman, who once
saw a corpse in her church, asked the preacher: "Will I look just
so when I am dead?," was told: "Just so," and to the preacher
said – but there is no final word, no final note, only, natural-
istically, "a very loud scream." [92]

VII. CONSERVATISM AND MAGIC

One-step melodies have a universal distribution all over the
globe. The majority occurs – and often to the exclusion of other
styles – among extremely archaic peoples: Californian as well
as Northwest Indians and, in South America, East Brazilian
Botocudos and Fuegians of Patagonia; Bushmen and other
pygmies and pygmoids, both in Africa and Asia; and Solomon
Islanders in Melanesia.

But one-step melodies are by no means limited to Stone Age
civilizations; they are found on essentially higher levels: in the
oldest form of Indian Veda cantillation, in the modern Pacific,
in Muhammedan countries: [93]

Ex. 25*

and in the folksong of eastern Europe, as in Bulgaria, Rumania,
Lithuania.

The European habitat is, once more, an evidence of palaeolithic survival in the midst of European civilization, which has a
striking parallel in "the occasional appearance of Palaeolithic
physical types in the present European population."[94]

Such survivals are by no means paradoxical or even confusing.

---

* Transcr. C. S.

[91] About animal dirges: G. Herrlinger, *Totenklage um Tiere in der antiken Dichtung*,
1930.

[92] Published in Arthur Palmer Hudson and George Herzog, *Folk tunes from
Mississippi*, New York, 1937, no. 43.

[93] From *EFw* FE 4469 (P 469) II 1 (Kurds).

[94] Ralph Linton, *The tree of culture*, New York, 1955, p. 27.

Nor do they lure us into misdating cultural traits; for the method of prehistory has taught that "it is by the appearance of *new* forms that a stage is recognized, not by the survival of old types." [95]

Thus, we need not wonder at finding here and there a chronological disharmony between music and other elements of a civilization: "the integration within cultures is loose enough so that some parts of a culture may be highly evolved while others have remained simple." [96]

This fact has a bearing upon one much contested problem in the situation of Polynesia: the utterly simple style of Hawaiian music. Helen H. Roberts attributed it to influences from the cantillation of the old-Indian Veda texts.[97] With all due respect it must be said that her suggestion is not acceptable. The supposed migration and diffusion from India through half of Asia and half of the Pacific is hardly convincing, on account not only of the enormous geographic distance, but also of an enormous difference in religion, culture, and musical styles.

Farther to the west, "the extremely primitive" character of Carolinian melodies surprised George Herzog as "a fact unexpected within the partly high civilization of the Caroline Islanders." [98] Tentatively, he suggested [99] that the luxuriant poetry of Micronesia and Polynesia might have enslaved their melodies and killed their musical development. This idea, if not exactly conclusive, has a certain merit. It is a well known fact that poetry and music, though mated by nature and often inseparable, have their latent frictions and open conflicts. Up to the twentieth century, the histories of western song and of opera provide examples on every page: musical drama, as Gluck's and Wagner's, stands against common opera, one proclaiming the mastery of drama, and the other, the dominant rights of music; and, in a similar way, the song inspired by a poet's accents, thoughts, and words, as Hugo Wolf's *Lieder*, avoids and opposes the neutrality of melodies that fit the

---

[95] Sonia Cole, *The prehistory of East Africa*, London, 1954, p. 113.

[96] Ralph Linton, *o.c.*, p. 56.

[97] Helen H. Roberts, *Ancient Hawaiian music*, in *Bernice P. Bishop Museum Bulletin* 29, Honolulu, 1925, pp. 378–380.

[98] George Herzog, *Die Musik der Karolinen-Inseln*, Hamburg 1936, p. 263.

[99] *ibid.*, p. 279.

different stanzas of the same poem or even different poems as happens so often in anthems and hymns. It is characteristic that Goethe, as a poet, liked the simple and neutral settings of his friend Karl Friedrich Zelter better than the illustrative, meddlesome interpretations of Schubert.

How strict this domination of poetry over music can be – and here we return to our primitive ground – appears in the unbelievably simple recitation of national epics. We think of the Georgian *mestwirebi* and their recitations of myth and of history:

Ex. 26

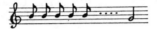

of the Finnish *kalevala*,[100] the Balkan epics of the *guslari*,[101] or the Arabian Abu Said romances, with their wearisome, hardly varied melody patterns as a vehicle for many thousands of lines; of the archaic cantillation of Persian and Yemenite Jews; [102] and of the medieval French *chansons de geste* whose sections or *lais*, up to fifty verses long, obeyed each the same melody before the last broke loose to form the cadence.[103] And we may assume that the Homeric epics were no exception. Such melodic scraps can be repeated for hours and hours without annoying a listener exclusively interested in the narrative.

A SECOND REASON for inertia is the kind of majority archaism that we can best observe in Europe. While the leading composers, often in a breathtaking tempo, hurry from style to style, the idiom of our anthems, hymns, and many of our hits has basically not changed since the eighteenth century. We take development, evolution, and revolution for granted in the concerthall and on the operatic stage, but resent the simplest ninth chord in the settings of popular music. The ages of the machine, of electricity,

[100] A. Launis, *Ueber die Art, Entstehung und Verbreitung der estnisch-finnischen Runenmelodien*, Helsingfors, 1910.

[101] Gustav Becking, *Der musikalische Bau des montenegrinischen Volksepos*, in *Proceedings of the International Congress of Phonetic Sciences 1932* (1933). – Walther Wünsch, *Die Geigentechnik der südslawischen Guslaren*, Diss., Prag, 1934.

[102] Curt Sachs, *The rise of music in the ancient world*, New York, 1943, p. 83.

[103] Curt Sachs, *Our musical heritage*, 2nd edition, New York, 1955, pp. 71 ff.

and of the atom may have remodeled our thought and our vision, but have not touched the ears of our majorities. If this is true of our own civilization, how much more does it apply to the primitives whose balance of change and perseverance is almost always in favor of tradition.

A THIRD REASON for the tenacity of archaic music applies in particular to primitive civilization. There, only material equipment is in need of change and advance. Weapons and tools must never lag too much behind the ones of hostile neighbors; and a change of climate and habitat can force a tribe to readapt its whole material existence.

Immaterial traits are exempt from such competitive adaptation. The help that music might give in battle, hunt, and personal crises of life, to be sure, is of a magic and therewith practical, almost material nature. But magics as well as advanced religion depend essentially on faithful accuracy in the sense of unadulterated tradition rather than on change, experiment, or so-called progress. Should the songs of the Apache shaman not be sung in the right way, "the masked dancer would fall down like a man knocked out by a blow." [104] (Which brings to mind the fatal consequences that Hindu mythology ascribes to the unskilful singing of hallowed *rāgas*).[105] "As a matter of fact, the high standard of accuracy facilitates continued belief in the powers of the medicineman and his ritual; the stock explanation for failure to cure is that a mistake must have been committed in the ceremony or the singing." [106]

To avoid this, accuracy was often enforced – as strictly as possible. "On the island of Gaua in the New Hebrides it is said that formerly the old men used to stand by with bows and arrows and shoot at every dancer who made a mistake." [107] And this formidable discipline applies to music, too: "Newly initiated Wasuto (South Africa) boys are beaten with specially plaited grass switches for mistakes in singing." [108] Which is certainly a

---

[104] Morris Edward Opler, *An Apache life-way*, Chicago, 1941, p. 107.

[105] Curt Sachs, *The rise of music in the ancient world*, New York, 1943, pp. 173 ff.

[106] George Herzog, *Speech-melody and primitive music*, in *The Musical Quarterly*, vol. 20 (1934), p. 462.

[107] Curt Sachs, *World history of the dance*, New York, 1937, p. 219.

[108] Hugh Ashton, *The Basuto*, London, 1952, p. 51.

gentle rebuke when compared with the methods of Polynesia,
where carelessness in performing a ritual "was usually dis-
couraged by executing the one who made the mistake." [109]

It is less serious and yet within the same ideology when in
French Upper Guinea a visitor trying to enter the retreat of
newly circumcised boys must first intone a circumcision song
which the boys in the hut take up. If the guest or the boys make
a mistake, the culprit must pay a moderate fine.[110]

The solicitous regard for pure tradition is not just 'pagan.'
The sacred cantillations of Brahmans, Buddhists, oriental Jews,
and Muhammedans are all archaic; and the Catholic Church
has been anxious to preserve the Gregorian chant and to restore
it to its pristine austerity whenever practice swerved from
authenticity. The same is true of the Eastern Orthodox Churches.

The oneness of material and immaterial culture, which we so
easily take for granted, often falls a victim to the extraordinary
inertia of music. Civilization as a whole would change its contents
and its forms, but musical instruments, much as they are
connected with ideas and customs, change at a lesser speed,[111]
and music as a whole might stagnate.

Where this is fully intentional, inertia has magic connotations.

THE WORD MAGIC conjures up an all-important complex of
mental functions overwhelmingly active in the primitive world
and still alive within and without religious rites of the highest
civilizations, however weakened they may be by scientific
knowledge and reasoning.

Primitive man is exposed to countless occurrences whose
causes he fails to see; all his life he suffers destinies whose
reasons of being are hid from his eyes. Conception and childbirth, sickness and death, abundance and want, rainstorms and
dearth – who makes, who sends them? What can man do to
avert misfortune? How may he summon health and copious
food?

Primitive answers to these questions are not rational; being
unscientific, they ignore deduction, test, and hence the lawful

   [109] Ralph Linton, o.c., p. 192.
   [110] André Schaeffner, *Les rites de circoncision en pays Kissi*, in *Etudes Guinéennes*,
no. 12 (1953), p. 44.
   [111] Cf. André Schaeffner, *Les Kissi*, Paris, 1951, p. 6.

processes at the bottom of nature and life. Instead, all that which befalls a man, his livestock, and his crops, must be the intentional doings of benign or malevolent beings, be they demons or mortals; and, in the ever-present dangers of existence, he tries to call, appease, or combat these powerful shapers of fate.

In doing so, his strongest and often exclusive weapon is magic, "a supernatural technique," in Malinowski's short definition, "by which man can, in his conceit, bring about all that which his rational technique fails to accomplish." [112]

The ideas and practice of magics take up an incredible space in the lives of men and of peoples – far beyond the primitive level; and special libraries have been founded to house the gigantic literature devoted to this form of approach to the secrets of our existence. Here, we cannot give a comprehensive survey of this field; but a few principal forms connected with sound and with music must be mentioned.

Charms against sickness are supreme among them. In many civilizations, certain rites are performed by an intelligent, excitable, and often psychic [113] spokesman of the tribe whom we know as the medicine man, witch doctor, or shaman. In a state of self-inflicted trance he acquires the superhuman power to foresee the future, to heal, and to chase the evil forces. He dances with clattering anklets, shakes the seed-filled, rattling gourd, strikes his shallow, circular drum, and sings or bawls his hectic incantations for hours and hours until complete exhaustion silences him.

The strength of believing in these nerve-wrecking rituals even in the midst of a western environment and in the face of American doctors, can be judged from a recent case of seventy frightened Navaho Indians, tuberculosis patients in an Arizona sanitarium, who during a thunderstorm had to be quieted by the magic herbs and the 'sing' of a native medicine man flown to the hospital.[114]

An Amerindian healing song, breathless and breathtaking, is reprinted in my 'Rise of Music' on p. 22.[115]

[112] Bronislaw Malinowski, *The dynamics of culture change*, New Haven, 1945, p. 49.
[113] But cf. A. P. Elkin, *Aboriginal men of high degree*, Sydney, 1944, pp. 22 ff.: "Medicine-men are normal." – Psychoneurotic: Paul Radin, *The world of primitive man*, New York, 1953, chapter 4.
[114] Associated Press report, quoted from *The Boston Herald*, Aug. 17, 1955, p. 16.
[115] After Erich M. von Hornbostel. – Cf. also Frances Densmore, *Music in the treatment of the sick by American Indians*, in *Hygeia*, April 1923, pp. 29 ff.; *The Musical Quarterly*, vol. 13 (1927), pp. 555 ff.; *Scientific Monthly*, vol. 79 (1954), pp. 109–112. Also: *EFw* FE 4525 (P 525) A 14 (Eskimo).

After sickness – death.

There are funeral rites in the primitive world with the noble pathos of deepest emotion; nothing could be more strongly moving than the dirges of North American Indians. But oftener the rites derive from terror and the fearful anticipation of imminent danger, be it through the hostile spell which must have caused the present death, or through mischievous acts of the deceased himself. From such peril the living must be protected by magical practices. Inversely, the magical acts may serve the interests of the dead, especially in cattle-driving societies where the living try to safeguard life in the beyond.

In planter civilizations, everybody's existence depends upon the mysterious growth of the seed. Thus it is protection of life, too, when tillers bridge with magical rites the critical time between the seasons of sowing and reaping. Processions cross the fields or walk around them with sacred songs and often with a shell trumpet, which, coming from the water, must unfailingly attract the needed rain. Or else the boys leap over the pastures with shouts and tinkling bells to drive the evil spirits away. Peasants in Europe still cling to the old tradition, and the blessing of the crops is part of Catholic no less than of Hindu and Malay rites.

Nowhere are such ceremonials more beautiful than in Indonesia. To sow the rice, planters advance in solemn dance steps and open the ground with pounding poles whose rattle tops are tuned each to one note of the scale; the women follow and drop the grains in the pits. On the evening of the harvest sacrifice, the maidens hit the soil with seed-filled bamboos and to their rhythm sing the charming ditty: "Stamp, ye friends, for we look down, look down to the praying, the praying new rice."

The dull and hollow-sounding shell trumpets and the seed-filled bamboos (as many other instruments) belong in the province of homoeopathic sorcery, which, based on a presumed affinity and attraction of phenomena equal or similar, forces nature to imitate what is done in its face. Pounding the soil with seed-filled tubes must act on the seeds interred in the ground and makes them thrive when their time has come. The charms for wind and rain must be of an analogous kind of homoeopathy. The rainmaker ties a narrow, thin-cut slab of wood to a cord and whirls such a 'bull-roarer' round his head; size and speed make it whistle like a squall or roar like a thunderstorm. Squall and storm, irresistibly attracted by their own characteristic noises, must come and bring the rain that the crops require. Mere whistling with the mouth has the same effect.[116] Again, should there be too much rain, the charm is simply reversed. The Zulu shaman climbs a hill when an undesired thunderstorm nears, blows a squeaking fife of bone, and shouts: "Ye sky, be gone, I hold nothing against you, I will not fight!" [117]

EVERYTHING THAT SOUNDS, be it in the cruder form of frightening noise or the organized patterns of music, bears the brunt of mankind's eternal strife against the hostile forces that threaten his life and welfare; and, just as well, nothing better than sound can summon the powers of luck and prosperity. Songs, say the Melanesians, can have *mana*, or a hidden supernatural energy, and the Polynesians "chanted hymns which had *mana* because of the things which they recounted and the rhythmical, forceful way in which they were recited." [118] The songs of American Indians, too, "were believed to come from a supernatural source and their singing was connected with the exercise of natural powers." [119] Sound, as we mentioned, affects our nervous system more than other sense perceptions; and since the primitives project their own emotions onto the invisible forces around them, these too must succumb to the unique mysterious spell of timbre, rhythm, and tune.

Even language stresses the unity of singing and magics as the Latin word *incantatio*, 'magic formula,' derived from *cantare*, and the English *charm*, from *carmen*.

WHEREVER SINGING is an act of ecstasy and depersonalization, it moves away from ordinary human expression. The voice is often remote from being as 'natural' as we believe our own execution to be. It is colored by pulsating, yodeling, ventriloquizing, or bleating. One screams, yells, squeaks, mumbles, and

[116] Leslie Milne, *The home of an eastern clan*, Oxford, 1924, p. 231.
[117] Henri A. Junod, *The life of a South African tribe*, vol. II, Neuchâtel, 1913, p. 291.
[118] William Howells, *The heathens*, Garden City, 1948, p. 234.
[119] Frances Densmore, *The study of Indian music*, in *Smithsonian report for 1941*, Washington, 1942, p. 540.

nasals. Some people set such mannerisms strictly apart according to the purpose of singing; the Sioux, for instance, reserve a nasal intonation for love songs; [120] on the Orinoco in northern South America the singing women pinch their noses when the gruesome mask dancers make their appearance; [121] and Yemenite Jews use a boy's high-pitched voice to chant the *targumim* or Aramaic translations of the Bible.[122] If this last example is not exactly a mannerism, it is a special coloring for a special purpose.

Scattered all over the world is the queer nasaling caused by a tiny membrane which screens the voice and colors it in co-vibration. Its original form, a simple tree leaf stretched out in front of the mouth, has survived in practice and in the otherwise inexplicable German phrase: *kein Blatt vor den Mund nehmen,* which means literally 'to hold no leaf against the mouth,' or, in idiomatic English, 'to be plain-spoken.' The membrane, whatever its substance, form, or frame, is indeed a concealing agent; more specifically, it is used as a sound mask to deperson-alize the singer's voice just as visual face masks dehumanize the ritual dancers.

Similar 'kazoos' are described in my earlier books.[123] There are pseudo-trumpets serving as megaphones, or drums held at a certain angle in front of a shaman's mouth, or conch shells to make a chieftain's voice suprahuman, hollow, and eerie. The strangest device is the *nyāstaranga* of India: a singer presses two trumpet-like tubes right and left against his throat, and the vibrations of the vocal chords are caught by a membrane in the 'mouthpiece' of the trumpet and reinforced by its tube. Two further examples, not mentioned before, might be added: according to Tacitus' *Germania,* c. 100 A.D., the Germans sang their battle songs against the shield to make them more raucous and frightening; and in a curious game little Eskimo girls bend down and whisper into a kettle words in strict, strong-breathing eighth and sixteenth notes ($\jmath$ = c. 108 MM) which irresistibly

[120] Frances Densmore, *Chippewa music*, Washington, 1910, p. 61.

[121] Alain Gheerbrant, *L'expédition Orénoque Amazone*, Paris, 1952, p. 125.

[122] Johanna Spector's tape recordings and her paper *On the trail of Oriental music,* in *The Reconstructionist,* vol. 18 (1952), p. 11.

[123] Curt Sachs, *Geist und Werden der Musikinstrumente,* Berlin, 1929, pp. 106 ff. – id., *The rise of music in the ancient world,* New York, 1943, p. 23. – Cf. also: Curt Sachs, *The history of musical instruments,* New York, 1940, pp. 462 ff. – EFw FE 4451 (P 451) I 2 (Cameroons).

remind of jolting railway imitations [124] (cf. ex. 15 on page 62). Therewith we have entered the realm of voice mannerism.

VIII. VOCAL MANNERISMS

The impersonalization of the human voice in magical rites does not explain the total of distinctive mannerisms in singing styles all over the world. The neat notations of non-western music that we are offered to read, withhold from us one salient fact: that nowhere outside the modern West do people sing with a voice for which we have coined the honorific title of 'natural,' [125] that, to the western ear, all oriental and primitive singing is unnatural and seasoned with strange, unwonted mannerisms; and that these regional differences in handling the voice are often more significant than tonal ranges and structures. How people sing is no less meaningful than what they sing. An American Indian, a Japanese or Korean, an Arab, a Negro – let them sing a couple of notes, and they cannot escape recognition.

VOCAL MANNERISM is the hardest and most neglected branch of our studies. For expressing what we hear, we have no proper classification or terminology beyond the arbitrary lingo of western voice teachers.

The difficulties grow when we face a phonograph recording instead of the voice itself. Although the most recent methods of phonography with microphones and tapes diminish the danger of distortion and mishearing, even a first-class modern loud-speaker still might leave the listener in doubt as to whether the singer is a man or a woman.

There is a pioneering practical guide through this field in an album of Ethnic Folkways Library,[126] which Henry Cowell has compiled and introduced under the title *The World's Vocal Arts*. Unfortunately, for us, the stress is on the word Arts: all the singing styles of American Indians, African Negroes, and Australo-Pacific peoples, in short the Primitives, are excluded from this collection.

[124] *EFw* FE 4444 (P 444) I 8.
[125] But cf. Douglas Stanley, *Your voice*, New York, 1945, pp. 295 ff.
[126] *EFw* FE 4510 (P 510).

The weighty problem of voice mannerism entered our field
of vision at first when Erich M. von Hornbostel, going beyond
the previous exclusive interest in melodic and rhythmical aspects,
drew our attention towards the vocal style of the Amerindians
and described its emphasis and over-accentuation, its sharp
staccato, indeed, its puffing steam-engine quality, with the
characteristic break-up of longer notes in even pulsation.[127]

More recent is Merriam's description in a monograph on the
Flathead Indians: "Using a tight, though open throat but without employing full resonance possibilities of the upper nasal
caveties, a penetrating quality is produced in the style often
labeled as the 'clenched-teeth' or 'ventriloquistic' style.[128]

Tenseness and emphasis recur in Siberia, from which the Red
Man first migrated to the American continent from twelve to
fifteen thousand years ago.[129]

One more connection between the musical styles of Indians
and East Asia (Japan) is the frequent upwards drive, especially
of higher notes. It is particularly clear in the *Navajo Creation
Songs* recorded by Harvard's Peabody Museum. But McAllester
emphasizes rightfully that the Navaho style "is not as tense, as
throat-splitting, as Sioux singing." [130]

Indeed, an (essentially smaller) part of the Indians, "the
Yuman tribes, the Pima and Papago, and the Serrano and
Cahuilla," have no share in the typically American technique.
The area of these dissenters "corresponds to those of the mythical,
dreamt song series, of a certain simplicity of the melodic develop-
ment, and of the prominent use of the gourd rattle." [131]

---

[127] Erich M. von Hornbostel, in Theodor Koch-Grünberg, *Vom Roroima zum
Orinoco*, vol. 3, Stuttgart, 1923, p. 408. – id., *Ueber ein akustisches Kriterium für
Kulturzusammenhänge*, in *Zeitschrift für Ethnologie* (1911), pp. 601 ff. – id., *Fuegian
songs*, in *American Anthropologist*, N.S., vol. 38 (1936), p. 363.

[128] Alan P. and Barbara W. Merriam, *The ethnography of Flathead Indian music*,
in *Western Anthropology* no. 2 (1955), p. 13.

[129] Ralph Linton, in the *Scientific Monthly*, vol. 72 (1951) and in Hoebel, Jennings,
Smith, *Readings in anthropology*, New York, 1955, pp. 48 ff. – "The somatic and
cultural affiliations of the American Indian and the Siberian aborigine are today
taken for granted; archaeological research has made steady progress toward docu-
menting the route of aboriginal migration to the Americas across the Bering Straits
and the Aleutian Islands." (Melville J. Herskovits, *Franz Boas*, New York, 1953,
p. 19).

[130] David P. McAllester, *Enemy Way music*, Cambridge (Mass.), 1954, p. 55.

[131] George Herzog, *Musical styles in North America*, in *Proceedings of the twenty-
third International Congress of Americanists*, 1928, p. 457. – id., *The Yuman musical
style*, in *Journal of American Folklore*, vol. 48 (1928). – id., *Maricopa music*, in
Leslie Spier, *Yuman tribes of the Gila River*, Chicago, 1933, pp. 271–279.

Beside these two fundamental styles, the American Indians perform their love charm songs in a completely different way. Supposed to derive from flute melodies, these songs have indeed a distinctly instrumental character. They are slow, unaccented, nasaling, and often fluttering under the impact of a waving hand before the mouth.[132] In a similar way, we learn from an eighteenth century source that the (now extinct) Abipón in South America changed their voices in a manner consistent with the text. [133]

Few regions have completely unified styles and mannerisms. Polynesians, alike, adapt their voices to changing purpose of singing: the Tuamotu in the West make their voices breathy, low, mysterious for chants to exorcise the evil spirits.[134] But they also know a strait and steady singing and, alongside, a quavering manner, which at times becomes a trill on two pitches.[135]

In the South of Polynesia, the Maori of New Zealand performed their war songs prestissimo in a lashing microtonic falsetto, which to the unprepared listener may well sound like excited cackling in a barnyard (at least in the phonograph). Incantations, although in a similar high-strung style, give this impression much less.[136]

The excited treatment of the voice reaches across the Tasman Sea to Australia. The Australians, so tells us a report from the 1860es, sing every note with a kind of (strong) expiration. All the time they gasp with a convulsive quaffing (*Schlürfen*), only to waste their wind with an obvious effort.[137] But Australian, as well, is a strange abdominal grunting hardly heard elsewhere.[138]

Even in a comparatively small territory like Uganda, so we learn from Wachsmann,[139] voice production is very different; women in the extreme North tap their throats with the finger tips, while others ululate, yodel, or sing in glissando.

Classic singers in the Far East are trained in "seven different

---

[132] George Herzog, *Special song types in North American Indian music*, in *Zeitschrift für vergleichende Musikwissenschaft*, vol. 3 (1935), pp. 5 ff.

[133] Martin Dobrizhoffer, *Geschichte der Abiponer*, Wien, 1783, vol. 2, p. 577.

[134] E. G. Burrows, *Native music of the Tuamotus*, in *Bernice P. Bishop Museum Bulletin* 109, Honolulu, 1933, p. 57.

[135] *ibid.*, p. 58.

[136] *EFw* FE 4433 (P 433).

[137] Hermann Beckler, *Die Corroberri*, in *Globus*, vol. 13 (1868), p. 82.

[138] A. P. Elkin, *Arnhem Land music*, in *Oceania*, vol. 25 (1955), pp. 322, 326, 329 (reprinted as *Oceania Monograph* No. 9, Sydney, 1957).

[139] K. P. Wachsmann, *Folk musicians in Uganda*, Kampala, 1956, p. 4.

vocal styles; one for each of seven emotional situations, instead of one voice placement as in the West." [140]

This is correct as far as it goes. Actually, the modern West has an official style as well as a crooning, a torch, and a *diseuse* or diction style.[141]

From these motley pictures we learn that many tribal groups have several voice mannerisms according to sex, geographic situation, and the singing occasion. No attempt must be made to ascribe the individual styles to 'races,' whatever this word may mean. They are not biologically conditioned and hence not inherited but purely environmental, that is, cultural. An attempt at classifying vocal styles in the framework of *Kulturkreise* has been made by Herbert Hübner.[142] But the field is marked off too narrowly; it comprises nothing but the islands of New Britain and New Ireland; a solution requires a broader basis and a careful avoidance of the dangerous ground of pre-conceived theories.

'A QUAVERING MANNER' appears in our description of Tuamotu singing. This mannerism is still important on the high level of India's culture: in the classification of Nārada's *Sangītamakaranda*, her melody patterns or *rāgas* were divided into three groups: "the first includes those sung with a quivering voice throughout; the second, those with partial quivering; the third those without any quivering." [143] Indeed, two symbols in the neumatic notation of Gregorian song, *quilisma* and *pressus*, indicated in early times a singing *"tremula voce"*; and Magister Lambertus, the 'Pseudo-Aristotle,' mentions a third neume, the *plica*, as due to half-closing the *epiglottis* or glottal valve, combined with a *repercussio* of the throat itself.

There seems to be a connection with the bleating technique that reaches from Mongolia to the East.

[140] Henry Cowell, *l.c.*, p. 2.

[141] "Coon shouting, blues singing, torch singing come from an uncoordinated, or mixed, lower register and a mouth resonance adjustment ... Crooning is a throaty, mixed falsetto screaming". (Douglas Stanley, *Your voice*, New York, 1954, p. 7). – "Diction singer (*diseuse*) is one who concentrates on the words with complete disregard for the music or import of the composition. Each and every syllable is carefully and deliberately articulated and one syllable is sung at a time. The consonants are over-articulated ...." (*l.c.*, pp. 23 ff.).

[142] Herbert Hübner, *Die Musik im Bismarckarchipel*, Berlin, 1938.

[143] Sachs, *The Rise of music in the ancient world*, New York, 1948, p. 182.

Beyond all these mannerisms we find, as the most remarkable fact, in many parts of the world an emphasis on the higher register of man. Real barytones and bassos are generally absent. This seems to have been the case in the European Middle Ages, too. Guillaume Dufay, in the fifteenth century, was commended for having expanded the lower limit of the musical tessitura by a fourth from *G* to *D;* in the Trent Codices, principal repository of fifteenth century music, only six percent of all voice parts follow the bass clef; and bass instruments were not manufactured before the end of the 1400s.

BEYOND SUCH GENERALITIES and single traits expressed in a vague, inconsistent terminology, the method we need for future research is strictly physiological. There is essentially only one question to answer: which muscles, between diaphragm and face, are used in the cases to describe?

Such detailed analysis from continent to continent cannot be carried through in this general study. It must be left to a specialist, and even the specialist will need the pioneering work of many monographs before he surveys the globe as a whole.

Being neither a physiologist nor a trained singer, I must step back and leave the work to scholars better prepared. For obtaining at least a sample of the method I visualize, I enjoyed the competent help of Rose Brandel, who, as an ethnomusicologist and a singer, was infinitely better equipped to analyze foreign singing styles. Here is the analysis of the Japanese *no* style, which is essentially due to her empathy and knowledge.

The Japanese *no* style is to a high degree guttural, nasal, and impure in its low register. Physiologically, the word guttural means the extreme tension of the *constrictor* muscles of the throat; and nasaling, the tension of facial muscles (though not the resonance of the nasal cavity). Japan's low or chest register is not (in our western sense) coordinated with the upper, head, or falsetto register; and the tension of the laryngeal muscles has little balance. The back of the tongue blocks the pharynx almost completely, so that the mouth provides the resonance. Breathing is extremely shallow; and no vibrato enlivens the voice. Once in a while we hear the short and sudden leap to and from the upper register for which there is no name (since it does not occur in western music) and which we might adequately call a spasm or jerk.

Beyond the sample of Japanese singing, our discussions found evidence of an enormous province, reaching at least from the Far East to Negro Africa, with the common characteristics: guttural obstruction, lack of vibrato, shallow breathing, closed pharynx, and mouth resonance.

These scanty sentences are meant to show an acceptable method of avoiding an unfounded terminology and unfounded impressions. But the way is long, and the going rough.

THE ELUSIVE QUESTIONS of tempo and intensity should at least be touched upon.

Shamans accelerate their songs very often in order to increase the excited and exciting character of the healing act. But an increase of speed might occur under other circumstances as well. John Ross, discoverer of the Smith Sound Eskimo in 1818, mentions that these people sang accelerando and with an ever shriller voice. Strangely enough, R. Stein, wo accompanied Robert W. Peary to Greenland in the 1890es, reports the contrary: these same men sang in "a low tone, inaudible thirty feet away" and refused to raise their voices.[144] Neither do the Batak in Sumatra tolerate loud voices; they "even subdue the tone of their gongs."[145]

Here, too, we should take to heart the moral of that classic example given by two South American Indian tribes of the same race and living side by side on the same spot of the northeastern Gran Chaco. One of them excels in wildest dance leaps, vigorous rattle swinging, and violent singing. The dances of the other tribe are "a hesitant, indolent weaving to and fro; their musical instruments sound weak and timid; their drum, as though muffled; and their flutes, never shrill; and even their war horn makes less noise than a toy trumpet ... No effervescent enthusiasm appears in their melodies. Their singing is soft and listless."[146]

A similar example has in later years been reported from two tribes of the Bororo Fulah in the Sudan: one of them shows

---

[144] Christian Leden, *Ueber die Musik der Smith Sund Eskimos*, in *Meddelelser om Grønland*, vol. 152, no. 3 (1952), p. 10.

[145] Raden Suwanto, notes to *EFw* FE 4406 (P 406).

[146] Curt Sachs, *Rhythm and tempo*, New York, 1953, p. 53 after Herbert Baldus, *Indianerstudien im nordöstlichen Chaco*, Leipzig, 1931, p. 106.

more youthful vigor in its dances, more freshness and nerve than the other one, and the tempo of its songs is markedly faster.[147] In Uganda, some tribes delight in a slow tempo; others disdain it and prefer to hurry so much that "the sung words are often unintelligible on account of the pace." [148]

The ultimate cause of such a contrast within the same people is unknown. But it cannot be racial, cultural, or climatic.

Physiologically conditioned intensity has been exemplified earlier in this book: true tumbling strains start always in fortissimo and weaken until the bottom note is sung in pianissimo.

In the same paragraph I mentioned the psychological change of loud and soft in the one-note litanies of the Maori.

IX. INSTRUMENTS

The knowledge of instruments, although important enough in every chapter of music history, is vital in its primitive and oriental branches: ten thousands of years have left us no other musical relics.

This book can give them but limited space. For a more comprehensive presentation, the reader is referred to my *History of Musical Instruments* [149] and to my German *Geist und Werden der Musikinstrumente*,[150] which specialize in primitive, folk, and oriental instruments and their problems.

To supplement such studies by audible illustrations, the author has compiled an album of two records with sixty-seven selected examples from the non-western world (1956).[151]

LET US ONCE MORE REMEMBER that the beginnings of music were purely vocal. Peoples representing a particularly pristine phase of man's evolution, like the Vedda in inner Ceylon, the East African Wanege, the Siriono of eastern Bolivia, and most Patagonians, have no instruments. When, in a later

---

[147] Zygmunt Estreicher, *Chants et rythmes de la danse d'hommes Bororo*, in *Bulletin de la Société Neuchâteloise de Géographie*, vol. 51 (1954–'55), p. 68.
[148] K. P. Wachsmann, *Folk musicians in Uganda*, Kampala, 1956, p. 3.
[149] New York, 1940.
[150] Berlin, Dietrich Reimer, 1929.
[151] *EFw* FE 4525 (P 525).

phase, instruments begin to appear, they do so in rudimentary forms without any attempt at melodic achievements.[152]

The use of instruments goes back to late palaeolithic times. A number of instruments – strung, beaded rattles, scrapers, bullroarers, and bone flutes – have been excavated at least from Magdalenian strata, which represent the ultimate steps before reaching the end of the Older Stone Age.[153]

In early periods, the reasons for using instruments were totally different from those of singing. Early vocal music had carried words as a mere vehicle or else burst forth as a powerful discharge of passionate feeling. But instrumental music, at first remote from passion, began in general as a percussive act of the body: slapping the buttocks, the belly, the thighs, or clapping the hands, or stamping the ground. Its cause was a muscular urge concomitant to the nervous tension of those who sang or listened to singing; its aim was audible order. Against the basically melodic character of vocal music, the beginnings of instrumental music were basically rhythmic. Singing is allowed to be free, and the warbling bird does not obey a conductor's baton; percussion, like any recurring motion of the body, invites, indeed, demands a regular time: *rhythmus in corporis motu est*, states Marcus Fabius Quintilianus, the orator, around the year 100 A.D.

Percussion stands seldom alone; rhythm, as a regulator, becomes nonsensical where there is nothing to regulate, be it a melody or at least the steps of dancers and marchers. Thus, early percussion acts mostly as an accompaniment, although we shall see that in quite a number of cases the drums keep a rhythm and tempo totally different from that of the voices.

But our narrative is still rather far from times when drums were used. Incidentally, the drum as a criterion of chronology must be dealt with very carefully. We can more or less exactly determine when the drum appeared; but the lack of drums in

---

[152] For a classification of musical instruments cf. Erich M. von Hornbostel and Curt Sachs, *Systematik der Musikinstrumente*, in *Zeitschrift für Ethnologie*, vol. 46 (1914), pp. 553–590. – Abridged in Curt Sachs, *The history of musical instruments*, New York, 1940, pp. 454–467. – Contradictory: André Schaeffner, *Origine des instruments de musique*, Paris, 1936, and Hans-Heinz Dräger, *Prinzip einer Systematik der Musikinstrumente*, Kassel, 1948.

[153] Otto Seewald, *Beiträge zur Kenntnis der steinzeitlichen Musikinstrumente Europas*, Wien, 1934.

some civilizations does not necessarily indicate an earlier stratum. In Polynesia, for example, drums were once in use, but have in many islands been abandoned.[154]

In a long evolution, early man increased the effect of pristine body percussion by replacing the struck or striking part of the body with a harder object taken from nature or made by human hands. Clapping the hands was superseded by the wooden click of boomerangs; stamping the ground was reinforced by rattling nuts or hooves strapped around the ankles, indeed, by using some resonant, hollow bamboo as a pestle. Such 'extensions,' as the anthropologists call them, led from the bare, uncovered body in a slow evolution to the actual instruments of later times and the present.

Extensions of the limbs were not the only beginnings of instrumental music, and intensified rhythm was by far not its sole purpose and meaning. There were the many objects, mute themselves, but able to make a section of the air vibrate and thus to provide sounds. A hollow branch or reed or conch distorts the hum or howl of those who press it as a loudspeaker against the lips; an eagle's bone becomes a screaming whistle; the bull-roarer – a flat slab of wood whirled around the head on a twine – roars like a motor propeller. Eerie, non-human, terrifying were those sounds and roused emotions and the imagination of man beyond whatever slapping, clapping, or pounding could do. Rather, this horrific, awe-inspiring din stands for the voices of spirits and demons, as we behold them in the gruesome masks of demon-dancers. "A cold sweat," confesses Gheerbrant, "had broken out of all my pores and run down my body. The hairs on my skin had stood upright. The blast of the trumpets had shaken the walls, the roof of the hut, and the very ground itself. The sounds had seemed full of sweat and smoke, and they had moaned and howled as though they really were the voices of spirits, simple animal spirits of the heaven and the earth. They rose from the ground and echoed from the walls and the roof; they went through my vitals like beasts roaring in the forests." [155]

Once more we find ourselves in that proto-religious and pre-scientific world in which both outlook and action obey the paralogical laws of magic.

[154] E. G. Burrows, *Native music of the Tuamotus*, in *Bernice P. Bishop Museum Bulletin* 109, Honolulu, 1933, p. 71.

[155] Alain Gheerbrant, *Journey to the Far Amazon*, New York, 1954, p. 104.

The role of instruments in magic-ridden cultures is confusingly manifold. Instruments, as the only objects, have not only meaningful shapes and colors but also meaningful sounds and even significant substances. The ensuing connotations are often in agreement and sometimes contradictory. All of them can be reduced to one of the two universal principles: through the worlds of men and beasts, across all groups and families, a great divide leaves, left and right, what Chinese cosmology has called the *yang* and the *yin*, the male sex and the female sex as the fundaments of all organic life. Not even divinities are exempt from this elementary dualism – the skies and the underworld have their gods and their goddesses: Zeus with Hera, Osiris with Isis, Odin with Frigg. Differing and complementing each other in their anatomical, physiological, psychical, social traits, the sexes are in their polarity important, indeed, indispensable to ascertain the survival of society and procreation. The impact of this dualism has been so strong, essential and consistent on the human mind that the universe in all its manifestations, as planets, seasons, liquids, colors, numbers, pitches, seemed to be an interplay of male and female qualities. If in these cosmological juxtapositions the sun and daytime, blood, color red, odd numbers stood on the masculine side, the moon, and nighttime, milk and color white as well as even numbers stood across on the feminine side.

Musical instruments were vitally involved in this sex dualism.

Masculine, in unimpaired purity, is the trumpet – even in its pristine, pre-metal form when, made of reed or wood, it served solely as a megaphone or voice-disguising mask without requiring the resilient tension of the lip muscle characteristic of actual trumpeting. With its aggressive, menacing sound, it is clearly virile; as a tube, it has definitely phallic connotations; often it is painted red, and even into the twentieth century it has in military bands been adorned with tassels in red or wrapped in felt of the same color. In virtue of such masculine symbolism, it became in later civilizations an instrument for war and princely pomp; but in more archaic cultures it was confined to rituals of a male and solar nature. It acted as a charm for rebirth or resurrection after death or when in rites at dusk and at dawn the sun must be forced to reappear in the morning. Women who happened to see a trumpet were often put to death.

The role of the flute is originally as virile as that of the trumpet. Owing to its tubular shape, it represents the penis; and the sound is male enough; the flutes are either long and wide and yield a subdued roar, or they are short and narrow and have the shrill agressiveness of a whistle. Often, in this latter case, they are made of bone which, once more, has generally a phallic significance. Accordingly a flute must, in many archaic civilizations, not be seen by uninitiated strangers, women, or children. In New Guinea, sacred bamboo flutes, up to six meters long, are actually used as penes for ritual cohabitations with the chieftain's wife; they are played in the forest while a widow is compulsory sleeping with a relative in the degree of kinship that the tribal law requires; and girls are deflowered in front of them in the ceremonial house of the village.[156]

The flute seems to be a love charm everywhere. Ernest Hemingway, in *A Farewell to Arms*, makes one of the soldiers tell how at home in the Abruzzi mountains young men were not supposed to play the flute in serenades "because it was bad for the girls to hear the flute at night." Among American Indians, the flute belongs greatly to lovers and love; but we do not know whether or not its effect is still considered magic. Often, as among the Sioux, young men in love learn the flute so they may woo their girls in the proper way; playing the flute amounts to a proposal;[157] and many love songs are derived from flute melodies.

Flute melodies are dangerous not only to girls. Herdsmen of the Gikuyu in East Africa are sometimes forbidden "to play the flute while the flock is in the grazing field, for it is feared that sweet melodies might invoke evil spirits and thus bring defilement to the herds. It is also taboo to play a flute or to whistle inside a hut, because it is believed that sweet music can easily attract the attention of wandering evil spirits and lure them to come and cause mischief inside the homestead."[158]

Stringed instruments, rather scarce in primitive civilizations, are on the feminine side. Originally struck with a slender stick (before being plucked or bowed), they render a frail, subdued, and quite unaggressive sound so weak that some resonance

[156] Richard Thurnwald, *Bánaro society*, in *Memoirs of the American Anthropological Association*, vol. 3 (1916), pp. 261, 269.

[157] *EFw* FE 4505 (P 505) II 6 (ed. Henry Cowell).

[158] Jomo Kenyatta, *Facing Mount Kenya*, London, 1953, p. 95.

cavity is necessary to make it audible to others – a pit in the
ground, an earthen vessel, a gourd, or even the player's mouth;
and this resonator gives them a womb-like cavity. They are
allotted intimate, introvert roles: the musical bow or a hunter's
bow whose string is gently struck with a slender stick has here
and there the reputation of inducing contact with benevolent
spirits.[159] Among non-stringed instruments, a widespread importance in courtship is assigned to the jaw's harp, whose elastic
tongue vibrates between the player's jaws and receives pitch and
resonance from the changing form and size of his mouth.[160]

SOME INSTRUMENTS have conflicting characteristics of either
sex and thus are ambiguous or contradictory in their connotations.
A trumpet made by cutting off the apex of a conch shell is
masculine in virtue of its aggressive, frightening sound; but as it
derives from a water animal and in its slit and lips reminds of
a woman's sex organ, it is feminine as well. Thus being andro-
gynous, it serves at one place for solar, and at another place
for lunar cults, here for boy's initiations and there for women's
mystic dances which a man is forbidden to see.

The change can also occur through a clash of form and playing
action: drums and wooden slit-drums, rounded and hollow, are
feminine as forms, but masculine because the primitive sees in
the beating act a symbol of cohabitation. Either instrument
develops from feminine to masculine connotations, from the
predominant consideration of form to that of the act.[161]

But even without any changing or conflicting sex characteristics, all instruments become in their connotations in-
creasingly weaker with the weakening or reversing of magic
beliefs. They then assume new social rules, be it within their
indigenous environment or in foreign places to which they have
been exported.

Two impressive examples of revaluation are the bull-roarer
and the gourd rattle.

On the lowest cultural level of Australia, the bull-roarer, as a
ghost's voice, frightens the women away when boys are being

[159] Curt Sachs, *l.c.*, pp. 56 ff.
[160] e.g. A. L. Kroeber, *Peoples of the Philippines*, 2nd ed., New York, 1943, p. 221.
– R. F. Fortune, *Sorcerers of Dobu*, London, 1932, p. 29.
[161] Sachs, *l.c.*, ch. 1.

circumcised in the bush; a woman who has happened to see the instrument must be killed. Indeed, the bull-roarer is supposed to hold the forces of ancestors and to fecondate the wombs of women. But in New-Guinea, on a somewhat advanced level, girls (!) having reached maturity whirl it around as a love charm to secure a young man's affection. In early planters' civilizations, it serves as a weather charm to attract both wind and rain; in Malaya, it frightens elephants away from damaging the plantation; and in a village on the Lido near Venice I once saw a boy with a simple school ruler spun round on a twine. Here is, in one short paragraph, the gamut of meaning from utmost secrecy to open magic, and over sheer utility to children's fun.

The gourd rattle runs through a shorter gamut. Where shamanism comes to an end or women no longer shake the rattle in their original feminine rites, they leave it to the infants as an irresistibly fascinating toy – its way from places of worship to cribs in the nursery is but one step.

How quick the transition to a children's toy can be is clearly shown by a custom in French Upper Guinea: newly circumcised boys, dismissed from their retreat, perform a ceremonial dance which they accompany with a kind of sistrum especially made with little disks of gourd stringed on a shaken bow. Then they drop their instruments to be picked up by the children.[162]

THE ALL-DOMINATING CONTRAST of the sexes also lends a hand in shifting certain instruments from the pristine concepts of mere sound to the pre-melodic contrast of high and low, even if these two qualities have not yet definite pitches or a definite distance from one another. On the Orinoco, Gheerbrant saw all instruments in pairs of unequal lengths, "the male and the female."[163] The dwarfish aborigines of Malacca have in either hand a stamping bamboo tube; the right tube, higher in pitch, would give one blow quickly followed by three beats of the left and low-pitched tube. The higher tube, a little shorter, is called father or man, the lower and taller one, mother or woman. This is bewildering: we, today, would invert the names and give the

---

[162] André Schaeffner, *Les rites de circoncision en pays Kissi* in *Etudes Guinéennes*, no. 12 (1953), p. 52.
[163] Gheerbrant, *l.c.*, p. 94.

male connotation to the taller, low-pitched tube, since men are higher in stature and lower in voice. The aboriginal ideas are different: the primitives are, above all, aware of the aggressiveness of higher pitches and the passive, more subdued character of a lower one. The same is true of quite a number of regularly coupled instruments: in the New Hebrides, the biggest slit-drum is called the mother (which may also be due to matriarchal concepts), and in the Islamic belt the larger of two kettledrums is defined as female (this time in the absence of matriarchal connotations). Only late did the sex connection reverse itself.

The two sexes lend their names even to the two lips of a slit-drum (although they are originally, seen from an anatomical viewpoint, strictly feminine); drum sticks and the very beats follow the same dualism: the Japanese call the right stick 'male' and the left stick 'female'; [164] and American jazz percussionists call the left-hand 'hard' beat *mama*, while the right-hand 'soft' beat is the *daddy*.[165] The Olombo of the Upper Congo dub the open string of their two-stringed zithers *nyangó* or mother,[166] evidently without bestowing the name of father upon the other string which is meant to be stopped.

Nor should we forget that in the Far East the twelve pitches within an octave (*lü's* in Chinese) are alternately male and female and, with them, the stone slabs, bells, and pipes in which they materialize; that the *ryo* mode on *C* is male, and the *ritsu* modes on *D* are female; that the *saléndro* gender of Java is male and the *pélog* gender female; and that the melodic speech inflections of China are subdivided into male and, a tone lower, female groups.

A generally accepted western remainder of sex dualism as a metaphor are the 'masculine' and 'feminine' word endings in rhymes of our poetry, according to whether the accent is on the last or the penultimate syllable – probably because the accented ending sounds stronger and more decisive.

THE MALE-FEMALE CONCEPT illustrates an important stage in the history of instrumental music. While on an archaic level

---

[164] F. T. Piggott, *The music and musical instruments of Japan*, 2nd ed., Yokohama, 1909, p. 162.

[165] Cf. Harold Courlander introducing *EFw* FE 4502 (P 502).

[166] John F. Carrington, *A comparative study of some Central African gong-languages*, Ph.D. diss. Univ. of London, Brussels, 1949, pp. 37 ff. (Courtesy Rose Brandel).

instruments serve basically to mark rhythm or to utter mere
sounds without vying with voices to produce melodies, we watch
in the stage of sex contrasts an enrichment of the instrumental
language by opposing high and low. The 'father' and the 'mother'
of a pair of stamping tubes might produce them; or the two lips
of a slit-drum; or the two sections that a stopping finger creates
on the string of a musical bow.

It will not always be easy to decide whether or not this pre-
melodic distinction and enjoyment of high and low is a natural
evolution from one-tone concepts to melody or rather the retrocessive adaptation of higher, melodic forms from some advanced
civilization down to the lesser needs and potentialities of primitives. The conclusive criterion will probably be provided by
some alien detail in the non-musical workmanship of the
instrument. Where every trait conforms with the primitive level
of the home civilization, the musical feature is almost certainly
genuine; where an ornamental carving betrays foreign influence,
the indigenous character of the music is open to doubt.

Of actually melodic instruments we meet, among the first,
the ubiquitous flutes. At that stage, they are not too long and
not too short, not roaring and not shrill, but soft-spoken and
of medium size; and one feature lifts them to a level where they
can compete with human voices and begin to sing: fingerholes,
opened and closed, vary the pitch-producing length of the flute
and allow it to play in melodies, brisk and longing, staccato,
legato, by steps and by leaps, in tender pulsations and foamy
cascades.

The holes appear in strange arrays. It is obvious – as every
violinist or guitarist knows – that two musical steps of equal
width require different strides on the instrument, with the
second smaller than the first one, and so forth. This applies to
finger holes as much as to frets: their progression should be, in
mathematical language, 'harmonic' rather than 'arithmeti·.'
But no array of holes proceeds in a harmonic progression; the
holes are equidistant throughout or else arranged in two groups,
either one with equidistant holes and separated from one another
by a somewhat larger space. And often the holes begin only in
the exact middle of the flute and leave the upper half intact.
This is a strange abdication of the aural to the visual sense. It

would be incomprehensible were not the individual holes quite
often musically 'corrected' by increasing or diminishing their
normal sizes. It is, to be true, not only the visual but
also the tactile sense to which the ear must yield: the holes
are always at an easy fingering distance, not excluding the
larger gap between the two groups of holes, which is exempt
from fingering concerns, since either hand is assigned to one
group.

The easiest fingering distance, not too long and not too short,
is about an inch – a fact that shifts the whole question from the
visual, tactile, and acoustical to the metrical field. All over the
ancient Orient, the measuring unit was the foot with its nine,
ten, or twelve inches as the subdivisions. Far from being a merely
utilitarian device, as it is in our own civilization, the ancient feet
were venerable symbols of order, rule, and cosmic unity important enough to be engraved as *etala* on the socles of royal
statues in Mesepotamia; and, forcibly expressed in figures and
ratios, they reflected the mystic power of numbers, immanent in
the tenets of both religion and philosophy from the Pacific to
the Mediterranean. Philo, the Jewish-Hellenistic thinker, who
lived in Alexandria at the beginning of the first century A.D.,
has given this short formulation of numeric control: "Whatever
is not considered worthy of being conceived by a number, is
profane and not sanctified; but whatever is based on a numerical
value is recognized as already proved." [167]

But feet and inches were rarely consistent; the feet had
different length and a different number of inches. They changed
from country to country, from dynasty to dynasty, from ruler
to ruler. As a consequence, the flutes as well were substantially
different in length and fingerhole distances. In many cases, a
careful comparison with the various ancient feet and inches in
metrological records allows to identify the provenience and
approximate date of a flute. On the other hand, many flutes have
undergone a disturbing diffusion from high to lower civilizations
which themselves had no conception of measuring standards.
Where such was the case, the flutes lost exactness to thoughtless

---

[167] Philo, *Posterity of Cain*, 28, quoted after Hanoch Avenary, *Magic, symbolism
and allegory of the old-Hebrew sound-instruments*, in *Collectanea Historiae Musicae*,
vol. 2 (1956), p. 23.

copying and to casual measuring by the maker's digits and span.[168]

Even outside the concern of hole-drilling, tuning seems to be a visual and tactile procedure. Panpipes, those rafts or bundles of stopped flutes without fingerholes, each rendering one different pitch, are adjusted without reliance on the ear; the players rather introduce a measuring rod to take their sounding (a word particularly inadequate in this case) and rests satisfied when the depth is exactly like the one of the model pipe. To quote the best example: on the Solomon Islands in Melanesia this is carried out in several days of ceremonies by reproducing painstakingly the paragons in the possession of the grand-chieftain.[169] As late, culturally speaking, as the European Middle Ages, all the many treatises on organ building or the casting of bell chimes simply teach to proceed from pipe to pipe or from bell to bell at the ratio of 9 : 8 for the wholetone distance (or of 3 : 2 for the fifth, and so forth), measuring there the mere lengths and here the mere weights. Actually, pitch depends on more than just a single measuring unit, and musically such unilateral way of tuning can never yield satisfactory results.

It is important to stress these facts. Any attempt at measuring a couple of ancient or exotic flutes for the purpose of finding the 'scale' used in a certain age or by a certain people must ultimately fail. If there is such a scale, it is the player's, not the maker's concern, even when the two are one person. He achieves it with the strength and direction of his breath, with the tension of his lips, with a movement of his tongue, and with a complicated fingering that might cover the lowermost hole only in part or open one hole between two closed holes. The musical imperfection of a non-musically perforated instrument allows the flutist – almost paradoxically – a welcome freedom of intonation which

---

[168] An excellent description of such measuring and burning procedures in East Africa can be found in (Margaret Trowell and) K. P. Wachsmann, *Tribal crafts of Uganda*, London, 1953, p. 339. – Cf. also, for the Provençal *galoubet*, Claudie Marcel-Dubois, *Extensions du domaine d'observations directes en ethnographie musicale française*, in *Les Colloques de Wégimont*, vol. 1 (1954–'55), Paris-Bruxelles, 1956, p. 109.

[169] Erich M. von Hornbostel, *Die Musik auf den nordwestlichen Salomo-Inseln*, in R. Thurnwald, *Salomo-Inseln und Bismarck-Archipel*, vol. 1, 1912. – id., *Die Maassnorm als kulturgeschichtliches Forschungsmittel*, in *Festschrift für Pater Wilhelm Schmidt*, 1928, pp. 303 ff. Curt Sachs, *Les instruments de musique de Madagascar*, in *Université de Paris, Travaux de l'Institut d'Ethnographie*, vol. 28, 1938, pp. 14–23.

no player of a modern Boehm flute enjoys. He is independent of the tyrannic authority of a preconceived, demanding system.

THE OLDEST FOOT of China that we know measures 230 mm; a stopped pipe of this length produces a pitch very close to *f'* sharp. Erich M. von Hornbostel found this pitch so often on panpipes and other wind instruments between East Asia all the way across the Pacific to South America that he safely excluded mere coincidence. Indeed, he found that all over this enormous territory the scales available on individual instruments were different from ours but conspicuously similar among themselves. He saw an explanation in the two assumptions that (1) to tune the canes of a panpipe the easiest way is overblowing the largest cane and thus producing a twelfth which, transposed down by an octave, provides the fifth; and that (2) this overblown fifth in stopped pipes is slightly shorter than the perfect fifth, so that any tuning due to a cycle of fifths and fourths yields of necessity steps shorter than 'Pythagorean.' [170]

This sensational *Blasquintentheorie* was contradicted by the late Manfred Bukofzer, whose physical measurements showed that overblown fifths have very different degrees of deviation from perfect fifths according to their size.[171] Another weakness of this ingenious theory is that the way of tuning, wherever described, consists in comparing the lengths of tubes, not their pitches.

Nevertheless, even with methodical flaws, the agreement in tuning over such enormous stretches is impressive enough to forbid a mere shelving of Hornbostel's astounding results.

THE TUNING OF STRINGS and chimes follows other principles. Stringed instruments are on the whole of two kinds: those with open strings and those with stopped strings. Lyres, harps, and zithers belong to the first group, and lutes to the second. There are however lyres, harps, and zithers with strings occasionally

[170] Von Hornbostel's first communication in *Anthropos*, vols. 14/15 (1919), pp. 569 ff.

[171] Manfred Bukofzer, *Präzisionsmessungen an primitiven Musikinstrumenten*, in *Zeitschrift für Physik*, vol. 99 (1936), pp. 643 ff. – id., *Kann die Blasquintentheorie zur Erklärung exotischer Tonsysteme beitragen?*, in *Anthropos*, vol. 32 (1937), pp. 402 ff. – id., *Blasquinte*, in *Die Musik in Geschichte und Gegenwart*, vol. 1 (1951) col. 1918 ff. – Jaap Kunst, *Around von Hornbostel's theory of the cycle of blown fifths*, in *Koninklijke Vereeniging Indisch Instituut, Mededeeling 76*, Amsterdam, 1948.

stopped, and lutes with open strings. Since most of all these instruments are post-primitive, it might suffice here to say that the first group is usually tuned by ear in a cycle of fifths and fourths, and the second group is ruled by a 'divisive' system, half the string yielding the octave of the 'open' note, a third of its length the fifth, a quarter the fourth, a fifth part the major third, a sixth part the minor third.[172]

But there are many more ways of tuning, and some of them quite unexpected. In Uganda, harps are not only 'well-tempered' but also 'isotonic': one Ganda people divides the octave into five, in principle equal, steps of around 240 cents, which corresponds to the *saléndro* gender of Java's and Bali's *gamelan* orchestras. We might call this tuning 'iso-pentatonic.' Another Ganda people divides the octave into four equal steps, of a minor third each, which makes it 'iso-tetratonic.' This, of course, is highly suspect of oriental influences, although we are not yet able to trace their exact diffusion routes.

To achieve isotony, one could (1) start from the octave as a given whole and divide its tonal space into equal parts, four or five; or else (2) advance in equal steps until the octave is reached. The first procedure is not feasible; the ear in all its frailty cannot divide an octave into a given number of equal parts. The second course is problematic, too; a unit which, multiplied by four or five, leads to a perfect octave is not easily found. And yet this second method is a fact. The performer proceeds from the unit to the octave, which however yields approximations only and requires subsequent corrections.[173]

In a special paper,[174] K. P. Wachsmann, then curator of the Uganda Museum in Kampala, describes the actual procedure to the last detail. The harpist pulls the highest string to about g'. Next, he tunes the adjacent string to a distance of about 240 cents without any standard other than his tonal memory and goes this way down over all the eight strings. This method, it is true, requires control and adjustment. To achieve it, the player rapidly plucks the strings 1, 2, 3, which in succession yield

[172] Curt Sachs, *The rise of music*, New York, 1943, pp. 71 ff., 75 ff.

[173] K. P. Wachsmann, *l.c.*, pp. 4 ff.

[174] K. P. Wachsmann, *An equal-stepped tuning in a Ganda harp*, in *Nature*, vol. 165 (1950), pp. 40 ff. – id., *A study of norms in the tribal music of Uganda*, in *Ethnomusicology*, Newsletter no. 11, Sept. 1957, pp. 11 ff.

about 480 cents or almost the 498 cents of a perfect fourth. He continues in a similar way with 2, 3, 4 and 3, 4, 5 down to 6, 7, 8, all these groups being expected to affect the ear as nearly identical fourths. An easy second control tests the octaves between 1 and 6, between 2 and 7, between 3 and 8. With all this reliance on mere hearing accuracy, the maximum deviation from normal that Wachsmann found with the help of a modern stroboscope was, on any string, no more than fifteen cents or the negligible 13.6th part of a tone.

THE ISOTONIC TUNINGS in Uganda have astonishing parallels in African xylophones: two South African peoples, Bapende and Chopi, give their xylophones an 'iso-heptatonic' arrangment with seven equal steps of about 171 cents in an octave, which amounts exactly to the current genders of Siam and Burma, that is, of another region in Southeast Asia. This striking coincidence has of course attracted attention.[175]

From a methodical viewpoint, it is instructive to hold the Chopi xylophones, as they actually sound, against H. A. Junod's very different notation of the eighteen nineties, which makes believe that these instruments are tuned in a neat European tonality, be it *E flat* minor or *G flat* major, however you want to read it.[176] Such comparison amounts to a good warning of the treachery of our ears as well as of western staff notation, and hence, alas, of most of our printed music examples.

These South African xylophones lead us into a third domain of melody-carrying instruments: percussive chimes, or sets of ready-made elements, be they slabs, bells, gongs, bowls, and here and there even drums, each element rendering one single note and all together constituting a scale. The set is finished by the instrument maker to the minutest detail; the player must obey his tuning, although he is allowed to make a few minor

[175] Cf. Jaap Kunst, *A musicological argument for cultural relationship between Indonesia – probably the Isle of Java – and Central Africa*, in *Proceedings of the Musical Association*, Session 62 (1936), translated into German as *Ein musikologischer Beweis für Kulturzusammenhänge zwischen Indonesien – vermutlich Java – und Zentral-Afrika*, in *Anthropos*, vol. 31 (1936), pp. 131 ff. – Hugh T. Tracey, *Chopi Musicians. Their music, poetry and instruments*, Oxford, 1948, pp. 121 ff. – Ernest Haddon, *Possible origin of the Chopi timbila xylophone*, in the *African Music Society Newsletter*, vol. 1 No. 5 (1952), p. 61. – In a more reserved attitude: K. P. Wachsmann, *Musicology in Uganda*, in *Journal of the Royal Anthropological Institute*, vol. 83 (1953), pp. 50–57.

[176] Henri-A. Junod, *Les Ba-Ronga*, Neuchâtel, 1898, p. 264.

alterations during changes of temperature by adding appropriate lumps of wax or by chiseling matter away.

The roots of chimes reach down to prehistoric, pre-melodic levels, when two or three and exceptionally more rough-hewn slabs were loosely laid on the stretched-out legs of a person sitting on the ground and struck with two knobbed sticks. But whether these primitive leg xylophones, in Melanesia and westward to Indonesia, are actually beginnings or rather retrogressive forms is hard to decide. Nor do we know from reports at hand whether or not a genuine, well-tuned scale is planned. Where on the contrary the slabs are shorter, more numerous, and solidly assembled in some portable framework or on a cradle-shaped resonance box, as in the Southeast of Asia, in Africa, and in Negro-America, we can be sure of a careful tuning in the scale-system of the country (usually done by cutting out the surface of the slab, which is done in the middle for flatting the tone, and near the end, for sharping it). This applies to the principal stations along the great migration route: from Indonesia to Southeast Africa and from there with the black slaves across the Atlantic to Central America, plus minor branches to Japan and Europe.

Everywhere the playing technique is highly developed; and the often incredible virtuosity of the performers has created a genuine, idiomatic instrumental music which we can best compare to our western keyboard toccatas. In this respect, the next of kin of the xylophone – the lithophones, metallophones, and crystallophones – lag somewhat behind; and so do the second cousins: the drum chimes, porcelain bowl chimes,[177] gong chimes, and bell chimes. The unmuffled resonance, particularly of the metal, excludes the uninhibited, agile technique that the dry and short-breathed wooden slabs invite.

As an aside: metallophones and gong chimes, chief instruments of Indonesian music, do not occur in Madagascar,[178] which was an Indonesian colony. Since the last wave of Malayo-Polynesians seems to have reached the island off Southeast Africa as late as the fifth century A.D.,[179] we must presume the non-existence of bronze sets at that time.

[177] *EFw* FE 4409 (P 409) II 1 (India).
[178] Curt Sachs, *Les instruments de musique de Madagascar*, in *Université de Paris, Travaux et Mémoires de l'Institut d'Ethnologie*, vol. 28, Paris, 1938.
[179] Ralph Linton, *The tree of culture*, New York, 1955, p. 203.

THE SUBJECT OF LITHOPHONES cannot easily be examined without a glance at the curious stones, excavated early in 1949 in Indochina and shipped to their present quarters in the *Musée de l'Homme* at Paris.[180] Rarely, musical instruments have been given a publicity like this one; musicological periodicals and even dailies have view in conferring on these venerable stones a "megalithic" age and "a complete Eastern or Javanese pentatonic scale."

After such magniloquence, it is almost a disappointment to read the more cautious report by André Schaeffner, music curator of the Musée de l'Homme.[181] Schaeffner is careful enough to say that (from his viewpoint) nothing allows to date the stones; they may be a few centuries old or several millenniums.

In the discussion of these stones we face two apparently contradictory qualities; they have been chipped and hence prepared in a technique officially known as palaeolithic; but tuned chimes, to the best of our present knowledge, nowhere occur before the Bronze Age.

The conflict might be alleviated by the modern loosening of the time-honored equations: chipped stone = palaeolithic, polished stone = neolithic. "This classification was one of the first to break down." [182] We know well-polished implements from the Magdalenian (late Palaeolithic) and, inversily, chipped artifacts from the Neolithic, and Linton mentions expressly that Southeast Asia's Neolithic still knew chipped stone implements, much as they were rare and crudely shaped.[183]

As to the stones of the *Musée de l'Homme*, the archaeologists leave no doubt that their find is neolithic *"de facture bacsonienne."*

The musical side of the question is still more complicated. The trove itself consists in eleven disconnected, chipped slabs of sonorous stone in various sizes, the largest being 101.7 cm long. As to the allegedly pentatonic scale, we must for the time being rest satisfied with non-committal and contradictory measure-

[180] G. Condominas, *Le lithophone préhistorique de Ndut Lieng Krak*, in *Bulletin de l'Ecole Française d'Extrême Orient*, vol. 45, 2 (1952), pp. 359-392. – Cf. also: Bernard Fagg, *The discovery of multiple rock gongs in Nigeria*, in *Man*, vol. 56 (1956), pp. 17-18, and *African Music*, vol. 1, 3 (1956), pp. 6-9.
[181] André Schaeffner, *Une importante découverte archéologique: le lithophone de Ndut Lieng Krak (Vietnam)*, in *Revue de Musicologie*, vol. 33 (1951), N.S. pp. 1-19.
[182] Melville J. Herskovits, *Cultural anthropology*, New York, 1955, p. 43.
[183] Ralph Linton, *The tree of culture*, New York, 1955, p. 174.

ments taken at the museum, which in their divergences can perhaps be explained by the quantity of irregular partials above the actual, intended pitches. The two measurements taken with undisclosed apparatuses, but not with an electronic counter, by three scholars and published by Schaeffner, vary at times by no less than 134 cents or two thirds of a wholetone; and among the steps from slab to slab one distance reaches only 18 (or, in the other measurement, 24) cents, which amounts to more or less a tenth of a tone and does not fit in any conceivable system of tuning, pentatonic or non-pentatonic. Possibly, it has been suggested, the stones do belong to two lithophones, not just to one.

Moreover, we read in the archaeological report: [184] "It is possible that originally the longest slab was even longer," and: "It is hard to say whether one of the slabs (lame XI) is not the remnant of a more important element or a defective, broken slab, or whether it represents in itself a piece of which we ignore the role." And on the following page: "Two slabs present important breaks. One end of slab V is completely broken, and the accident has taken away two other pieces on either edge of the slab; one of them has left a cut 17 cm long, and the other one 15.5 long – a break, it seems, posterior to the manufacture of the slab and causing a false sound. Slab II is damaged on either end ..."

Therewith, any discussion of a scale becomes mere speculation.

As matters stand, I am at this stage inclined, not to doubt [185] whether these stones were a musical instrument, but whether it was meant for actual musical performance. They were found in an unsuitable, upright position against the wall; they have apparently none of the forms known from other sounding stones discovered between the Carolines in Micronesia, the Far East, Chios in the Mediterranean, Ethiopia, and Venezuela; [186] unlike anyone of them – the *kawa* bowls on Ponape (Carolines) excepted – they have no hole for passing a suspension-cord. The makeshift playing arrangement that the *Musée de l'Homme* has given them – horizontal on two longitudinal supports like those of a xylo-

---

[184] Condominas, *l.c.*, p. 6.
[185] As does Fritz A. Kuttner, *Nochmals: Die Steinzeit-Lithophone von Annam*, in *Die Musikforschung*, vol. 6 (1953), pp. 1–8.
[186] Curt Sachs, *Geist und Werden der Musikinstrumente*, Berlin, 1929, pp. 119 ff.

phone – does nowhere occur where stones are involved. All considered, the only musical datum is the fact that these like many other stones yield definite, different tones when struck with a hammer. Even if they were meant to be struck and to sound in some ritual, there is no indication that they were used in scale-like tuned chimes.[187]

BEFORE DISCUSSING INSTRUMENTAL MUSIC, we should briefly touch upon the problem of general distribution. A panoramic view discloses a number of areas strangely distinct in their instrumental possessions and predilections in spite of diffusion from country to country and across the seas.

Indonesia shows the sharpest outline: tuned idiophonic sets, like xylophones, metallophones, and gong chimes, have an uncontested leading role and (together with one single drum), often unite to form the famous *gamelans* or orchestras. Strings, and wind instruments are by no means absent but mostly due to Muhammedan incursions around the middle of the second thousand years A.D. and hence of minor importance. In the Far East and westward to Burma and India, idiophonic chimes occur but have an essentially weaker position. Only the xylophones, hardly used in the Far East and unknown in India, crossed the ocean, reached Negro Africa, and from there were taken to the West Indies and Central America.

India gives a leading musical role to the drum. This role is slightly weaker in the Middle East and more or less accessory in the rest of the world.

This statement excepts Black Africa, where the drum in solos and ensembles seems to be almost indispensable. Yet there is a strong possibility that in Africa the drum belongs in a later

[187] Since then, however, there have been found in the same region (the remnants of) two more of such lithophones. One of them, originally heptatonic (but one of the slabs was totally crushed by the bulldozer that brought the instrument to light) is now in the possession of Mr. Claire Omar Musser, Los Angeles. Mr. Musser who is an expert in acoustics, sent me the measurements of the intervals, made with a Strobokonn. The scale has nothing in common with the Parisian instrument:

$$1473.6 \quad 1241.09 \quad 1173 \quad 1008.7 \quad 959.2 \quad 841.3$$
$$\text{I} \quad 297 \quad \text{II} \quad 97\tfrac{1}{2} \text{ III } 261\tfrac{1}{2} \quad \text{IV} \quad 87\tfrac{1}{2} \quad \text{V} \quad 227\tfrac{1}{2} \text{ VI}$$

The other instrument, according to the population of the village where it was found, originally had had six slabs, three of which had been lost in the course of the years. The remaining three slabs were held in high honor and awe and were sounded only at special occasions. (J.K.)

stratum; in several cases we hear that a certain tribe owes its drums to an import from the north. "Indeed, among the Bashi no particular emphasis seems to be placed upon drums and drumming; these percussion instruments are relatively rarely used ... One seldom hears drums being played about the countryside ... Singers, with some exceptions, do not call for drums nor seem particularly pleased when a drummer happens to be present." [188] Among the Gikuyu in Kenya "the use of drums as musical instruments has been adopted only in recent years; the idea was borrowed from the Wakamba, who are the eastern neighbours of the Gikuyu." [189]

Below this possibly later stratum of drums, we behold a strange prevalence of stringed instruments, from the simplest musical bows, ground harps, and ground zithers way up to lyres, harps, and zithers in many forms and hybrids. A number of them are clearly dependent upon old-Egyptian and Arabian diffusion; but many types do not occur anywhere else and must be considered indigenous.

Once more, we see old Europe in a certain agreement with Negro Africa: the earliest literary sources mention harps and lyres in the north; prehistorians have found the strangest horns of bronze-age character, as the Baltic *lurer* and the side-blown instruments from ancient Ireland; modern folk usage still knows zithers and fiddles as well as rustic horns, trumpets, and flutes. Incidentally: the side-blown Irish horns have their only parallels – in antler and ivory – all over Negro Africa. Oboes and clarinets are originally absent from either region.

The Pacific Islands, including Australia, are comparatively poor in instruments. With the exclusion of panpipes, their instrumental music is not important enough to settle in definite patterns. The same applies to American Indians with their strong predilection for flutes and their apathy to stringed instruments if we except the Spanish import of recent ages.

Altogether, the diffusion of instruments across the seas and along the caravan routes has been more essential than the diffusion of singing styles, as they are material goods. We can

---

[188] Alan P. Merriam, *Musical instruments and techniques of performance among the Bashi*, in *Zaire*, vol. 9, 2 (1955), pp. 123, 131.
[189] Jomo Kenyatta, *Facing Mount Kenya*, London, 1953, p. 95.

follow their traffic from Prehistory up to the modern regrettable, destructive trade in accordeons and mouth organs all over our globe.

Further interpretation of this sketchy survey must be left to future detail research.

THE ORIGINAL CONCEPTS of vocal and of instrumental music are utterly different. The instrumental impulse is not melody in a 'melodious' sense, but an agile movement of the hands which seems to be under the control of a brain center totally different from that which inspires vocal melody. Altogether, instrumental music, with the exception of rudimentary rhythmic percussion, is as a rule a florid, fast, and brilliant display of virtuosity. Unlike the distinct and clearcut melodies of voices, it consists of quick figures and passages, which often remind the listener of seventeenth century 'divisions.' Quick motion is not merely a means to a musical end but almost an end in itself, which always connects with the fingers, the wrists, and the whole of the body: the inventive power of a drummer, for instance, depends on the nature and particularly on the beating position of his drum and therewith on the position of the hands and their striking arc. A drummer who holds the drum like a hobby-horse between his legs plays rhythms different from those which he would perform on a drum he squeezes under his shoulder or carries horizontally in front of his abdomen.

Consequently, the vocal and the instrumental expression of a tribe are never one in style. They shape two separate arts.

Nevertheless, the beginnings of instrumental music remind in a way of the early vocal one-step melodies. We find this one-step pattern in the female-male contrast of two stamping tubes or the two slabs of rudimentary xylophones in Melanesia. Strangely enough, the one-step music has been preserved all the way up to the most sophisticated xylophones. The *amadinda* of Uganda, for example, is played by three men, one of whom faces the other two; and while two of them perform their complicated parts, the third plays only on the two highest keys about a wholetone apart.[190]

[190] Joseph Kyagambiddwa, *African music from the sources of the Nile*, New York, 1955, p. 117 and examples 101–162.

The same applies to the Negro regions of Madagascar. The xylophone of the Sakalava in the west consists in an unusual number of disconnected slabs arranged across the stretched-out legs of a woman. A second woman, sitting at right angles, beats only two of the slabs, while the third and the first one strike the melody proper. [191]

Even *zanzas* (cf. later in this book) follow in Central Africa the principle of a one-step upper voice part. In a piece of the Batwa in Central Urundi, transcribed by Rose Brandel, the first of three cooperating *zanzas* plays nothing but *a–b* (excepting one single *g*). [192]

Yet another elementary form of instrumental music is the one-sided, scale-like advance from neighbor to neighbor, from slab to slab, from fret to fret, from fingerhole to fingerhole.

X. RHYTHM AND FORM

Rhythm and form are the two organizing powers of melody. In recurrent patterns they dam and divide its flow; they control its tension and relaxation; they balance its law and its freedom.

The concepts of rhythm and form overlap and cannot be strictly kept apart; rhythm is as much a form quality as form is a rhythmical quality. But in current terminology, we speak of form when we want to discuss the organization of an entire piece or movement, and of rhythm, when we analyse a smaller section which we easily perceive and remember.

Rhythm in its beginnings is extra-musical.

Melody does not of necessity depend upon rhythm; like the songs of many birds, it can exist without recurrent, strictly gauged patterns of organization. Solo singing on the oldest levels confirms it; in many cases "we are at a loss to detect a binding principle or pattern in any western sense except for an emotional stress here and there or for the to and fro, however irregular, of tension and relaxation." [193]

The inroad of rhythm is due to ourselves, to our bodies and

---

[191] Curt Sachs, *Les instruments de musique de Madagascar*, Paris, 1938, pl. XIII.
[192] Transcribed from Riverside: Voice of the Congo, RLP 4002, Bd. 9.
[193] Curt Sachs, *Rhythm and tempo*, New York, 1953, p. 36.

our minds. To the voices Plato assigned melodic structure or, as the Greeks called it, *harmonia;* but rhythm he allotted to the artful motion of bodies. We saw a similar antithesis in a quotation from the Roman rhetor Marcus Fabius Quintilianus. Almost two thousand years later, Karl Bücher, the sociologist and economist (d. 1930), stated in his often reprinted *Arbeit und Rhythmus* that rhythm was basically not a quality inherent in music or poetry but only in bodily movement. Rhythmical structure of verses and melodies, as a consequence, was nothing but a transfusion from the moving body, although, we might add, from a body consciously moving under the firm control of the mind.

Rhythm springs from man as a slowly developing psycho-physiological urge. Its physiological part is the impulse to equalize continuous, regular movements, such as walking, dancing, running, or rowing. Psychological is the awareness of greater ease and gusto through constant evenness in motion. Hence we experience the often irresistible need to impose such evenness on every succession of acts and movements, if they can be automatized and removed from wilful change (which excludes all ordinary speech and any doings that demand the worker's permanent, watchful attention).

To those interested in rhythmical problems, poetry might be the most familiar carrier of regular rhythm. But taken in its precise, metronomical sense, poetical rhythm would drown the verses in a soulless, meaningless, antipoetic scanning. All versification depends on irrational respiration with a meaningful lengthening and shortening of individual syllables. As a spoken art, it requires a freedom in which both the stresses and the meters are little more than merely suggested.

But the central field of rhythm is music. Singing and playing are indeed successions of acts; they can to a certain degree be called automatic; and they have a high degree of ease and gusto both as a cause and as a result of rhythm. Consequently, even the most primitive music has a trend towards regular time units or *chronoi protoi*, albeit not always in the sense of a ticking metronome. This irresistible regularity retroacts upon man, its creator, and, by way of his mind, to the muscles. The archaic Vedda in inner Ceylon allow us to behold the beginnings of such reciprocity; they accompany their songs with a slightly rocking trunk or a leisurely moving toe.[194] Needless to say, dances, too, belong in the field of kinetic reaction.

Early, an urge develops to make the bodily reaction an influential part of music: the muscles no longer follow in silent co-movements, but are used to produce a noise and, in another retroaction, to increase, by this noise, the equalization and effectiveness of melody. Out of this reciprocation, mankind proceeded to a sonorous, audible movement of the body, be it slapping the buttocks or the chest or the flanks, stamping the ground, or clapping the hands – activities of which the last two are still common in Western folksong and in the kindergarten. On a higher level, the striking limbs or the beaten body yield to extensions: natural or artificial replacements intensify the result. The numberless varieties of rattles and clappers, of pestles and stamping boards, of tapping sticks and beaten gourds are extensions of the hands, the feet, and the torso.

Rhythm, in music (as in poetry and the dance) an organization of lapsing time, is based on the keen awareness of time units, equally spaced and ever repeating like the monotonous ticktack of a clock. Such uniform and mostly rapid ticking is often found in percussion, in clapping, rattling, and drumming, along with the song or in an independent tempo of its own as "an inexorable and mathematical background to the song." [195] It may be open to discussion whether or not such rhythm as an aesthetic experience demands a transformation of purely mechanical pulses into characteristic, stimulating patterns. But in our field it is unavoidable to accept the rhythmical quality of any simple pulsation, albeit on the lowermost level.

RHYTHMIC ORGANIZATION into clear-cut patterns – in music as in poetry – assumes essentially three different, however overlapping, forms.

One form of rhythm – not the earliest – is purely numerical. It consists in counting out and repeating again a number of time units (or several numbers in a characteristic arrangement),

---

[194] Max Wertheimer, *Musik der Wedda*, in *Sammelbände der Internationalen Musikgesellschaft*, vol. 9 (1909), p. 300.
[195] A. M. Jones, *African rhythm*, in *Africa*, vol. 24 (1954), p. 28.

without depending on accent or meter, although such qualities might be present or at least be suggested. In the Orient – as this section will show – such counted rhythm is common in the Far East. The West knows the counting principle from the *endecasillabo* or eleven-syllable verse of Italian poetry, as in Dante, and musically, from the folksong of Russia.[196] In the primitive world, numerical rhythm has hardly any importance.

Another form of rhythm relies on actual or merely suggested stresses; it groups a series of even-spaced pulses by accenting the first of two or more of them. This is the common form of later western 'time' with its two-four, three-four, four-four:

$$. . . . .$$
$$x . x . x . x . x . x . x$$
$$x . . x . . x . . x . . x$$
$$x . . . x . . . x . . . x$$

Ties, syncopations, triplets, counteraccents may disturb the basic time-pattern as added spices; there also may be conflicting episodes in some different rhythm for the sake of contrast. But the straight and simple 'time' is always clearly recognizable and can be easily beaten with a baton – most western music throbs in even pulses.

In primitive music, two-four or binary time prevails, unless some surplus syllable in the text expands it to ternary time. All over East Asia two or four-beat rhythms are almost exclusive; man's two-foot stride might account for it. They rule supreme in the Far East; and only Korea uses three beats here and there.

Binary rhythms, with ♫ as the nucleus, play an all-important role in children's and women's music. Their normal length is eight units in a line, most often in 4 + 4.[197]

Quintary rhythms are exceptional. Among the Kwakiutl on Nootka Sound, the half-initiates of the Sparrow Society strike the sounding boards in front of the dance-house "in five part rhythm, which is called 'one beat between.'"[198] As Franz Boas,

[196] Curt Sachs, *Rhythm and tempo*, New York, 1953, pp. 29 ff.

[197] Cf. Constantin Brailoiu, *La rythmique enfantine*, Paris-Bruxelles, 1956. – Robert Lachmann, *Jewish cantillation and song in the isle of Djerba*, Jerusalem, 1940, pp. 72 ff. – id., *Musik der aussereuropäischen Natur- und Kulturvölker*, in Ernst Bücken, *Handbuch der Musikwissenschaft*, Wildpark-Potsdam, 1931, p. 8.

[198] Franz Boas, *Ethnology of the Kwakiutl*, in *Bureau of American Ethnology*, 35th Report (1913–4) part 2, Washington, 1921, p. 1168.

the reporter, was familiar with music, we must accept this statement as correct; evidently there are five beats in what we would call a measure; and according to the native term in single quotes, this quintary time seems to be an irregular rhythm in the eyes of the Kwakiutl. Incidentally, their neighbors, the Nootka [199] and the Bellakula, have also drum-accompanied songs in strictest 5/8 time,[200] which might confirm the report on the Kwakiutl.

Downbeat and upbeat – the stress on the first or on the second beat of the melody – carry in primitive music by far not the significance granted them in the West of today. An overwhelming majority of pieces start on the downbeat, and an analysis of the civilizations in which the upbeat occurs is not yet possible. The situation is surprisingly reminiscent of earlier music in Europe, where the upbeat has no evidences before the fourteenth century.[201]

Binary beats are occasionally submitted to 'metric alteration'; the first of two presumably even notes is slightly lengthened at the cost of the second, just as it was in Europe up to the eighteenth century.[202]

Metric alteration can be inverted, by shortening the 'good,' accented notes and lengthening the 'bad,' unstressed ones. This so-called Scotch snap, in which the second note so to speak recoils from the first note, is common among American Indians and Siberians in their 'rumbling' styles. It also is common in Hungarian folk music. Alteration appears sometimes in the form of the Greek amphibrachic meter or 'short on both sides,' as ♪♩♪

Altogether, Indians and Siberians (as well as Norwegians and other folk musicians) are particularly fond of dotted and double-dotted, craggy rhythms in whatever form.

THE WORD METRIC, in these last few paragraphs, leads to the third type of rhythmical patterns.

The vocables metric and meter fall all too easily victims to a

[199] Helen H. Roberts and Morris Swadesh, *Songs of the Nootka Indians*, in *Transactions of the American Philosophical Society*, N.S. vol. 45, part 3 (1955).

[200] C. Stumpf, *Lieder der Bellakula-Indianer*, in *Vierteljahrsschrift für Musikwissenschaft*, vol. 2 (1886), p. 413, reprinted in *Sammelbände für Vergleichende Musikwissenschaft*, vol. 1 (1922), pp. 94, 95.

[201] Curt Sachs, *l.c.*, pp. 111 ff., 124, 261 ff.

[202] *id.*, *l.c.*, pp. 296–301. – Cf. *EFw* FE 4419 (P 419) I 2.

lax and irresponsible terminology which gives them without the slightest justification to measures from barline to barline (as '3/4 meter') and to 'time' or accentual rhythm. A four-four or a three-four are 'times,' as they obey a 'time-signature'; meter, on the contrary, belongs exclusively to some characteristic pattern of longer and shorter notes. The longer ones may extend over one pulse of the ticktack or more; the short ones may subdivide such pulse into halves, thirds, or otherwise. The well known verse feet of ancient Greek poetry (and vocal music) provide the standard examples with their trochees and iambs, dactyls and anapaests, spondees and paeons. But while Greece, at least in theory, gave every short syllable the length of one time unit or pulse, and the long one two of them, other countries, such as India ancient and modern, give the long note from two to seven units and feel entitled to assign to the short note more than one unit if necessary, as, for example, in the dactylic pattern of $7 + 2 + 1$ units (an ambiguity that later recurred in the western Middle Ages as *longa perfecta* and *imperfecta*, and *brevis altera* and *recta*), the former two measuring three and two breves, and the latter ones, three and two semibreves.

Meter, though often divisible by two or three like a divisive stress rhythm – as in the cases of the Greek *dactyl* (long-short-short) or the *molossos* (long-long-long) is in principle 'additive.' It can be best, and often exclusively, described as the sum of different amounts of time units, such as $2 + 3$, $2 + 4$, $3 + 4$, $3 + 3 + 2$, or $2 + 2 + 1 + 1$. Such metrical patterns are found quite early in percussive accompaniments. On the Carolines in Micronesia, for example, percussion would sometimes proceed in $1 + 2$ or $1 + 3$ halves, that is, in an iambic meter.[203] The finest Amerindian examples are found among the Nootka in Vancouver.

Outside India and the Middle East, such additive meters are most important and vital in Bantu Africa. The Zulu have a $9 + 7$ meter,[204] as

$$x..x.x... + x.x..x.$$

More frequent and of greater historical interest is the common

[203] George Herzog, *Die Musik der Karolinen-Inseln*, Hamburg, 1936, *passim*.
[204] *EFw* FE 4506 (P 506) III 45 b.

pattern of $7 + 5 = 12$; twelve time units are grouped this way:

$$x.x.x.. + x.x..$$

The $7 + 5$ recurs in the Arabian poetical meters of seven and five time units and in the strange caesura of Roman hexameters, such as, in Virgil's Aeneid:

Arma virumque cano / Troiae qui primus ab oris

or, inversely,

Infandum regina iubes / renovare dolorem

And it again recurs in the Far East. Japan distinguishes poems in the *haiku* form, with three lines of five, seven, and five syllables, and in the *tanka* form, with five, seven, five, seven, seven syllables.[205] In Chinese music, the combination of five and seven beats appears even where the text follows some other organization:

Ex. 27*

These parallels, reaching from Japan to Bantu Africa, are startling. But it seems premature to try an explanation.

Keeping quite independent from the singer's melody, rhythm, and tempo modifications, the clapping hands or the drum repeat such patterns over and over again, even if their beating falls between two syllables of the text.

---

* After Van Aalst.
[205] Curt Sachs, *l.c.*, p. 56.

Africa also favors the ubiquitous meter $3 + 3 + 2$:

x..x..x.   x..x..x.

(in which the members can be exchanged, as $3 + 2 + 3$ or $2 + 3 + 3$).

This "Fascinating Rhythm" – title of one of Gershwin's piano pieces – has an important key position in nearly every chapter of music history, from the Orient way up to our twentieth century with hot jazz and the Charleston.

Whatever the rhythm, percussion seldom starts together with the voice; it enters a few notes after the singer, or it precedes him.

All these patterns, though, are later developments; and if we hesitate to derive them from the Orient, because they play an eminent role also in Africa, we should realize that in this case as in others the Sudan and Bantu Africa are parts of the oriental rather than of the primitive world.

Next to Bantu Africa, additive rhythm prevails in Muhammedan countries and in India – not only in art music, but also in folk songs. In southwestern India even children sing in rapid $4 + 3 = 7$ units (our example 1). A majority of Turkish pieces follow a nine-eight measure in the arrangement $3/4 + 3/8$; the three eights do not form a triplet, as they would in ♩ ♩ ♩ ♪♪♪, but three exact half-quarters as in ♩♩♩♩.; other Turkish pieces have seven eights: ♩♩♩. or five eights: ♩♩.

To thispicture we must add the intricate meters of Southeast Europe:

Ex. 28*

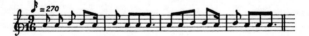

in Bulgaria, Macedonia,[206] Rumania, and Hungary, with up to twenty one units.

Here as elsewhere we face the weighty question: does this folk music derive from art music or vice-versa? I discussed it in an earlier book without arriving at a convincing solution.[207] The

---

* After Christo Obreschkoff, *Das bulgarische Volkslied.*

[206] Yury Arbatsky, *Beating the tupan in the Central Balkans*, Chicago, 1953.

[207] Curt Sachs, *l.c.*, pp. 93–95.

question itself might be due to the bias of the modern West. In our civilization, the two worlds of art and folk music are rigidly separated. Art music – the product of desk work by men of intellect and systematic instruction – has little in common with illiterate 'folk' melodies. This gap is almost non-existent in the Orient. Music in all social layers is practically scriptless and non-intellectual, as tradition rules at court as well as on the village level. The roots are the same, even if there are shades of refinement. The Muhammedan Orient is most characteristic in this respect: the best trained and most highly regarded 'art' singers perform regularly, not in concert halls, but in urban coffee houses for a thoroughly mixed audience, effendis no less than common people, and the music they offer is the highest available. In many cases the music that we are inclined to dub 'folksong' is rather 'tribal' and rural or belonging to one of the ethnic minorities which often preserve a more archaic style of melody.

ONE MORE QUESTION arises: is there a law, or at least a principle, to determine the growth or change of rhythm? Does rhythm tend to become simpler and more regular within a certain civilization, or does it on the contrary move to an ever greater complexity?

Let us test a few examples.

In certain Amerindian communities, 'modern' songs are said to have a more regular rhythm (and a smaller range) than the 'old' ones.[208] There is no reason for doubting the statement as such. Still, the contrast of old and recent within a primitive man's quite personal memory is too insignificant where we deal with traditions of ten-thousands of years. We should here refrain from generalizations, and the more so as modern songs might easily be influenced by white-American tunes.

Growing rhythmic rigidity, however, also occurs elsewhere. Rhythm was free in the archaic style of India's *Veda* cantillation; but in the more recent style of this chant, dating from about 400 B.C., uniform meters and regular structures prevail.[209]

---

[208] Frances Densmore, *Chippewa music*, Washington, 1910, p. 59. – *id.*, *The study of Indian music*, in *Smithsonian Report 1941*, Washington, 1942, pp. 568 ff.

[209] Cf. Erwin Felber und Bernhard Geiger, *Die indische Musik der vedischen und der klassischen Zeit*, in *Sitzungsberichte der Kais. Akademie der Wissenschaften in Wien, Phil.-Hist. Klasse*, vol. 170 (1912) no. 7.

Maybe we should not take our examples from Primitives or Orientals, but rather from the West, where the historical development is to the last detail familiar in the sequence of its cycles.

In Graeco-Roman antiquity, Plutarch speaks of the motley patchwork in the rhythms of older Hellenic music, and especially in its instrumental parts. Later masters, he says, gave up such rhythmic complication and turned once more to melodic emphasis. Indeed, he contrasts the two groups of composers as the older 'rhythmophiles' and the subsequent 'melophiles.' The fact is clearly stated; but an interpretation can hardly be given, since we neither know the time that Plutarch had in mind nor the musical circumstances.

In the Middle Ages, the best visible rhythmic event was the change from the rational, meager *modi* of the thirteenth century to the most incredible complication with its climax around 1400. This luxuriant sunset of the Middle Ages was a typical end-of-a-cycle trait. That the nascent Renaissance discarded these excesses in the interest of austere simplicity was a just as typical start-of-a-cycle trait.

In our own century, we behold the crisis of 1910, when the uniform 4/4 and 3/4 of the eighteenth and nineteenth yielded almost suddenly to the rhythmical wealth of jazz and of Stravinsky's and Bartók's scores. This impressive revolution contradicted the plausible events of 1400, giving rhythmic simplicity to the end of a cycle, and complication to the beginning of a new one.

The way out of this confusion is indicated by the changing role and character of rhythm. Around 1400, rhythm was the principal carrier of an end-of-a-cycle sophistication. Around 1910, this inevitable sophistication devolved upon the colors of harmony and orchestration. Rhythm, starving under their impact, had to begin the coming cycle in a primitive freedom, which was not sophistication, but the elemental force of a start-of-a-cycle. Hence, a general rule as to the direction in which the form of rhythm moves does not, and cannot, exist.[210]

STRICTNESS AND FREEDOM of rhythm are nevertheless by no means developmental stages. Often the same civilization uses

[210] For all details: Sachs, *l.c.*, *passim*.

the two types alongside, even in the same piece, with freedom in the song and strictness in the instrumental accompaniment.

Sometimes, the freedom of rhythm depends on the singer's sex. On Pur in the West Carolines, women's songs are rhapsodic, but men's, strictly rhythmical.[211] This is no general rule. On the contrary, where such a difference in sex behavior has been observed, men are usually freer, while neatness and strictness belong to the women, who, within or near the house, do their regular, rhythmical chores, as cradle rocking, kneading, grinding, pestling, seeding, and weaving.[212] In the villages of the Northwest Siberian Vogul – to mention one example – the men, who do almost all the singing, keep melodies free in rhythm and structure, while the women arrange their tunes in simple and regular verses of the kind already mentioned.[213]

RHYTHMIC OVERALL PATTERNS, well known and highly thought of in medieval Europe, are by no means absent from primitive music. Such advanced form of rhythmic organization shows even in 'isorhythm.' This we find in the repertory of the Menomini and other North American Indians (and elsewhere) as well as in the Gothic age of France among Machaut's and Dufay's works. There, in compliance with a rhythmic drive more dominant than the melodic urge, a characteristic metrical pattern, maybe four measures long, is forced, not upon a percussive accompaniment, but upon the melody itself. If this melody has a span of, say, twelve measures, the "patternization' divides it into three groups with the same arrangement of halfnotes, quarters, and eighths to whatever ups and downs the melodic line might turn. "Measures 5 and 9, though melodically different, have the exact metrical organization of measure 1; and measures 6 and 10 follow just as strictly the metrical pattern of measure 2; and so forth, with measures 7 and 11 after 3, and 8 and 12 after 4." [214]

Along with this description an example from the Menominee west of Lake Michigan is given in my book. Other examples are provided by the Arapaho in the Great Plains.[215]

---

[211] George Herzog, l.c., p. 277.
[212] Sachs, l.c., p. 50 ff.
[213] A. O. Väisänen, *Wogulische und ostjakische Melodien*, Helsinki, 1937, p. 3.
[214] Sachs, l.c., pp. 47 ff.
[215] Bruno Nettl, *Musical culture of the Arapaho*, master's thesis, Indiana University, Bloomington, 1951. Also in *The Musical Quarterly*, vol. 41 (1955).

Isorhythm, though, is a dangerous term. If the example from the Comanche Indians that Bruno Nettl calls isorhythmic because every measure is built on the same short pattern, then we must of necessity call isorhythmic everyone of the numberless recurrent patterns, such as the meters of Greece and the *modi* of the Gothic age, the *rāgas* of India and the Radetzki March. Nobody would go that far. All the metrical patterns just mentioned – the Greek term polypodies might be a good common label – have a strong and immediate motor appeal. This is hardly ever the case in medieval isorhythmy. Most of its patterns do not strike our sense of rhythm; and in many cases, we must actually parse the score to come to an isorhythmic diagnosis. But without motor appeal and immediate perceptibility, such a repeated pattern moves from rhythm in a narrower sense to a unifying articulation, that is, to a structural device. I think it would be preferable not to confuse the two types by a distorting oversimplification.

BEFORE LEAVING the manifold questions of rhythm, we pause for a last panoramic view.

The styles of rhythm, as do the families of instruments, have settled in a few distinct areas. The first one, almost without exception, is the whole stretch of East and Southeast Asia with a regular, monotonous four-four time. The second, with rich and complicated additive meters, is the enormous region from India through the Middle and Near East to Negro Africa. Ancient Greece presents an attractive blend of these contrasting types of rhythms: it has additive rhythms up to the epitritic meters of $3 + 4$ units as a gift from the Orient, whose music determined to a great extent the music of Hellas; but it also has a distinctly binary attitude in many meters and their combinations – probably due to the concept of Greek orchestics as the common ground of music, poetry, and the dance.

Ancient Europe is strangely problematic. There is no trace of percussion and hence a strong suspicion that rhythm played a minor role. A confirmation of this belief can be seen in the bewildering fact that the central field of medieval music, the Gregorian chant of the Catholic Church, despite its rather strict supervision by ecclesiastic authorities, lost its rhythmic tradition within a couple of centuries and became arhythmic already in the eleventh century. Indeed, around 1300 Johannes de Grocheo stated explicitly that no monophonic melody – including the Gregorian chorale as well as the songs of the courtly *troubadours*, *trouvères*, and *minnesinger* – was precisely measured.[216]

This intentional lack of precision must have kept the earlier notations from indicating metrical values; both the neumes and their offshoot, the plainsong script, bypassed them: and even the 'mensural notation,' developed in the thirteenth century for giving such values to the plainsong symbols, struggled almost three hundred years before being able to express them in a clear and unambiguous form. The fight of strict against free rhythmization extended at least into the Renaissance: the Italo-Flemish polyphony, though strictly formalized, still shows two characteristically conflicting trends: on the one hand, the inexorable binding time unit in the form of the handbeaten *tactus* and in its augmentations and diminutions under the telling title *proportiones* (at least in principle) and, on the other hand, a free-flowing melody in all the voice parts without evenly spaced stresses or regular additive patterns. This conflict leaves the modern editor all the time in doubt as to where to put the barlines in. Only with the decline of polyphony after 1600 and probably in the retinue of the ever more influential social dancing in the seventeenth century did simple four-four and three-four win out.

FORM, as the beginnings of this section define it, is the organized flow of a musical piece as a whole.[217]

A very general statement must head this examination: practically all the forms that we meet in primitive, oriental, and western folk music are surprisingly short-winded. Even an African Negro, otherwise so outstanding in musical achievements both vocal and instrumental, can play the same phrase for a whole day or a week if he is fond of it, without any signs of fatigue.

---

[216] The Latin text and a German translation: Johannes Wolf, *Die Musiklehre des Johannes de Grocheo*, in *Sammelbände der Internationalen Musikgesellschaft*, vol. 1 (1899), p. 84.

[217] Wilhelm Heinitz, *Strukturprobleme in primitiver Musik*, Hamburg, 1931, covers much more ground than mere form.

Scholars have blamed this deficiency on a still undeveloped mentality, and this reasoning has doubtless its merits; birds go hardly beyond the one call of their species, and children display an irritating endurance in repeating a tiny scrap of melody again and again. But the argument can certainly not apply to the sophisticated music of high oriental civilizations, which all the eloquence of Hegelian evolutionism is unable to relegate to mankind's childhood. The growth of musical forms that we observe in Europe from the seventeenth century on seems to be connected with the growing separation of music from social life and extra-musical claims. Contents, sizes, and forms underwent an obvious change when music became self-contained, to be listened to in public concert halls and opera houses by audiences wholly devoted to its artful elaboration.

It might be helpful to take into consideration Radin's ideas on the contrast of the man of action and the thinker, of whom the former category, *homo faber*, is among the primitives much more frequent. "His mental rhythm is characterized by a demand for endless repetition of the same event or, at best, of events all of which are on the same general level. Change for him means essentially some abrupt transformation. Monotony holds no terrors for him." [218]

Just as tools and implements of pristine manufacture are often decorated with a simple, unassuming row of ever recurring uniform dashes without the aesthetic need of a change, much primitive music is but a mere seriation of tiny groups of notes.[219] It must be conceded, however, that there is a flaw in this comparison, inasmuch as visual ornaments are easily taken in as a whole, while musical ornaments are singly heard after each other.

Examples abound. Pygmoids in Central New Guinea repeat persistently two notes a fourth apart: [220]

Ex. 29

(After Kunst)

[218] Paul Radin, *The world of primitive man*, New York, 1953, p. 39.

[219] Cf. also: Robert Lach, *Das Konstruktionsprinzip der Wiederholung in Musik, Sprache und Literatur*, in *Sitzungsber. Akademie der Wissenschaften in Wien, Phil.-Hist. Kl.*, vol. 201, Wien, 1925.

[220] Jaap Kunst, *A study on Papuan music*, Weltevreden, 1931, pl. II.

and so do little Eskimo girls [221] (our example 15). The Botokudos, a truly palaeolithic people in eastern Brazil, would sing seven times, without variation, one group of four notes: g ʄ g ʄ, so that actually the secondal *step* g–ʄ repeats no less than fourteen times; [222] on a recording at the *Musée de l'Homme* in Paris, a women's chorus on Lifou, one of the Loyalty Islands in southwest Polynesia, iterate twenty times a very small motif of four notes; [223] H. A. Junod heard Baronga lilts of two or three measures ten, twenty, fifty times in a stretch; [224] Lagu Muna women in North New Guinea endlessly repeat a scanty five-beat melody; and a medicine man of the Taulipang Indians in northern Brazil dwells mercilessly on a tiny motif of a rapid triplet with a sustained note a semitone higher, the whole in a frantic accelerando. [225]

This last example draws our attention to another probable cause for at least some cases of primitive shortness and repetition. The enervating, ceaseless recurrence of an identical sense perception no longer interesting in itself, affects, indeed intoxicates us in either one of two opposite ways, as a potent stimulus or, inversely, as a narcotic. Such impairing or even deadening removal of man's unfettered volition is appropriate in cultures whose thoroughly magic orientation assigns to much of their music the role of depersonalization and release from normalcy. Widely known examples are the trance and ecstasy of Derwishes and other Muhammedan brotherhoods under the impact of musical monotone and Koran reading.

Unassuming repetition, whatever its cause and reason may be, occurs in many parts of the world, including the folksong of Europe, as the following ditty from Rumania shows:

Ex. 30*

* After Riegler-Dinu.

[221] *EFw* FE 4444 (P 444) II 1.

[222] J. D. Strelnikov, *La música y la danza de las tribus indias Kaa-Ihwua (Guaraní) y Botocudo*, in *Proceedings of the 23rd Congress of Americanists 1928*, New York, 1930, p. 801.

[223] Transcribed in Curt Sachs, *The rise of music in the ancient world*, New York, 1943, p. 50.

[224] Henri-A. Junod, *Les chants et les contes des Ba-Ronga*, Lausanne, 1897, p. 33.

[225] Sachs, *l.c.*, p. 22 in E. M. von Hornbostel's transcription.

Herewith, we face the remarkable parallels between primitive structures and the secular forms of the Middle Ages in Europe.[226]

To begin with, the repetition form appears in medieval epics of the so-called litany type: each line of the text was sung to the same melody: AAA ... [227]

A step further is taken in the rather recent Ghost Dances of the Plains or Buffalo Indians like the Algonquin and the Sioux: "every phrase is rendered twice." Such paired patterns or paired progression, as George Herzog has called this arrangement,[228] are equally well known to the historian of western music; they form the *lai* or *sequence* (as AA BB CC ...) so often used in the Gothic Middle Ages.

An advanced type of this medieval *lai*, the instrumental court dance *estampie*, repeated the musical phrase in a more flexible way; instead of a strict AA BB CC, it answered the *overt*, or half cadence, of the first line by a *clos*, or full cadence, in the second line of each of its pairs.[229]

This principle has been known in the very earliest layer of music still preserved. The first line and its repetition were twinned but provided with different endings: the first time, the voice rested on a non-final level that kept the listener's ear in suspense; the second time, it shifted to the final level to give a satisfactory conclusion. "To put it technically: the first phrase ended on a semi-cadence, and the second, on a full cadence ... By uniting two phrases with cadential distinction to form what musical theory calls a *period*, primitive peoples at a very low level of civilization had created the most fertile of musical structure schemes, the *lied* form." [230]

Early examples are as archaic as Vedda and Patagonian music.[231] Later, we find them in the liturgies of Oriental Jews, for instance the Song of the Red Sea from Gen. 14 : 30 in the Yemenite version.[232]

[226] Sachs, *Our musical heritage*, 2nd edition, New York, 1955, p. 71.

[227] Cf. Gustav Becking, *Der musikalische Bau des montenegrinischen Volksepos*, in *Archives néerlandaises de Phonétique expérimentale*, vol. 8/9 (1933); and Felix Hoerburger, *Westöstliche Entsprechungen im Volksepos*, in *Die Musikforschung*, vol. 5 (1952), pp. 354–361.

[228] George Herzog, *Plains ghost dance and Great Plains music*, in *American Anthropologist*, vol. 37 (1935), p. 404.

[229] Sachs, *Our musical heritage*, l.c., p. 72.

[230] Sachs, *The rise of music in the ancient world*, pp. 34 ff.

[231] Sachs, *ibid.*, p. 34.

[232] Sachs, *ibid.*, p. 83.

Iteration can also be enriched by repeating a short motif at a different pitch – a practice exemplified in the Rain Dance of the Navaho Indians: [233]

Ex. 31

Such shifted iteration, as we shall call it, would be a sequence in western terminology. But for the sake of clarity it seems wiser to avoid so ambiguous a word, as it also covers the *lai* and a closely related form of Catholic Church music.

The section on medieval forms in *Our musical Heritage* discusses after the litany and the *lai*, as the last one, the round-dance, *rondeau*, or refrain type, characterized by the coöperation of a solist and a chorus: "a leader sang the stanzas, and the chorus of the dancers answered with the refrain." [234] In primitive music, the regular alternation of a chorus in response to a solo 'verse' is quite general. It is natural enough to occur in all continents and archipelagos but is most vital in Negro Africa.

Next comes the stanza form, in which the lines have different melodies. On Dobu in the western Pacific, the lines follow in one of the arrays:

A B C A   A D E F C

or

A B A   C D E A

or in some other arrangement.[235] A, repeated at the beginnings and often at the ends of half-stanzas, serves as a refrain and leads us to the following type of structure.

The response principle can assume a variety of forms. In the

[233] George Herzog, *Speech-melody and primitive music*, in *The Musical Quarterly*, vol. 20 (1934), p. 458.

[234] Sachs, *Our musical Heritage*, 2nd. edition, New York, 1955, p. 72.

[235] Cf. R. F. Fortune, *Sorcerers of Dobu*, London, 1932, ch. VII.

simplest, the same verse melody (v) alternates steadily with the chorus refrain (R), like:

v R v R v R ....

Elsewhere, the verses have different melodies in alternation with an unchanging refrain, as in the well-known form of the western instrumental rondo:

R a R b R c R ....

to be repeated as often as necessary and desired.[236]

The answering chorus often performs in dance steps; sometimes it sings meaningless syllables and occasionally in a faster tempo.[237]

H.-A. Junod shows in a diagram the way of staging responses in the Delagoa Bay in eastern South Africa.[238] The whole array is semicircular: silent dancers move in an outer semicircle; an inner semicircle belongs to young girls, who sing the refrain and clap the rhythm; the soloist, between the two semicircles, dances and sings the verses; and in the common center of these three semicircles, a drummer takes care of the leading rhythmical patterns.

Sometimes, the responding chorus interjects two notes without affecting the line of the soloist, as it so often occurs in our passions, cantatas, and oratorios. Indeed, in Africa the choral responses would follow so breathlessly that the soloist and the chorus almost clash in a two-part polyphony, in which the short quartal motifs of the chorus act as an *ostinato* (cf. later), just as in certain French motets of the thirteenth century. Such a two-part polyphony is actually achieved in Uganda.[239]

While response is the alternation of a song leader or cantor and an answering chorus, we call antiphony the alternation (and occasionally merger) of two half-choruses.[240] The two principal forms of antiphony are: (1) line by line the second chorus repeats the melody of the first one; (2) the lines are

[236] Cf., e.g., Erich M. von Hornbostel, in Günther Tessmann, *Die Pangwe*, Berlin, 1913/1914, vol. 2, no. 2, pp. 334 ff. Also: no. 3, pp. 336 ff.; no. 5, pp. 340 ff.

[237] Cf. e.g., Cora Du Bois, *The people of Alor*, Minneapolis, 1944, p. 136.

[238] Henri-A. Junod, *Les Ba-Ronga*, Neuchâtel, 1898, p. 271.

[239] Joseph Kyagambiddwa, *African music from the sources of the Nile*, New York, 1955, p. 48.

[240] Nguyen Van Huyen, *Les chants alternés des garçons et des filles en Annam*. Paris, 1934. – Sachs, *The rise of music in the ancient world*, pp. 50, 59, 92–95, 101.

alternately sung by one chorus, the odd-numbered by the first, and the even-numbered by the second chorus, although they might join forces at times.

The answering forms, response and antiphony, are intimately and often exclusively linked with group dancing. But here and there this connection breaks. When such is the case, music seems to be the surviving partner, whereas the dancing crumbles away. This happens in primitive societies [241] as well as it occurs in the West – from the musical *rondeaux* of the Middle Ages to recent times with their pavanes, sarabandes, courantes, or minuets divorced from the ballroom.

CONSTANT REPETITION often defies the patience of singers and listeners even within alternating patterns. To break the wearisome sameness, the variation form comes up as the most natural remedy: the melody or theme repeats in a modified version, different enough to keep the interest awake and similar enough to secure familiarity and oneness. Being at once a faithful rendition and a free improvisation, the procedure of variation is indeed one of the oldest and most persistent of formal principles; it has been omnipresent without interruption from the earliest strata up to western twentieth-century music.

Variations may follow the original in its course and size. But they also are flexible enough to undergo expansion or contraction.

To show variation incipient and mature, it is best to juxtapose the word-conditioned changes of the earliest strata and the free elaborations of later instrumental music. The word-conditioned changes occur whenever two lines of the text have a different number of syllables. This primitive type of variation is hardly consciously conceived and has aesthetical values at best as a starting point for later, imaginative treatments of a given theme.

Variations of the very finest kind are played on an exclusively Negro African instrument, in general known as the *zanza*. Pressed against the performer's chest, is a small resonance box, usually of wood, to which a set of carefully tuned rattan or iron lamellas are tightly strapped with their lower ends so that the

---

[241] Verrier Elwin & Shamroo Hivale, *Folk-songs of the Maikal Hills*, London &c., 1944, p. xv.

slightly deflected upper ends can freely vibrate when plucked with the two thumbs. A. M. Jones is right when he feels "something soothing and restful in the constant reiteration of a short piece of beautiful music, whereas any possibility of monotony is removed by the delightfully light and airy nuances produced by the subtle variations." [242]

Incidentally: it is bewildering to find in the latest musicological literature of Germany this refined virtuoso instrument somewhat discourteously described as a *Klimper*. This neologism is completely inadequate, as it derives from the verb *klimpern*, 'to thrum,' denoting a very strong derogatory connotation of poorest, incompetent bungling on the keyboard. But Mr. Jones, who writes so enthusiastically about this little instrument, is in his terminology no paragon either. The disdainful and often cynical nicknames that old-time travelers or colonials bestowed on instruments are by now discredited; the obsolete misnomer Kafir Piano has long been the laughing stock of scholars. By no stretch of the imagination does this delicate, pocket-size instrument resemble our pianos, either in sound or construction; and the Kafirs are an arbitrary, tiny segment of the untold millions of Bantu who play the zanza in the enormous span between 10° N. to 25° S. all across Africa, which amounts to the expanse of the North American continent.

BESIDES ALL serial or additive forms, although less often, primitive music knows *da capo* or ABA structures. Polynesia provides very fine examples with, in the middle of a piece, a contrasting passage in a contrasting tempo.[243]

The rare occurrence of ABA is understandable. All the other forms of primitive music are open, additive, repetitive, be they the simple seriation of some tiny group of notes or, more elaborately, *lais*, *estampies*, *lieder*, *rondeaux*, responses, antiphonies, variations. ABA is the only form that does not permit an endless addition of similar groups. It is a symmetrical, closed, and self-sufficient configuration superior to repetitive forms.

[242] A. M. Jones, *African music*, Livingstone, 1949, p. 27. – To be heard on *EFw* I 3 (from Equatorial Africa) and on English Decca (collected by Hugh T. Tracey) LF 1084 I 1.

[243] E. G. Burrows, *Songs of Uvea and Futuna*, in *Bernice P. Bishop Museum Bulletin* 183, Honolulu, 1945.

Our knowledge of primitive form is altogether more than limited. The phonograms, our principal source, are unduly short – be it for economic or technical reasons. We seldom know that which precedes or what follows; and the side of a record or, worse, the band on a side represents at best a sample rather than a complete structure.[244] That the almost ceaseless singing during day- or night-long feasts takes often the shape of compound forms out of coherent, though contrasting movements cannot be doubted. In an earlier section I mentioned a cantata describing a hunt in Uganda, which is a definite compound; and the cycle of the *Hako* ceremony, as held by the Pawnee Indians, was published in a valuable volume more than fifty years ago.[245]

But it seems doubtful whether these aggregates are forms in the sense of this chapter. We certainly speak of a symphonic form, embracing, as a superstructure, all the four movements in their changes of tonality, rhythm, and mood. But this overall pattern is a pale configuration when compared with the individual types, as the sonata form of the first movement, the variations of the adagio, the ABA of the scherzo, and the rondo form of the last movement. The night-long span of a primitive ceremony does hardly alter the short-winded forms of its components. Nor are the complex liturgies of Good Friday or the Day of Atonement musical forms.

---

[244] Cf. Gilbert Rouget, *A propos de la forme dans les musiques de tradition orale*, in *Les Colloques de Wégimont*, vol. i, p. 132 ff. (1954–1955).
[245] Tracy's transcription in Alice Fletcher, *The Hako ceremony*, Washington, 190

THREE

ON THE WAY

GROWTH, PERSONALITY, ART

The oldest music described in the preceding sections has no claim to pristine purity. We know from modern anthropology that in itself "every culture element is essentially a range of variation." This fact contributes "very considerably to the flexibility of cultures and their capacity for under-going numerous changes and stresses without actual disruption." [1]

Even beyond such innate capacity for change, the very oldest music cannot be thought of without admixtures of later or foreign elements. But two types of melodies (treated in Sections Five and Six) keep rather near to the ideal of unadulterated purity: the tumbling strains in an earlier state of organization and the one-step melodies out of shortwinded and endlessly repeated motifs. Examples come from every continent and from the islands in between, and though survivals occur in many higher civilizations, it is no undue generalization to state that all the oldest cultures partake in these, and no other, styles. This cannot be a consequence of diffusion or influence from group to group. Such diffusion would suppose an intercontinental globe-girding cosmopolitanism in palaeolithic ages and a subsequent isolation in mesolithic or neolithic times. This does not make sense. Our oldest music must be a general, innate, compulsory quality of palaeolithic man.

There are not enough such compulsory qualities to permit speaking of mesolithic or neolithic music. On the contrary: after the Palaeolithic, we are confronted with a good many different styles, which cannot be assigned to definite ages and therefore have been attributed to 'races,' to geographic provinces, to culture patterns, or to *Kulturkreise*. Most of these ascriptions are doubtful or incorrect, and reluctantly we have to leave an

---

[1] Ralph Linton, *The tree of culture*, New York, 1955, p. 34.

acceptable solution to later generations of ethnomusicologists.

Instead, we face another question: what forces form a musical culture and lead it from palaeolithic stage to post-palaeolithic levels?

There are two such forces: influence from outside and change from within.

Influence from outside or 'diffusion' is natural and does not need explanation or justification. Preceding sections of this book referred repeatedly to the inevitable contact with neighbors in trade and intermarriage and to clashes with foreigners during the ceaseless migrations of hunters and cattle drivers. That in spite of continual influences native styles have to an amazing degree preserved their distinctive qualities, derives from the fact that every group opens easily up to influences homogeneous enough to be assimilated, but is hermetically closed to indigestible, 'outlandish' traits. "Borrowing is always selective." [2]

Borrowing could not have occurred if mankind everywhere had strictly, exclusively stuck to its palaeolithic heritage. Most societies must have had a latent urge and the versatility to change traditional patterns. We do not know the causes; just as we do not know why almost of a sudden the polyphonic ideal of the European Renaissance yielded to the *stile recitativo e rappresentativo*. Very little in music can be fully traced to social and technical changes, and any attempt to unveil the inner process of art creation is doomed like a search for the soul with the anatomist's scalpel.

The only experience we can rely upon with confidence is this: every creation in the arts is a personal act but must be prompted and supported by collective needs. Nobody else could have accomplished in exactly the same way what Leonardo, Raphael, and Michelangelo did; but they themselves could not have achieved what they did, and how they did it, without the powerful upheaval that we call the Italian Renaissance. Rembrandt is unique in his unmistakably personal style; and yet he could not be imagined outside his native Holland and outside the early seventeenth century. And this is true of every genius. In the primitive world, with its tightly knit society and social responsibility, the prompting and supporting power of the

[2] Clyde Kluckhohn, *Mirror for man*, New York, 1949, p. 59.

collective is even considerably stronger than it could be in the
individualistic culture, of the Later West.

THE ANTI-INDIVIDUALISTIC COHERENCE of primitive life and
the purposeful character of music within a world of magic ideas
seems to remove all primitive music from the concept of art
that we hold in the modern world. The question of sufficient
and insufficient skill and our complicated gamut of aesthetical
values can not apply where a predominant part of music is meant
to be powerful in a social, magic, or religious sense and to impress
the good and the evil forces in nature much more than the
audience on the village square. In a like manner, nobody would
expect or wish the intoning priest in a Catholic church to strive
for the laurels of opera tenors; nor is a congregation anywhere
supposed to sing with the discipline and tonal beauty of a well-
trained concert chorus.

"The first empirical and detailed exploration of the inter-
connections between esthetic values and the more pervasive
standards and value orientations of a particular culture is,"
in Clyde Kluckhohn's words, "due to David P. McAllester's
study of social and esthetic values as seen in Navaho music." [3]

The primitives themselves, at least on a post-neolithic level,
distinguish very definitely between a good and a poor performer
and good and poor compositions. They often admire a singer's
expanded range [4] or, as in Hawaii, his deep and powerful chest
resonance; [5] and on the North Pacific Puget Sound, certain
singers are said to have too rough a voice for love songs.[6] In
Kenya, the Gikuyu women – who themselves do not play the
flutes – listen with keenest interest and present a successful
flutist with food and drink as a sign of appreciation.[7] "In the
Trobiands (due SE of New Guinea), as with us, a tenor or bary-
tone is sure of success with women. As the native put it: 'The
throat is a long passage like the *wila* (cunnus) and the two

[3] Clyde Kluckhohn's foreword to David P. McAllester, *Enemy Way music*, Cambridge (Mass.), 1954.
[4] Frances Densmore, *Chippewa music*, Washington, 1910, pp. 59, 61.
[5] Helen H. Roberts, *Ancient Hawaiian music*, Honolulu, 1926, p. 71.
[6] Erna Gunther, in Willard Rhodes, *Music of the American Indian Northwest*
(*Puget Sound*), Washington, 1955, p. 10.
[7] Jomo Kenyatta, *Facing Mount Kenya*, London, 1953, pp. 94 ff.

attract each other. A man who has a beautiful voice will like women very much and they will like him.' " [8]

An interesting statement on the people of Alor (East Indonesia) tells us that "an inadequate performance is not publicly ridiculed, but there is a certain amount of snickering behind the performer's back. Those with real ability persist in their efforts and may be admired performers by the time they are in their late thirties or early forties. Abilities naturally vary. By rough estimate perhaps 10 per cent of the mature men are recognized as good singers." [9]

Such distinction gives primitive music qualities of an aesthetic order, indeed of art; it makes it independent from personal, sexual, social, and religious functions: "the search for beauty is universal in human experience." [10]

The author found a similar development in the realm of the dance, where an involuntary motor discharge, a state of frenzied movement, and a ceremonial rite, were gradually transformed "into a work of art conscious of and intended for observation. ... The individual participant in a ceremony of this kind which becomes a work of art cannot repudiate for himself the corresponding evolution into an artist." [11]

It also constitutes a step towards art when groups within a village or from neighboring communities celebrate competitive singing or playing feasts and the winners are awarded enthusiastic applause or even material gifts (although in these games the text is often more important than the melody). We know of many such contests. They reach from Central Asia to Iceland,[12] from the Eskimo to South Africa (here both vocal [13] and on antelope horns).[14] The Alps, Corsica, Brittanny play an outstanding role; and in ancient Greece the *agones* or competitive festivals gave a prominent place to musical contests; indeed, Hellenic mythology relates the cruel penalties that Thamyris, Marsyas and Midas had to pay for challenging the Muses and even Apollo.[15]

[8] Bronislaw Malinowski, *The sexual life of savages*, London, 1929, p. 478.
[9] Cora du Bois, *The people of Alor*, Minneapolis, 1944, p. 136.
[10] Herskovits, *Cultural Anthropology*, New York, 1955, p. 234.
[11] Curt Sachs, *World history of the dance*, New York, 1937, pp. 218 ff.,
[12] E. Emsheimer, *Singing contests in Central Asia*, in *Journal of the International Folk Music Council*, vol. 8 (1956), pp. 28–29.
[13] Cf., e.g., Hugh Ashton, *The Basuto*, London, 1952, p. 97.
[14] Henri-A. Junod, *Les Ba-Ronga*, Neuchâtel, 1898, p. 147.
[15] Curt Sachs, *The rise of music in the ancient world*, New York, 1943, pp. 271 ff.

The use of the word art, in its turn, raises an inescapable, embarassing question: can primitive music, so manifestly based on inexorable tradition and collective mentality, ever have the personal quality that we connect with the concept of art?

Yet this personal quality in music is expressly attested on various levels of culture. Many melodies already in common use show individual differences when performed by different singers (who in scriptless civilizations are often the composers, too); and in some of the higher cultures, a personal variant can be so distinctive that fellow countrymen recognize the author. This often goes beyond the life span of the inventor; in Central Asia the melodies of great singers of the past are sung to this day, "and they are given a name that unequivocally indicates their authorship." [16] The same applies to Arnhem Land in North Australia.[17]

Anthropology teaches in fact that every single culture "includes individual and social poles which are distinguishable, but not actually separable." The common social heritage of a tribe must not "mislead us into overlooking the role of the individual in modifying or adding to his cultural heritage. Individuals not only fail to conform to ideal social patterns but also initiate many changes which later become universally accepted." [18]

'Practical anthropology' is no less outspoken on this point than 'theoretical anthropology.' "Every man," says Herskovits, "lives as a member of a society, ordering his behavior and shaping his thought in accordance with its pattern; yet except in the rarest instances, this is not the whole story. At some time in his life, however brief the moment, in some mode of conduct, however slight its import, he asserts his individuality." [19]

In art, "the directives laid down by any traditional style govern the artist even as he introduces change into its art forms. In every society the artist is the experimenter, the innovator, the rebel. But he is an innovator only within bounds, for he is all unwittingly influenced by factors that guide him in his creative

---

[16] E. Emsheimer, *l.c.*, p. 28.
[17] A. P. Elkin, *Arnhem Land music*, in *Oceania*, vol. 24 (1953), p. 97, reprinted as *Oceania Monograph* no. 9, Sydney, 1957.
[18] David Bidney, *Theoretical anthropology*, New York, 1953, p. 28.
[19] Melville J. Herskovits, *Franz Boas*, New York, 1953, p. 73.

experience, as they guide the behavior of all human beings in every aspect of their lives ..."

"It is important to stress this function of the artist in inducing change, where the art of nonliterate peoples is under discussion, because stability, rather than change, is generally emphasized when these art forms are being considered." [20]

In music – and this fact, too, stands on the side of individualism – we are often told that the oldest songs [21] and dances [22] of a community were inspired in dreams. Here, we should remember that in primitive societies dreams are more intimately interwoven with the realities of life and are more strongly under their influence.[23] Whatever the exact nature of this gift of the subconscious, it seems to be closely akin to the 'inspiration' of a creative artist in the West. It makes up the unique and personal character of a contribution, different from mere tradition and also different from a mechanical, uninspired com-position of conventional elements.

In a friendly chat with Eric Werner, we remembered that Richard Wagner had expressed exactly the same idea when, in the third act of the *Meistersinger*, Hans Sachs encourages young Walter:

> *Des Menschen wahrster Wahn*
> *Wird ihm im Traume aufgetan,*
> *Und alle Poeterei*
> *Ist nichts wie Wahrtraumdeuterei.*

> (Man's vision in his dream unfolds
> That what his inner eye beholds,
> And all poetization
> Is merely dream interpretation).
>
> (transl. C. S.)

MUSICAL INVENTION is in many archaic civilizations a matter of course. It was hardly an exaggeration to call the Eskimo a

---

[20] *id.*, *Cultural anthropology*, p. 255. – This complex question is brilliantly treated in A. L. Kroeber, *Configurations of culture growth*, Berkeley, 1944, particularly in the section on Genius, pp. 7–16.

[21] Frances Densmore, *l.c.*, p. 59. – id., *The study of Indian music*, in *Smithsonian Report for 1941*, Washington, 1942, p. 538.

[22] Curt Sachs, *World history of the dance*, p. 53.

[23] Richard Thurnwald, *Des Menschengeistes Erwachen, Wachsen und Irren*, Berlin, 1951, p. 121.

genuine people of musicians; every Eskimo must know the art of composition; [24] and, in supreme contempt, a jealous Eskimo woman would sneer at her rival: "She can't dance, she can't even sing ..." [25] In the South African Ila and Tonga regions it is incumbent on every young woman or man to compose personal songs: a groom is asked to sing a melody of his own on the day of his wedding,[26] and Tonga men, when possessed by an evil spirit, must during exorcising rites intone 'their' songs.[27]

But it should once more be said: with all his creative abilities, the individual is "born and reared in a certain cultural environment, which impinges upon him at every moment in his life. From earliest childhood his behavior is conditioned by the habits of those about him. He has no choice but to conform to the folkways current in his group." [28]

The individual and the social pole are counterbalanced against one another when on the Andaman Islands in the Gulf of Bengal "every man composes songs, and the boys begin to practise themselves in the art of composition when they are still young. A man composes his song as he cuts a canoe or a bow or as he paddles a canoe, singing it over softly to himself, until he is satisfied with it. He then awaits an opportunity to sing it in public, and for this he has to wait for a dance. Before the dance he takes care to teach the chorus to one or two of his female relatives so that they can lead the chorus of women. He sings his song, and if it is successful he repeats it several times, and thereafter it becomes part of his repertory of songs that he is prepared to repeat at any time. If the song is not successful, if the chorus and dancers do not like it, the composer abandons it and does not repeat it. Some men are recognized as being more skilful songmakers than others." [29] The individual, then, creates; society accepts or refuses.

How personal, how anti-collective musical creation can be in

[24] Zygmunt Estreicher, *La musique des Esquimaux-Caribous*, in *Bulletin de la Société Neuchâteloise de Géographie*, vol. 54 (1948), p. 3.

[25] Diamond Jennes, *The people of the twilight*, New York, 1928, p. 124.

[26] A. M. Jones, *African music*, Livingstone, 1949, p. 14.

[27] Thurnwald, *l.c.*, p. 132.

[28] George P. Murdock, *The science of culture*, in *American Anthropologist*, vol. 34 (1932), reprinted in Hoebel, Jennings, Smith, *Readings in anthropology*, New York, 1956, pp. 314 ff.

[29] A. R. Radcliffe-Brown, *The Andaman Islanders*, Cambridge (Mass.), 1933, p. 132.

primitive civilizations, shows in another habit of the Andaman Islanders: "Every man composes his own songs. No one would ever sing a song composed by any other person." [30]

WE ARE SELDOM in a position to sense the personal contribution in a music so remote from ours – just as a range of mountains, seen from afar, appears to our eyes as a single compact and undivided massif. In the chants of Hawaii, native singers often point out distinct and personal traits where we, the foreigners, only hear the same eternal cantillation on one pitch with merely a cadential drop at the end of a poetical section. This lack of distinction, by the way, can be reversed: oriental musicians are generally at a loss when asked to distinguish between the personal styles, even a hundred years or more apart, of western composers. I remember a musician from the Middle East who after eleven years of musical studies in Germany confessed to me that he was unable to notice any difference between a Haydn and a Mahler symphony.

Only rarely are we allowed to witness creation at work. It happens when the original pattern of one single step grows to a two or three-step pattern. 'Growing' is understood as a timid, occasional trait before the novel, larger pattern has taken roots to stay. The new step, as a result of some personal urge, may appear only once at the end of a melody after the traditional one-step pattern has been safely established. Less often does the singer yield to his urge right at the beginning, only to shyly relapse into the conventional model.

The following section will discuss these developments in greater detail.

A COMPOSER, the Eskimo say, is, and must be, the exclusive possessor of his song, since it carries his inalienable soul.[31]

Such rights and restrictions are by no means rare or sporadic.

On Dobu in the western Pacific every man composes; "he is proud of his creation, proud of its originality, and he has rights to prevent others from using his song, at least for a while. The song-maker must give his permission before his song is used

---

[30] *ibid.*, pp. 131 ff.
[31] Zygmunt Estreicher, *l.c.*, p. 3.

for the dance." [32] In the primitive Northern Territory of Australia, the 'song-man' of each group owns all the melodies and
dances that he performs, and "no one can sing his songs without
his permission." [33] By the same token, a funeral song can be
the exclusive property of an Indian chief or group,[34] just as in
the Scottish Highlands a particular piper's 'lament' is the
property of a particular clan. One of the Pawnee songs in the
Indian's Book had been the property of a man; but one day he
gave it to his brother by mutual adoption (the closest human
relation), "bidding him to sing it when he needed help or protection." [35] The sollicitation of assistance through sounds
miraculously carried across unlimited space – as by playing the
'Magic Flute' and the horns of Oberon, Roland, and the de-
parting Lohengrin – this ancient motif of saga finds a new
evidence on Amerindian soil.

The idea, intimately connected with the motif of a *quid pro
quo* relation between man and melody – anticipating the personal
Leitmotive in Wagner's *Ring* – finds a diminutive variation in
Uganda: every man of the Lango people has his own whistle
motif, not to be misused by anyone else. "An infringement of
this rule will certainly cause a violent quarrel, and may even
lead to bloodshed." [36] Evidently, such motifs are the precursors
of our somewhat degenerated family whistle-calls.

On the other hand, all melodies, though strictly taboo to un-
authorized performers, may be legally 'copyrighted' for natural
heirs and for buyers.[37] Actually, persons may for money or any
equivalent acquire the right to sing the melodies or dance the
choreographic inventions of other men.[38]

In Australia, songmen often trade their songs because of some
close kinship tie. But whether songs and dances are passed on
to other tribes or not, "they do serve to link tribes in friendship.

---

[32] R. F. Fortune, *Sorcerers of Dobu*, London, 1932, p. 251.

[33] A. P. Elkin introducing *EFw* FE 4439 (P 439).

[34] Marius Barbeau, *Asiatic survivals in Indian songs*, in *The Musical Quarterly*,
vol. 20 (1934) *passim*.

[35] Natalie Curtis, *The Indians' Book*, New York, 1907, p. 111.

[36] Driberg, *The Lango*, London, pp. 124 ff.

[37] Frances Densmore, *Chippewa music*, Washington, 1910, p. 60. – Cf. also: Erna
Gunther, in Willard Rhodes, *Music of the American Indian Northwest (Puget Sound)*,
Washington, 1955, p. 10.

[38] Richard Thurnwald, *Die menschliche Gesellschaft*, vol. 1 of *Repräsentative Lebensbilder von Naturvölkern*, Berlin, 1931, p. 38. – Curt Sachs, *l.c.*, p. 219.

They are performed as mutual entertainment and as a way of maintaining, strengthening and extending social relationships. Thus music, while being aesthetic in content, is a social institution of positive value." [39]

One evening in 1930, when the sun was setting over the yellow sands of the desert, a dozen Nubian oarsmen who were taking me through the rapids of the Nile around the isle of Elephantine sang endlessly in response form to the rhythm of the rows.[40] I followed with my pencil as best I could, running a race with the night which so quickly falls in that latitude. But when I had disembarked in Aswan, they demanded an extra bakshish as I had written down their ditty and thus appropriated what – they said – was rightfully theirs.

How far the concept of personal melodies as a line of business reaches into oriental civilizations of the highest level, is told in the story of a once famous musician in India who, being in serious money difficulties, succeeded in mortgaging a certain melody or *rāga*, which was closest to his heart and a favorite of his maharaja. Soon thereafter, when ordered by the sovereign to sing it at court, he confessed what he had done. The deal, apparently unusual, amused the prince; generously he paid up the loan and, besides, rewarded the moneylender for his "keen appreciation of the value of music." [41]

Modern musical copyright was first enacted in 1831 at Washington D.C.[42]

In this context it might be appropriate to remember Herskovits' statement that "intangibles form an important category of property in all societies, as witness the economic value placed on patent rights, on good will, and on copyright in our own culture ... [An] example of the importance of incorporeal property includes an assortment of rights called *topati* by the Nootka of British Columbia – knowledge of family legends, a ritual for spearing fish, honorific names of many kinds, the right to carve certain designs on totem poles and grave posts, to sing

[39] A. P. Elkin, *Arnhem Land music*, in *Oceania*, vol. 24 (1953), p. 106. Reprinted in *Oceania Monograph* no. 9, Sydney, 1957.
[40] Music example 35 in Curt Sachs, *The rise of music in the ancient world*, New York, 1943, p. 95.
[41] Herbert A. Popley, *The music of India*, Calcutta, 1921, p. 66.
[42] Hans Abraham, in Willi Apel, *Harvard Dictionary of Music*, Cambridge, Mass, 1944, pp. 184 ff. (with bibliography).

certain songs, to dance certain dances, to perform certain specific parts of certain rituals ... In the South Sea, personal names, incantations, songs, charms, and family traditions all figure as family wealth." [43] Therefore, "for the most part, those who received training in composition, narration, and chanting were usually of noble birth." [44]

[43] Melville J. Herskovits, *l.c.*, p. 160.
[44] *id.*, *l.c.*, p. 189. – Cf. for social restrictions as discussed in this section also Jaap Kunst, *Sociologische bindingen in de muziek* (inaugural oration), The Hague, 1953.

FOUR

THE FATE OF
SECONDAL AND TERTIAL PATTERNS

While tumbling strains developed by inner consolidation, horizontal melodies chiefly evolved by enlargement. One-step patterns reached out, upwards and downwards, usually by giving citizenship to former occasional affixes. From there the process went on to a conquest of more and more of the musical space.[1]

A classical evidence of transition from a secondal one-step to a secondal two-step pattern are the two oldest of the successive styles in which the priests of India used to chant the sacred texts from the Vedas. Early in times B.C. the chant, almost certainly, knew only two notes or pitches; a higher one, *udātta*, a lower one, *anudātta*, and their legato succession or ligature, *svarita*. Pānini, patriarch of grammarians in the fourth century B.C., has stated this expressly. Later, the *svarita* changed into a third note which, appoggiatura-like, dropped to *udātta* from a tone or a semitone above but never fell directly to *anudātta*,[2] possibly to avoid an indesirable leap:

Ex. 32*

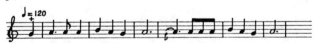

Similar arrangements occur in other oriental cantillations of high antiquity. A very fine example is the central creed of the Jews in its Babylonian version – *Harken Israel, the Lord our God, the Lord is One* – in which we readily distinguish the ap-

---

* Transcr. C. S.

[1] John Frederic Rowbotham, *History of music*, London, 1885, seems to have been the first to see this phenomenon.

[2] Erwin Felber, *Die indische Musik der vedischen und der klassischen Zeit*, in *Abhandlungen der K. K. Akademie der Wissenschaften*, Wien, 1912, no. 7. – *EFw* FE 4431 (P 431) I 3.

poggiatura-like B♭, being a quasi-*svarita*, the *A* as an *udātta*, and the *anudātta* on G (Example 24).

The process of widening the original one-step patterns is rather common in the history of oldest music. Even typically primitive tribes such as the Vedda in inner Ceylon often add a third note to the two already used. And in this case, as well, it will not do to simply count the notes. Such naive procedure will yield no chronology, no grade of perfection, no rate of civilization. A Vedda melody with three notes or two steps came no later than a Rumanian folksong with only one step; nor is it better; nor are the Vedda more advanced in culture than the Rumanians. The tune is simply more complex.

Often is the original one-step quite clearly audible, while the third note is just an addition without actual naturalization. A characteristic example from the Vogul follows:

Ex. 33*

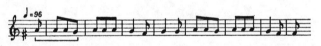

The famous epic songs of the Yugoslav *guslari* often lasting for an hour, also belong to this group, although the seconds are rather short.[3]

Sometimes we find group alternation, not just the alternation of two notes, but of two one-step patterns, like the following example from Bukaua in the Solomon Archipelago:

Ex. 34**

When in Hawaii either note sinks a semitone in the second half of the piece,[4] transposing might find an explanation – a possibly too rationalistic explanation – in the exhausting stretch

---

* After A. O. Väisänen, *Wogulische und Ostjakische Melodien*, Helsinki, 1937.
** After Erich M. von Hornbostel, *Die Musik auf den nordwestlichen Salomo-Inseln*, in R. Thurnwald, *Salomo-Inseln*, vol. i (1912).
[3] *EFw* FE 4506 (P 506) III 46.
[4] Helen H. Roberts, *Ancient Hawaiian music*, in *Bernice P. Bishop Museum Bulletin* 29 (1926), pp. 76, 81.

of Hawaiian cantillation. The eyes of old singers are reported to bulge with the effort.[5]

The tenacity of the nucleus is amazing. Affixes appear oftenest at the beginning of a song or at its end: the singer is bold and pioneering either at the start when he is quite himself or else in the coda when an audacious infringement does no longer endanger the identity of the pattern. But the main stretch of the melody follows tradition and is in many cases completely free of affixes.

On the other hand, affixes at the right place cannot fail to be eventually accepted with equal rights and to accrue the original nucleus. In the following example from Estonia the kernel is doubtless $bb-a$; but the affix c (much more than the less important infrafix g) has become strong enough to form the start and to usurp a few of the melodic stresses:

Ex. 35*

A TERTIAL NUCLEUS can be widened by appending a second, a third, or a fourth. But the most frequent, and a fascinating, form of tertial two-step melody is the one usually found under the doubtful nicknames 'fanfare' and 'triadic' melody.

In Europe, empty 'triads' are confined to the East, from the Lapps down the map to Greece; filled, they expand all over the continent. Both forms prevail in the two Americas and in Melanesia, while in Africa the filled type is more general. The Asiatic distribution includes, in either form, tribes as primitive as the Semang in Malaya, but it excludes the high civilizations of the Far East and of India.

The two current names 'fanfare melody' and 'triadic melody' are objectionable. The first is instrumental; it is too much reminiscent of the trumpet and the bugle to suit a vocal pattern. Neither is the second name to the point. Accepted musical terminology reserves the word triad for a chord of three simultaneous notes: a root or fundamental and, slightly less important,

---

* After Walter Wiora, *Europäischer Volksgesang*, Heemstede, 1952.
[5] *ibid.*, p. 72.

its third and its fifth. This would by all means be a pardonable loan – I myself do not hesitate to borrow from harmonic terminology when it facilitates quick understanding. But 'triad' misleads; the name refers at best to tonal anatomy, with no attention paid to the more important physiology.

Tonal physiology, as I see it, is less concerned with the static structure of a scale than with the distribution of moving forces and weight within a melody. It does not rest satisfied with finding out what the distances between the three notes of a triad are or in what order they appear, but also wants to know which note is the center of gravity and which of the two steps is allotted the greater shaping power. While anatomy speaks only of the major and the minor third that constitute a triad *C E G*, physiology demands an answer to the two specific questions: which of the three notes is the actual chief, and which of the two steps *C–E* and *E–G* has the greater importance?

As a start, we look for the first and the final note and, if possible, for cadential pauses inside. But we also must recur to mere statistics by counting how many time-units each of the three skeletal notes and their infixes (if any) is given. This sounds unpleasant to those who believe that music is a matter of the spirit and not of deadly numerical facts. But in test and counter-test the statistical method is with a few exceptions reliable enough as long as the analyst knows its limits.[6] A comparison of the starter-final and the statistical method will seldom lead astray.

Let us take three examples of empty triads without infixes or affixes. The first is a song of the Lapps:

Ex. 36*

The lowest note or root appropriates fourteen units or, in our transcription, eightnotes; the third, six of them; and the fifth, four or, including four rapid appoggiaturas, some more, say,

---

* After K. Tirén, *Die Lappische Volksmusik*, Stockholm 1942, p. 103 nr. 60.

[6] Cf. also: Linton C. Freeman and Alan P. Merriam, *Statistical classification in anthropology: an application to ethnomusicology*, in *American Anthropologist*, vol. 58 (1956), pp. 464–472.

six, units. No doubt the root prevails, and the two other notes are about equal in weight between themselves. As a confirmation, we find that the root acts as both the starter and the final. Thus, the three notes form indeed a genuine triad in root position.

A lullaby of the Slavonic Kashub:

Ex. 37*

consists of only eight notes per verse, to be repeated indefinitely. It gives five of them to the third, two to the fifth, and only a single one to the 'root'; the note g acts also as a starter; and from this principal note the melody reaches twice up to b and only once downward to e, which proves too little important to make it a root. This so-called triad is functionally just a centric melody of the kind to be examined in a following section.

Our third example, a song of the Vogul in northwestern Siberia:

Ex. 38**

starts on the fifth and repeats this note to the amount of 24 units, while only 14 go to the third, and 4 to the presumptive root. The fifth dominates; it forms a third with the middle note; and the lowest note is again an infrafix at the distance of a third.

Thus the same anatomical structure has three different physiological aspects, and the old suggestions that tribes who sing in so-called triads might have a "latent feeling of harmony" is Eurocentric and untenable. The 'triads' are simply double thirds.

Particularly convincing in this respect are melodies in which the so-called triad appears as two separated thirds: the first section alternates between the 'third' and the 'fifth,' and the

* After Tirén, *l.c.*
** After Väisänen, *l.c.*

second section, between the 'third' and the 'root.' [7] The double third that a mechanical addition of the two steps makes believe, is in fact a succession of two single thirds.

The general direction of a melody is an important factor, too. Double-third melodies of American Indians descend like tumbling strains, while similar European folksongs start as a rule on the lowest note.

Despite the non-triadic character of double thirds, the two adjoining thirds form often an organic whole. They have different sizes, one being (more or less) major, and the other one (more or less) minor; the two thirds together form an approximately perfect fifth. Non-perfect fifths, augmented or diminished, do hardly occur.

How strong the urge of the perfect fifth can be, appears from a klephtic (underground guerrilla) song of modern Greece:

Ex. 39*

Above the double third *f–a–c′*, still another third, *e′*, makes it a triple third. As this *e′* forms a so-called changing note with the affix *d′*, it is *via naturae* flatted; and being now an *e^b*, it entails an *a^b* below where there had been a natural *a* before.

This example leads from a two-step to a three-step pattern, from a double third to a triple third. The urge to expand the range and yet to cling to the same basic interval can indeed be so strong that singers feel compelled to enlarge their double third (or, as we shall see in the following chapter, double fourth) by adding, above or below, another third or fourth. In doing so, they create 'chains,' such as triple, quadruple, quintuple, and even sextuple thirds, and triple or quadruple fourths.

I call them chains, as our customary word scale would be a misnomer. An actual scale is an organic whole, in which every single note has a function of its own, as the tonic, the dominant,

---

* After Samuel Baud-Bovy, *La chanson clephtique*, in *Journal of the International Folk Music Coucil*, vol. 1 (1949), pp. 44 ff.

[7] For an example, cf. M. Kolinski, in Melville J. and Frances S. Herskovits, *Suriname folk-lore*, New York, 1936, p. 531, 1.

the subdominant, the leading note, the mediant, and so forth. Hardly one of such functions exists in a chain: while the singer moves from interval number one to interval two and from there to interval three, he often forgets about the first one and finds a new orientation. His chain is not an organic whole, but an unorganized concatenation of similar intervals. The intervals are similar, not identical, because the thirds in a chain are now major, now minor, to form every two a perfect fifth. It would be admissible to describe such a tertial chain as interlocking fifths.

TRIPLE THIRDS, in their two basic forms $C\ E\ G\ B$ and $D\ F\ A\ C$ have given music historians a troublesome problem to solve. Still unaware of the concept 'chain,' analysers of medieval melodies have operated with their old, familiar notions and, somewhat embarrassed, have called them mixtures of the Dorian and the Lydian Church mode or of our minor and major scales. In doing so, they ignored one basic fact: both the modes of the Church and of the world outside the Gregorian realm have octaval structures, while a triple chain is septimal. Actually, the triple thirds, universal and prevalent in Europe both in folksongs and in art music (including the Gregorian chant) were mostly discontinued during the sixteenth century when the major and the minor mode had been established to stay.[8]

An example from the so-called Turco-Sephardic version of the Jewish liturgy, a *Kol nidrei* to open the eve of the Day of Atonement, shows particularly well how a tertial nucleus, *G–B*, is first widened to the lower third *E* and eventually also to the upper third *D:*

Ex. 40*

We find similar triple thirds ever so often on archaic levels of Asia,[9] in North Africa,[10] in North and South America [11] way

* *EFw* FE 4505 (P 505) IV 14 (Transcr. C. S.).

[8] Curt Sachs, *The road to major*, in *The Musical Quarterly*, vol. 29 (1943), pp. 381–404.

[9] e.g. Flores: Jaap Kunst, *Music in Flores*, Leyden, 1942, p. 43.

[10] e.g. Berber (Morocco): Von Hornbostel and Lachmann in *Zeitschrift für Vergleichende Musikwissenschaft*, vol. 1 (1933), p. 4.

[11] e.g. Cocama (Upper Amazon): *EFw* FE 4458 (P 458) I 1.

up to the Eskimo [12] as well as in Melanesia, Polynesia, and New Guinea: [13]

Ex. 41*

One of the Asiatic examples is "the" strange melody pattern of the Palaung in Burma. All Palaung songs, we are told, are sung to this same melody, whether they are grave or gay; variations that we might hear are due to "the caprice of the singer." The tune as we read it in L. Milne's book is obviously written down by ear; but the transcription is convincing. Within scale *e g b c' d'*, the note *b* is three times held in long fermatas at the beginning of each phrase. The singer, she says, "first takes as long a breath as possible, in order to prolong the sound of the first note, which should be at least ten seconds in duration." [14]

QUADRUPLE THIRDS, requiring the wider range of a ninth, are conceivably scarcer. In the two basic forms, *C E G B D* and *D F A C E*, they are conspicuously absent from the Pacific; they do not touch Asia save in Turkey, and reach only a few North American tribes,[15] including the Copper Eskimo,[16] and also American jazz.

Inversely, they play an important role in Bantu Africa and are sung by the Hottentots as (usually unfilled) skeletons:

Ex. 42**

But their main habitat is Europe. Here, they occur as empty skeletons in Finnish folk music, while they are filled and diatonic

---

* Marind-anim, Southwest New Guinea, after J. Kunst.
** After Moodie.

[12] Helen H. Roberts and D. Jenness, *Songs of the Copper Eskimo*, in *Report of the Canadian Arctic Expedition 1913–18*, vol. 14, Ottawa, 1925, *passim.*

[13] Jaap Kunst, *De inheemse muziek in westelijk Nieuw-Guinea*, (*Mededeling XCIII of the Royal Tropical Institute, Amsterdam*), 1950, pp. 44–47.

[14] (Mrs.) Leslie Milne, *The home of an Eastern clan*, Oxford, 1924, pp. 303 ff.

[15] e.g., Quileute and Zuñi (Densmore).

[16] Helen H. Roberts and D. Jenness, *l.c.*

in other European countries. The pattern is so truly European that it reappears again and again in art music. One example comes from French polyphony of the mid-sixteenth century: in the motet version of Claude Goudimel's Psalm 10, the tenor cascades down from *g'* to *e'c'* and *a f*.[17] We have evidences even in contemporary music: a passage in Stravinsky's *Pétrouchka* (1911) ascends and descends in empty thirds from *a'* to *b''*; and the melody of the ninth *Ludus* in Carl Orff's *Catulli Carmina* (1935) scales in thirds from *d'* to *e''*.

QUINTUPLE THIRDS – C E G B D F or D F A C E G – are purely European. They occur in Iceland [18] and also in Serbia, although in the Serbian piece that comes to my mind [19] the lowermost fifth is not subdivided into thirds. Of quintuple thirds, as well, the polyphonic sacred music of the sixteenth century provides a startling sample: in the *French Mass* [20] of John Shepherd (d. circa 1563), the two upper voices unite to form the empty chain *d' f' a' c'' e'' g''*:

Ex. 43

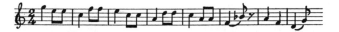

Indeed, late in the nineteenth century Mussorgsky gave to the Song of the Gnat in his *Boris Godunov* exactly the same chain in descending movement.

With all due reserve, mention could be made also of the 'old zither' *yamato koto* of Japan, whose six strings form a quintuple tertial chain – *d' f' a' c' e' g'* [21] except that the three last ones are tuned down by an octave.

Sextuple thirds do not occur in folksong, perhaps on account of a range overtaxing the possibilities of untrained voices. I found one in a *Fantasia a 5* by William Lawes (1602–1645), although to be a perfect example the lowest *B* should be flatted.

[17] Courtesy Eleanor Lawry.
[18] B. Thorsteinsson, *Folkelig sang og musik paa Island*, in *Nordisk Kultur* (1934).
[19] Communication from Danica S. Janković.
[20] ed. H. B. Collins, London, 1927.
[21] Sir Francis Piggott, *The music and musical instruments of Japan*, 2nd edition, London, 1909, p. 111.

It will be good to remember that quintuple and sextuple thirds are exclusively European. But (notwithstanding evidences from other parts of the world) quadruple thirds and lesser tertial chains are European as well as Bantu African. Once more: Europe and Africa, related in their preference given to thirds, both in melody and in chordal organization, were torn apart by a South Asiatic and Mediterranean wedge of quartal melodies.

MOST EXAMPLES, so far, were 'empty' skeletons. Only a few showed 'infixes' of the kind discussed in our chapter on One-step Melodies. Here, too, infixes mostly bisect the major thirds and leave the minor thirds intact. The result is a gamut of wholetones and minor thirds. But it should be realized that the infixes are fillers of inferior melodic importance and must not be joined with their two immediate neighbors above and below in what Hugo Riemann called a *pyknon* or density and believed to be the melodic nucleus. This it is not, since the central note is unmistakably a passage note without any structural significance.

This has not been the only mistake in interpreting the infixes in tertial chains. Minor thirds plus wholetones are on the surface so close to the so-called pentatonic scales that, alas, most authors have succumbed to the temptation of dubbing such chains pentatonic. Indeed, pentatonism is one of the obsessions in recent ethnomusicology. This is a dangerous misnomer. Pentatonic must be defined as an octave divided into five steps, be they equal or unequal, just as tetratonic, hexatonic, hepta-tonic scales are octaves divided into four, six, seven steps. Hence the term pentatonic applies perfectly well to Scottish, old-Greek, many Indian, and most East Asian scales, which are quartal in structure and use the octave as an organic and vital interval. But a tertial chain like $A\ C\ ^d E\ G\ ^a B$ has no octave in its skeleton or at best as a mere infix without a structural role. At a pinch, it is pseudo-pentatonic. The only similarity between the two organisms is the lack of semitones (which is not a necessary trait of pentatonic scales); they are, to use a Greek term, anhemitonic or 'without semitones.'

PENTATONISM AND HEPTATONISM – did they develop from one another? Are they independent? Do they reflect any racial idiosyncrasies? It means stirring up a wasps' nest to approach the question of their relations. Our literature is full of answers. But most of the opinions we hear are rash, contradictory, and, worst of all, 'plausible,' that is, as the writer at his desk thinks it could have been. The author begs to desist from summing them up [22] and to offer his own views for what they are worth.

Before giving an answer, albeit a tentative one, let us repeat with great insistence: the old and easy-going equation of pentatonism and anhemitonism is no longer admissible. The lack of semitones may occur in all kinds of structures, and, inversely, a wide-spread type of pentatonic melody has semitones (and major thirds). Unless this is clearly understood, we grope in the dark.

Any answer must have the support of our most archaic examples of primitive music. On thumbing through my own notations, I find in about eighty percent of all two-step melodies two different distances: when the nucleus is a major second, the other distance is either a minor third or else a semitone; when the nucleus is a minor second, the affix is generally a wholetone apart; when the nucleus is a minor third, the other distance is in most cases a wholetone or a major third. Evidently, there has always been an inhibition against equality, which is in a way reminiscent of the inhibition of artists against squares for the benefit of rectangles.

This elementary urge is even more obvious in three-step patterns. At random, I present two primitive examples which could easily be centupled. One comes from the Makushí in the Roraima Mountains, British Guyana. It has the four notes $a\ g\ f\ d;$ $g\ f$ is the nucleus, and the affixes keep at the distances of a wholetone and a minor third. The genus is definitely composed of minor thirds and wholetones, without any semitone.

The other example was sung by South African Lala. The four notes are $e\flat\ d\ c\ b\flat;$ the nucleus is $d\ b\flat;$ the infix c cleaves the major third into two wholetones; and the suprafix $e\flat$ keeps at a distance of a semitone.

The two examples prove not only the existence of mingled steps on a very early level. They also show that our two most

[22] A recent summary can be found in Constantin Brailoiu, *Sur une mélodie russe*, in Pierre Souvtchinsky (ed.), *Musique Russe*, vol. 2, Paris, 1953, pp. 329 ff.

frequent arrangements – anhemitonic and diatonic – have their origins in very archaic times, long before melodic patterns grew to the sizes of sixths and octaves.

It might be remembered that the word pentatonic can apply only where, by definition, an octave has five steps. This requires at least one structural fourth in an octave, that is, for example, $c\ e\ g\ c'$ or $c\ f\ g\ c'$. Chains of thirds with the major thirds filled in, as $c\ ^d\ e\ g\ ^a\ b$ .... are anhemitonic, but not pentatonic, since the octave appears as best as an infix but not as a structural tone.

The knowledge that anhemitonic and diatonic patterns are prototypes forbids us

(1) to establish a chronology of the two;
(2) to derive the diatonic gender from the anhemitonic gender by infixing two *piens*. The word and the fact apply to China only.
(3) to attribute the two genders to 'race.'

When we observe how again and again the Chinese attempted in vain to replace their pentatonic scale by introducing two *piens*, this is not evolution or progress, but simply an abortive change from an eastern to a western concept. And it is a matter of strongly traditional culture, not of race or 'blood,' as any American-born or American-reared Far Easterner will prove.

TWO OTHER FEATURES should be mentioned before we shelve the tertial chains. In Europe, the feeling for third catenation has been so strong that it led to some aspects inexplicable from our modern diatonic viewpoints.

The first one is the so-called German choral dialect of the Gregorian chant. When in the Roman chant a melody in the first mode (on *D*) reaches out beyond the fifth, only to revert at once to the latter, the singer makes instinctively this step up and down as short as possible; he reduces it to a semitone although this requires a flat against the purity of the mode. As the old cantorial rule expressed it:

una nota super la
semper est canendum fa

which meant, in medieval solmization, that the note above *a* must always be taken as *b♭*, as *fa* is the symbol of the semitone (*mi–fa*). But the Germans and Scandinavians, unaccustomed to semitones, replaced them by their traditional thirds. In other words, the Northerners transformed the typical pattern of the first Church mode, *d f a b♭ a*, into the equally typical triple chain of thirds, *d f a c a*. Inversely, melodies sung in the fourteenth century, and probably many of older times, too, avoided the *subsemitonium* or semitone below the tonic, as in our customary *g e c B c*, and preferred a minor third, as in *g e c A c*, which again opposes a tertial chain to a functional, modal scale with its seventh or 'leading note.' In this case we speak of a Landino third; but the great Francesco Landino (1325–1397) was by no means its inventor.[23]

I suggested long ago that in a similar way the four-line staff of the Gregorian chant reflects, not the system of the church modes, but the tertial chains of secular music: according to the clef prescribed, the lines

$$d f a c'$$
$$f a c' e'$$
$$a c' e' g'$$

while the spaces in between are literally intended for the empty spaces or the infixes between the skeletal notes.

IT MEANS MELODIC CONSOLIDATION, as opposed to the loose concatenation of the 'chain,' when the singer, starting from a double third, does not proceed to building a triple third, but reaches for a second only, be it major or minor. This second, in turn, leads the melody back to the original fifth – a case mentioned previously. Using our familiar terminology, the skeleton would be *F A C D* (*C*) in major and *A C E F* (*E*) in minor. Let us, once more, borrow from the nomenclature of harmony and call this grouping a six-five pattern.

But here, again, we must rely on musical physiology, even at the risk of disappointment. In most cases, as mentioned before, the sixth is simply a 'changing note' above the fifth and must be considered a suprafix. The given example:

[23] An example from English folksong in Constantin Brailoiu, *Sur une mélodie russe*, *l.c.*, p. 361, no. 107.

Ex. 44*

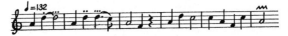

is a half-shouted *briolage* or incantation addressed to grazing cattle in the French province Le Berry. Many other instances are probably hybrids or concretions of two simpler patterns. In a song of Alu, one of the Solomon Islands, Melanesia:

Ex. 45**

the two elements are particularly obvious: a single empty fourth on notes 3 and 6, and a triad on 1 3 5.

It must have taken a long time before the sixth was firmly established in the skeleton as a part with equal rights and duties. This final stage is evident in the Gregorian chant and, probably deriving from plainsong, in Philipp Nicolai's *Wachet auf, ruft uns die Stimme* and similar Protestant chorales. But it is evident in Asia as well. It reappears at the other end of the world as the first of the Chinese modes or the Japanese *ryo;* and between these west-eastern extremes, there are many examples from Tibet and various parts of Europe, including the archaic Faroes due north of Scotland.

The Chinese occurrence of the six-five pattern has caused a fatal mistake in analysis. In China, so we are told even in recent books, all melodic modes derive from one original scale by top-tail inversions, the lowest note being in this process cut off and re-added an octave higher as the new top:

$$C\ D\ E\quad G\ A$$
$$D\ E\quad G\ A\quad C$$
$$E\quad G\ A\quad C\ D$$

This looks neat but is very questionable: scales 2 and 3 have quartal structures:

$$\overline{D\ E}\quad G\ A\quad C$$
$$E\quad G\ A\quad \overline{C\ D}$$

---

* *Pathé* Part. 5607; cf. J. Canteloube (ed.), *Anthologie des chants populaires français* (Paris 1951), t.IV, p.106

** After Erich M. von Hornbostel, *Die Musik auf den nordwestlichen Salomo-Inseln,* in Richard Thurnwald, *Salomo-Inseln und Bismarck-Archipel,* vol. 1 (1912), no. 41.

while the first scale, definitely non-quartal, constitutes a plain hexachord in six-five form. Since this latter pattern also appears not far from China, for instance in Indonesia to the south and in Tibet to the west, the *C* scale must be supposed to belong to some stratum different from that of the *D* and *E* scales.

ANOTHER FORM OF TRIADIC ENLARGEMENT is due to adding the higher or the lower octave instead of the sixth. In this case, the melody has the steps one-three-five-eight or, in the plagal form, low five-one-three-five, such as *c e g c'* or *G c e g*. We met with triadic octave skeletons in the section on tumbling strains. The triadic octaves of the present section are different: they do not cascade from the highest to the lowest note and therefore do not recapture the upper octave in order to repeat the pattern. Instead of stressing the octave, they usually rather accent the triad as their natural nucleus. Good illustrations come from New Guinea:

Ex. 46*

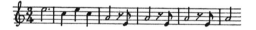

from Flores, the Amami Islands, and the western Bantu. A combination of the authentic and the plagal form – *D G B D G* – occurs in shaman's songs during the Peyote dances of the Huichol in Mexico.[24] Though the Mexican Indians have to some extent given way to white man's music, such influence is here quite out of the question: it would show in heptatonic melodies but not in a skeleton that at best may be heard on a bugle. The elimination of white man's influence is corroborated by the frequent occurrence of triadic octaves in songs of the Copper Eskimo.[25] But there, again, we should not be satisfied with the anatomical fact of a triadic octave, but proceed to the physiological facts. In such a skeleton as *C E G C* the bottom note *C* is not at all a root or a tonic; the functional stress is on *E*.

It is fascinating in this case of transition to watch the un-

---

* After J. Kunst, *A study on Papuan music*, Weltevreden, 1931, p. 25.
[24] *EFw* FE 4413 (P 413) II 3.
[25] Roberts and Jennes, *l.c.*, pp. 170 ff., 229.

certain, hesitant attitude of singers. Aiming now at the seventh now at the octave, they alternately create now a triple third now a triadic octave. The following is a curious example: a French *rondeau* from the *Roman de la Rose* (12th century) first establishes the triad, then turns to the seventh, but leaves it immediately to catch the octave, only to return in haste to the safer, wonted seventh.[26] A similar example of uncertain octavation will be described in the following section on the Fate of Quartal and Quintal Patterns.

A more primitive parallel, although in descending order, is the following song of the Buriat Mongols,[27] built on the quadruple third *e' c' a f d*. In one of its recorded variants it finishes correctly on *d;* in another one, the singer passes over the *d* and ends on *c*, which is the lower octave of the starting note:

Ex. 47

In a similar way, chains can be arrested in their growth as a step towards tonality. In an old German chorale, *Nun bitten wir den heiligen Geist*,[28] the principal note, starter as well as final, is *g*, and the structural skeleton, the tertial chain *e g b d'*. The melody, however, has a wider range; there are two additional notes, one above and one below. They could have been *c* and *f sharp*, making the whole a quintuple third. Instead, they abandon the tertial concatenation and repeat the highest note *d'* an octave below, and the lowest note *e* an octave above.

[26] Reprinted after Friedrich Gennrich in Heinrich Besseler, *Die Musik des Mittel-alters und der Renaissance*, Potsdam 1931, p. 104, ex. 61.

[27] Ernst Emsheimer, *The music of the Mongols*, part 1 (*Reports from the scientific expedition to the north-western provinces of China*, publ. 21), Stockholm, 1943, no. 1.

[28] From Constantin Brailoiu, *l.c.*, p. 365, after Charles Schneider.

THE FATE OF
QUARTAL AND QUINTAL PATTERNS

Double fourths, usually descending, can be paired in two different ways, either by 'disjunction' or by 'conjunction.' In conjunction, the two fourths share one central note, which thus becomes at once the final of the upper and the starter of the lower fourth. The total range of the double fourth is a seventh or heptad. In disjunction, the two fourths are separated by a wholetone, and the total range is an octave. Graphically:

conjunct: $\overline{d'\ a}$ e disjunct: $\overline{d'\ a}\ \overline{g\ d}$

In view of historical evidence, especially from the Far East, India, and ancient Greece, we can hardly doubt that conjunction marks an earlier phase of development than disjunction. Besides, conjunction shows a more limited planning: the performer considers one tetrachord at a time; and when the urge for enlargement creates another tetrachord, the new one starts where the first has left off, without a dividing space between itself and the older fourth, just as secondal and tertial patterns are conjunct. The two fourths are simply added, not integrated in any higher organization; the seventh is merely the sum of two conjunct tetrachords, not a melodic aim or a function. Except for a few examples from the Orang Kubu in Sumatra,[1] Mongolia,[2] and Finland:

Ex. 48*

* After A. O. Väisänen, *Wogulische und ostjakische Melodien*, Helsinki, 1937, p. 5.
[1] Erich M. von Hornbostel, *Ueber die Musik der Kubu*, in B. Hagen, *Die Orang-Kubu auf Sumatra*, Frankfurt a/M., 1908, Phon. 18.
[2] P. J. van Oost, *La musique chez les Mongols des Urdus*, in *Anthropos*, vol. 10/11 (1915/16), p. 364.

I do not know of any song where the voice leaps to the seventh without touching the conjunction at a fourth from either end of the heptad. Disjunction acts in a very different way. The two tetrachords are placed a wholetone apart (which, seen from a quartal viewpoint, is entirely arbitrary) because this distance integrates the two fourths in a higher organization: the octave.

With all due reserve, I want to draw the reader's attention to a Greek parallel. According to Plutarch, as a literary, and many vase paintings, as a visual testimony, the most archaic lyres of Greece had only three strings – called *netē, mesē, hypatē*, or the high, the middle, the low one – which were equally tuned in two conjunct empty fourths. A little later, but still in pre-classic times, the lyre had four strings tuned in two disjunct empty fourths: *d' a g d* against the previous *d' a e*. We do not know whether or not these fourths were used as bare as they appear or were stopped to provide all the notes of the older, microtone-less enharmonic gender.[3]

Otherwise, such empty heptads, consisting of nothing but the three skeletal notes occur quite often in Asia and in North America:[4]

Ex. 49*

Disjunct empty double-fourths exist in episodes inside Mongolian and Korean songs and also in religious recitatives of Italy.[5]

Mention of North American Indians and, in the footnote, of the Pawnee draws our attention to an odd trait of double-fourths, frequent everywhere, but almost to the exclusion of all other patterns in the *hako* ceremony of the Pawnee:[6] the

---

* Transcr. C. S.

[3] Sachs, *The Rise of Music, l.c.*, pp. 209 ff.

[4] Examples:

Asia: Tibet, Mongolia, Turkmen, Ostyak.

America: Iroquois, Hopi (B. I. Gilman, *Hopi songs*, in *Journal of American Archaeology and Ethnology*, vol. 5, (1908), Pawnee (transcribed by Edwin S. Tracy for Alice C. Fletcher, *The Hako*, Washington, 1904, p. 50).

[5] e. g. Constantin Brailoiu, *Sur une mélodie russe*, in Pierre Souvtchinsky (ed.), *Musique Russe*, vol. 2, Paris, 1953, p. 380, 381.

[6] Fletcher, *l.c., passim*.

voice leaps to the top note from the lower fifth, not, as one should expect, from the lower fourth. Obviously, the fifth is a better, more natural jumping board. This drive might ultimately be responsible for changing the double fourth into a fifth-on-fourth structure, as in the often printed *skolion* among the scanty relics of Greek music (Example 10).

It marks a definite victory of the octave when a heptad, although still unmistakable as such, must tolerate the accretion of an appendix or, with its official name in Greece, a *proslam-banómenos*, a 'to be taken-on one,' to convert the heptad into an octad. Appended above, it created in Greece a hyper-mode (like Hyperdorian, Hyperphrygian, Hyperlydian); added below, it gave rise to a hypo-mode (like Hypodorian, Hypophrygian, Hypolydian).

Good examples of pentatonic hypo-modes from outside Greece are provided by the Buriat Mongols:

Ex. 50*

While these can be regarded as traits of higher civilization, the accretion of an appendix was nevertheless prepared in the primitive world. The following example from the Iroquois Indians is a tumbling strain out of two empty, conjunct fourths with an appended bottom note, from which the melody leaps back to the upper octave: [7]

Ex. 51

A less solidified conversion of the heptad occurs both in primitive and in European music. In a melody of Bongili girls in French Equatorial Africa, the melody descends stepwise in a

* After Ernst Emsheimer, *The music of the Mongols*, part 1, in *Reports from the Scientific Expedition to the Northwestern Provinces of China*, publ. 21, Stockholm, 1943, no. 2.

[7] Cf. Gertrude P. Kurath, *Local diversity in Iroquois music*, in *Bulletin of the Bureau of American Ethnology*, no. 149 (1951), p. 119.

double tetrachord and then hesitates; it gropes its way one second further to reach the lower octave but, unsteadily, seems to probe the two possibilities.[8]

Ex. 52*

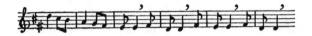

We saw a parallel case in the preceding section. This is an impressive illustration of what must have happened many times before the octave won out.

Quartal chains achieve their most impressive climax in the quadruple fourth of the Sioux,[9] which alternates between disjunction and conjunction and spans two full octaves. An infix subdivides each fourth into a (higher) third and a (lower) wholetone. From the central note, the melody leaps back to the upper octave for a new cascade: this pentatonic quartal chain is in reality a genuine tumbling strain.

Quartal chains in such a state of thorough pentatonic organization lead from the primitive world to higher and highest culture. They occur in a puzzling distribution: in the Indian reservations of North America:

Ex. 53**

as well as in the northern countries of Asia, such as China, Japan and Mongolia, and among the Chuvash, Vogul, and Cheremiss – and again, as was the case before, they belong to Mongoloid races. But for reasons yet unexplained, Scotland and Ireland join the Mongoloids, as does the Solomon island Nisan in Melanesia. This may be a warning to keep away from the slippery dallying with race theories.

Polynesia, Micronesia, Africa, and the European continent are excluded.

* Transcr. C. S.

** Iroquois, Tutelo, after Gertrude P. Kurath.

[8] *EFw* FE 4402 (P 402) II 1.

[9] Frances Densmore, *Teton Sioux music*, in *Bulletin of the Bureau of American Ethnology*, no. 61 (1918), ex. 43.

Heptatonic quartal chains are European – especially Greek, both ancient and modern, and Gregorian, as in the following Gloria ad lib. 1:

Ex. 54*

Altogether, the main territory of quartal structures in the primitive world is Indian North America. They appear seldom in Melanesia or Negro Africa and seem to be entirely absent from Micronesia and Polynesia. In the southern half of Asia, including the Caucasus and white African cities from Morocco to Egypt, the fourth is all-dominating. This statement, however, is true only of art music. The tribal music of Sumatra for example,[10] is entirely secondal and tertial, which seems to confirm that the quartal layer is more recent.

In Europe, parts of the East are quartal, but also Scotland and Ireland. And so is the (original) Gregorian chant. European fourths are single, double, triple, and, when double, either conjunct or disjunct; as a rule, they are not distinctly descending.

CHAINS OF FIFTHS are rare. The reason is evident: when a quintal melody expands, it cannot well afford to bypass the octave in order to pile up another fifth and hence prefers an octave-forming fourth above the initial fifth. In one melody of the Lapps we have seemingly the double fifth – *d–a–e';* but the *d* is only an appoggiatura in front of every single note and acts as a kind of interruped drone. Thus the singer leaps at the end up to the single *e'* in what amounts to a ninth.

The Lapps, indeed, make their voices often leap a sixth, a seventh, a ninth, and even a tenth; and in one of their melodies,[11] the two sections form a double sixth.

There is a definite example ˙from Annam, beginning on *d''*, descending to *g'*, and, via *d''*, ascending to *a''*.[12] This would be an unambiguous double fifth. But the *g'* occurs only one time,

* *Liber Usualis*, Paris/Roma, 1954, p.87.
[10] *EFw* FE 4406 (P 406) I 1–3.
[11] Karl Tirén, *Die lappische Volksmusik*, in *Acta Lapponica*, vol. 3 (1942), no. 246.
[12] *New Oxford history of music*, vol. 1, London, 1957, p. 158, after Gaston Knosp.

and the example, non-phonographic, is open to doubt and mistrust.

Otherwise, the urge to sing an ascending fifth is frequently satisfied by simply skipping one of the thirds in a tertial chain. This happens often in the Gregorian chant, as, for instance, in the initial formula of many melodies in the first mode or in the antiphon 7 for the second Sunday in Advent:

Ex. 55*

The missing third is however restored after some time and leaves no doubt that the pattern is a tertial chain. Similarities occur elsewhere: the map of distribution charts France, including Lorraine, fifteenth century Holland, sixteenth century Flanders, Germany, Italy, Rumania, and Albania; Ashkenazic and Yemenite Jews and Jacobite Syrians; Mongolia; Canadian and Iroquois Indians, and the Batwa pygmies in Congoland:

Ex. 56**

THE FREEDOM OF INDIVIDUALS mentioned in earlier sections and also the ever varying contacts of man cannot have left the melodies as 'pure' as our rough classification makes believe. Interpenetration of human groups, from single families to races, or even daily contact of the two sexes within one village must have led rather early to a duplicity, if not multiplicity, of melodic impulses in the same person, indeed, in the same melody. Often, tunes obeying two different impelling forces give an impression of uncertainty. We discussed such fluctuations in The Fate of Secondal and Tertial Patterns on page 149 when we saw the

* *Liber Usualis*, Paris/Roma, 1954 p.486.
** After Rose Brandel.

hesitant groping now for the seventh now for the octave in what had started as a conventional triple third.

In the semitone-over-third tetrachords described both in the One-Step Melodies and in the current section of the book, mere attentive listening combined with a careful statistic analysis shows vaccillation between the motor impulses of a fourth and a major third, as if the singer were not quite decided as to where to turn; and sometimes the fourth seems to be in competition with a semitonal pattern. Inversely, the interpenetration of two quite different urges is convincing in melodies of the Caribou [13] and the Smith Sound Eskimo:

Ex. 57*

where an (obviously older) one-step pattern g–f and a double third f–a–c are in strong opposition and contention. The Pawnee provide us with another informative example: of eleven measures, eight are taken from the single third a–f, and only three, in the middle, descend to d and c.[14]

The following Rumanian folksong shows clearly that a secondal impulse, yielding the step g–a, combines with a tertial impulse, materializes on g–e, which again leads to the second e–d. The melody is not secondal; nor is it tertial. As so many anthropological phenomena, it is due to two or three independent stimuli:

Ex. 58**

Some melodies from New Ireland, Melanesia, combine an

---

* After Christian Leden, *Ueber die Musik der Smith Sund Eskimos*, in *Meddelelser om Grønland*, vol. 152 (1952), ex. 19.

** *Boceta*, after Riegler-Dinu.

[13] From Zygmunt Estreicher, *La musique des Esquimaux-Caribous*, in *Bulletin de la Société Neuchâteloise de Géographie*, vol. 54 (1948), p. 5.

[14] Transcribed by Edwin S. Tracy in Alice C. Fletcher, *The Hako: a Pawnee ceremony*, Washington, 1904, p. 107.

(upper) second with a (lower) fourth,[15] and some from the Lapps, an (upper) second with a (lower) fifth:

Ex. 59*

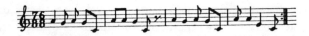

Add similar coalescences among the Celtic settlers of Cape Breton Island, Nova Scotia,[16] and the following gambling song of the Klallam (Yuki Indians, California) [17] which starts as a distinctly tertial pattern but changes in the third measure to an equally unmistakable tetrachord with the note *a* as the common pivot:

Ex. 60

The available mass of further examples defies enumeration. Hybrid from the static viewpoint of the classifier, these coalescences are important steps from pristine narrowness to a freer and richer expanse.

The most momentous form of coalescence, indeed of modulation, occurs in the province of quartal patterns. The term modulation, it is true, is taken from western harmony. It denotes a change of key due to the ambiguity of some chord: belonging to two or more tonalities (as most of our chords), it allows to continue in the old tonality as well as to glide into a new one. There is however no reason why we should not use the convenient word in a merely melodic context when a pattern unexpectedly changes to another one with the help of a common note in which the singer, though often unconsciously, gives a new interpretation within the melodic organization.

We saw that double fourths are sung both in conjunction and in disjunction and that the former one of these structures

* After Walter Wiora, *Europäischer Volksgesang*, Heemstede, 1952, p. 11.
[15] Herbert Hübner, *Die Musik im Bismarck-Archipel*, Berlin, 1938, p. 11.
[16] *EFw* FE 4450 (P 450) I 3.
[17] Frances Densmore in *Zeitschrift für Vergleichende Musikwissenschaft*, vol. 1 (1933), p. 31*.

represents most probably the older stage. Modulation appears quite often as a shift from conjunction to disjunction and vice versa. In this form it is well known in the Far East [18] and among the relics of ancient Greece, such as the so-called Cairo Fragment and the First of the Delphic Hymns.[19] But it also exists on a primitive level in songs of North American Indians (example 53).[20]

Altogether, we might venture this supposition: at times when disjunction was still less strongly settled than the older conjunction, the singer slipped at the turning point and relapsed into the original habit of conjunction. Of the initial derailment and uncertainty, later ages would have made a virtue in the interest of greater abundance.

THESE OPPOSITE URGES are part of the delicate problem of culture change. While the first half-century of Comparative Musicology was predominantly, indeed exclusively interested in the static aspects of traditional standstill, a younger generation of scholars investigate how this tradition is being challenged under the impact of a growing interpenetration of countries and cultures and the irresistible destruction of tribal life. The pioneers were basically concerned with the then present form of music and resented bitterly (and often rightfully) the anti-traditional transformations and distortions that music like all other forms of civilization of necessity underwent in the one-world trends of the day. All tradition – in today's conception – derives from a long process of influences and changes, both from within and from without. This process is as old as culture itself; and nowhere has it come to an end. Thus, the day we meet a tribe cannot be taken as a key-date; nor must we ignore the inevitable metamorphoses occurring under our very eyes.

This neo-historic concept is particularly strong in the United States; for here the clash of western and non-western music has been more vital and fateful than anywhere else.[21]

---

[18] Sachs, l.c., pp. 133 ff.   [19] ibid. pp. 244, 245.   [20] Kurath, l.c., p. 156.

[21] A bibl. excerpt: B. Malinowski, in L. Thompson, Fidjian frontier, S. Francisco 1940, pp. xvii ff.–id., The dynamics of culture change, New Haven, 1945. – A. L. Kroeber, Configurations of culture growth, Berkeley, 1944. – C. Sachs, The common-wealth of art, New York, 1946. – E. G. Burrows, Native music of the Tuamotus, l.c. pp. 97 ff. – W. Rhodes, Acculturation in N. American Indian music, in: S. Tax, Acculturation in the Americas, Chicago, 1952, 127–132. – A. P. Merriam, The use of music in the study of a problem of acculturation, in Am. Anthropologist, 57 (1955), 28–34. – A. Marinus, Tradition, evolution, adaptation, in Journ. of the Intern. Folk Music Council, IX (1957), 15 ff.

SIX

CENTRIC MELODIES

All the melodies we met so far, and indeed the overwhelming majority of melodic patterns, are steps or derive from steps. Only in the section on One-Step Melodies did we describe a recitativic variety of melodies based on a single, often repeated note. On a somewhat higher level, steps are by no means absent, but the melody, freely moving upward and downward, returns again and again to the same note in the middle, which is often starter and final as well as an ever recurring nucleus in the course of the tune. Let us call such melodies 'centric.'

I have no claim to lying bare this type of melody: Robert Lach defined it as early as 1913 [1] and called it 'perihelial.' I rather avoid this name. In the first place, it is incomprehensible unless the reader knows Greek; in the second place, it seems out of proportion to compare an often tiny strip of melody with the solar system; and lastly, the astronomer, in Webster's words, calls *perihelion* (the noun) "that part of the orbit of a planet or comet which is nearest to the sun"; and this is not at all what we want to express.

Historically, the centric melodies seem to be partly responsible for the later concepts of *finalis* and *confinalis* in modal systems and of tonic and dominant in harmonic music. These, too, have a steady 'function' in their melody, without being parts of some pattern of steps.

A plain example from the Lapps will easily show to what kind of melody we give the epithet centric:

Ex. 61*

* After Werner Danckert.

[1] Robert Lach, *Natur- und orientalische Kulturvölker* ('Studien zur Entwicklungsgeschichte der ornamentalen Melopoie. Beiträge zur Geschichte der Melodie,' *passim*), Leipzig, 1913.

Of the twenty-four eigth beats, sixteen go to the center *f*, and only four to either the upper note *g♭* and the lower note *e*. The central note assumes two thirds of the entire phrase; and it also serves as the starter and the final. No explanation is needed.

Many parallel examples can be drawn from the liturgy of Babylonian Jews. One, the creed Harken Israel, has been given earlier in this book as Example 24; we might add the beginning of the Song of Songs, as chanted by the same Oriental-Jewish group:

Ex. 62*

The relative chronology of centric patterns is in my opinion given by two facts. First: they cannot have existed in the stratum of one-step tunes, as they need at least one upper and one lower step with the center as the common basis and pivot. Second: we know enough examples of centric melodies with only three notes or two steps to provide a justification for placing the origin of the whole type in the two-step layer.

On hearing a melody of two steps with the middle note accented in weight, position, and frequency, we pause a moment to ponder two possibilities: (1) is it a truly centric melody, or (2) is it a one-step melody plus an affix above or below?

The example from the Lapps is unambiguous: the center has four times more importance than either of the outer notes. But other melodies present a different picture. Two examples come to my mind, one from the very primitive Vedda in inner Ceylon and one from the Mongolian lamas. Again we secure a correct answer by the statistical method: in what number of time units do the notes occur? In the Vedda song:

Ex. 63**

* After Idelsohn.
** After Myers.

the central note, in all its recurrences, extends over 22 units, the upper note over 6, and the lower note over 17. The evaluation cannot be doubtful; numerically, the upper note counts hardly at all, while the lower note moves in number so close to the middle one that the verdict is beyond hesitation: the Vedda melody is a one-step tune with a suprafix. This decision, it seems, is confirmed by the important fact that the lower, not the middle note is allowed to rest on a halfnote and even carries repeated *sforzati*. The Mongolian piece is in a opposite condition: the middle note has 19 units, the upper one 11, and the lower one a mere 3. This, too, is a one-step melody; but from time to time it has an infrafix:

Ex. 64

Only where the middle note is essentially more frequent than either one of the outside notes are we justified in speaking of centric tunes.

The distance from the centre to the outer notes is of no consequence. The Lappish example has a semitone above the central note, and a wholetone below; others, from the South Californian Luiseño Indians:

Ex. 65*

and also from German folksong, have a wholetone above and a minor third below. This quality places the little Russian melody, around which Constantin Brailoiu built his study of scales: [2] the center *g'* qualifies as such with its 9 units against the 4 units of *a'* and the three units of *d'*.

Innumerable centric tunes are double-thirds, concealed from correct diagnosis by the usual misnomers 'triads' and 'fanfares.'

---

* After Helen H. Roberts, *Form in primitive music*, New York, 1933, p. 24.

[2] Constantin Brailoiu, *Sur une mélodie russe*, in Pierre Souvtchinsky (ed.), *Musique Russe* II, Paris, 1953, p. 330 no. 1.

A case of particular interest is the double-fourth, in which the
central note, the 'dynamic *mesé*' of the Greeks, is the hinge and
meeting point of the two tetrachords. Ancient Greece provides
an evidence in the so-called Second Delphic Hymn, where the
center acts at once as the starter and as the final. Related
examples are frequent in the liturgy of the Syrian Jacobites [3]
and also in songs of Rumania and the Ostyak:

Ex. 66*

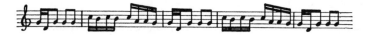

Although the center acts usually both as a starter and as a
final, this is not compulsory. At times, it begins the melody, but
does not conclude it; at times it ends it, but does not start it.
One of our most primitive examples, from Central New Guinea:

Ex. 67

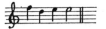

is a tiny motif of only four notes on three pitches; the two outer
notes, at the distance of a minor third, make the beginning with
a single beat each, while the central note is touched twice and
stands for three beats. The example is remarkable because the
central note comes last. But the two outer ones above and below
cannot be thought of without a mental anticipation of the
coming center.

A great many centric melodies can be safely derived from such
one-tone recitations as we met in the First Part of this book.
I think of melodic configurations whose central note is so often
repeated that any initial, intermediary, or final deviations are
almost negligible. Evidence of such centric repetition is nowhere
as strong as in the so-called Gregorian psalm-tones which provide
the models for performing the psalms in the Catholic Church.
The center, termed the *tenor*, *tuba*, or *repercussa*, is repeated as

---

* After Väisänen.

[3] Cf. no. 1 in A. Z. Idelsohn, *Der Kirchengesang der Jakobiten*, in *Archiv für Musikwissenschaft*, vol. 4 (1922), p. 369.

many times as the text requires; an *initium* precedes the *tenor* from below, a *flexa* allows the voice to relax on a lower pitch before the *mediatio* describes a semi-cadential turn around the center. Then, the tenor proceeds with the second line of the text and ends in a *terminatio:*

Ex. 68

These *tenor* melodies of the Catholic Church lead us from the simple two-step forms of centric singing to richer structures. We find them without going back to the Primitives or to archaic liturgies; there are many examples of two notes above and two notes below the center in the treasure house of the nineteenth century. One is the introduction of Schubert's Ninth Symphony, another, the slow movement in the First Symphony of Brahms:

Ex. 69

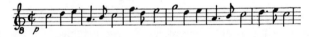

Therewith we have left the realm of simple two-step centricity – one step up, one step down. Practically, the number of circum-centric steps is illimited. A good illustration is the following prayer of the Jacobite Syrians [4] with the range of a minor seventh and the ever recurring center *C sharp:*

Ex. 70

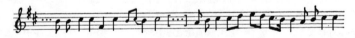

But in making our way through the province of wider centric melodies, we must make sure not to call a melody centric unless its focus is more or less in the middle of its span. It is not centric when in principle it reaches upward except for a leading note below the center.

[4] A. Z. Idelsohn, *l.c.*, p. 372.

The importance of the centric type in instrumental melodies has been mentioned at the end of our section on instruments.

The terminology of ancient musical instruments and their tunings and scalar systems seems to corroborate the vital impact of a tonal center. The Greeks expressed their musical system and the instrument on which they studied music by the same word *lyra;* they also called the string and the individual pitch by the same word *chordē;* and they arranged their whole material of pitches around a *mesē* or 'center,' which served as a common name to denote three different concepts: the middle string of the lyre, the center of the musical space (as the 'thetic' *mesē*), and the center of each of the modal octaves (as the 'dynamic' *mesē*). India knows in a similar sense a *madhyamā;* and even the modern West speaks popularly of 'middle *C*,' taken from the piano keyboard, as a more descriptive name for what otherwise and more professionally is called the one-lined *c'*. Frequently we find in early instrumental music a centripetal quality resulting from this middle position: a higher and a lower note, or several of them, play around a central note as butterflies play around an attractive flower. This even occurs where the player needs not lean over to hit the more distant slabs of a xylophone or metallophone; wind and stringed instruments are often fingered in a constant return to some immutable center.

Centering melodies reach a climax in the neckbreaking coloraturas in which oriental and Mediterranean pipers or fiddlers dissolve their tunes past recognition – provided that there is a melodic idea behind the foamy cascades. This dizzying, acrobatic style includes Pakistan and India and, no doubt, also ancient Greece, where one poet accused an *aulos* or oboe player for being 'loquacious.'

OUR CLASSIFICATION of melody patterns comes at this point to an end. An intricate system with all possible ramifications of melodic forms can be found in one of Kolinski's recent papers.[5] With all due respect for such courageous endeavors, I believe that detailed classifications are desirable and necessary in the

---

[5] Mieczyslaw Kolinski, *The structure of melodic movement, a new method of analysis,* in *Miscelánea de Estudios dedicados al Dr. Fernando Ortiz,* La Habana, 1956, pp. 881–918.

realms of nature objects and of human artifacts but impractical and useless in the immaterial world of human expression. Indeed, even if it were fruitful to catch static forms in a coherent system, dynamic, kinetic types elude classification beyond a mere minimum. Open to permanent change, growth, and mutation, they are doomed to lose their live individualities when dissected and labeled with a deadly terminology.

SEVEN

POLYPHONY

The word polyphony marks the performance and perception of more than one note at a time. Western terminology distinguishes two basic concepts of polyphony. One is 'harmony' or 'vertical' polyphony: we hear simuletaneous sounds or 'chords' in a lawful sequence of tension ('dissonance') and relaxation ('consonance'). The other concept is 'counterpoint' or 'horizontal' polyphony: we hear a lawful coëxistence of voice parts or simultaneous melodic lines. Actually the two concepts overlap: counterpoint obeys the laws of harmony, and good part-writing in harmony requires contrapuntal skill.

Both concepts have long been claimed for the medieval and later West exclusively and thought to be beyond the minds and means of Antiquity, the Orient, and the Primitive world. In a narrower sense this is true. When we speak of part-writing, we imply the salient point: most of our harmony and counterpoint depend indeed on notation and careful elaboration. They are, not exactly what the eighteenth century called 'learned,' but at least 'literate' music and therefore out of reach of non-western civilization.

In a wider sense, rudimentary polyphony as an improvised spice of simple monody is almost all-present. Way back to the Eskimo, there is hardly a single civilization without at least the rudiments of some sort of mingling notes and parts. Indeed, three large sections of the world,

(1) the Malayo-Polynesian area, including Melanesia, New Guinea, Indochina, and the ancient Far East,

(2) the Caucasian area with radiation to the northwest and the west,

(3) Central and South Africa,

have created polyphonies on a level to be compared with the part-writing of medieval Europe.

A study of these coincident sounds yields baffling results.[1]
Against our inherited misconceptions, today's monophony is
here and there in the oriental and primitive worlds an end
stage of what once was polyphonic. The Far East with its early
surrender of the polyphonic so-called Right Music [2] gives
examples as good as do the destinies of early Gregorian chant
and the transition from multipart to solo madrigals at the end
of the sixteenth century. And twice during the seventeenth and
eighteenth centuries European musicians abandoned a polyphonic *stile antico* for a monodic *stile moderno*.

Our documentation is far from exhaustive; strange things
have happened in reporting musical facts. To refer to a single
example: the northwestern Nootka Indians, so Morris Swadesh
relates, sing a sustained drone and two moving parts, which an
octave duplication by women might bring altogether six parts.[3]
But in the same book, Helen Roberts confesses that Edward
Sapir's phonographic recordings "do not offer conclusive
evidence as to what actually happens, since they were generally
given by only one informant singing into the recorder (!)." [4]

It is not possible to squeeze the many different forms of
simultaneous otherness into a neat historical sequence. Reaching
down into the primitive world of prehistory and up into the
western world of today, they overlap, grow complex, and again
yield to simplicity, so much so that any attempt at chronology
is doomed from the very beginning.

[1] Erich M. von Hornbostel, *Ueber Mehrstimmigkeit in der aussereuropäischen
Musik*, in *Kongressbericht der Internationalen Musikgesellschaft*, Wien, 1910.
   Marius Schneider, *Geschichte der Mehrstimmigkeit* I, Berlin, 1934. - *id.*,
Die musikalischen Beziehungen zwischen Urkulturen, Altpflanzern und Hirtenvölkern,
in *Zeitschrift für Ethnologie*, vol. 70 (1938), pp. 287 ff. - *id.*, *Kaukasische Parallelen
zur mittelalterlichen Mehrstimmigkeit*, in *Acta Musicologica*, vol. 12 (1940), pp. 52–61.
- id., *Ist die vokale Mehrstimmigkeit eine Schöpfung der Altrassen*, *ibid.* vol. 23
(1951), pp. 40 ff.
   Z. Estreicher, *La polyphonie chez les Esquimaux*, in *Journal de la Société des Ameri-
canistes*, N.S., vol. 37 (1948), p. 259.
   M. Antonowytsch, *Die Mehrstimmigkeit in den ukrainischen Volksliedern*, in
Kongressbericht der Internationalen Gesellschaft für Musikwissenschaft, Utrecht,
1952, pp. 55–64.
   EFw P 504 I 3.
   For a practically exhaustive bibliography see: Jaap Kunst, *Ethnomusicology*,
The Hague, 1959, p. 241 s.v. *multi part music*.
[2] Curt Sachs, *The rise of music in the ancient world*, New York, 1943, p. 46.
[3] Helen H. Roberts and Morris Swadesh, *Songs of the Nootka Indians of Western
Vancouver Island*, in *Transactions of the American Philosophical Society*, N.S. vol.
45, part 3 (1955), p. 324.
[4] *ibid.*, p. 222.

At random, we start from a type reminding, superficially, of western harmony and especially of the medieval *conductus:* Polynesian chords. The word chords is handy if inadequate, as nothing indicates a harmonic feeling in our sense, with the tension and relaxation of dissonance and consonance from chord to chord. On the western Polynesian islands, each note of a melody is often accompanied by a coincident bass note. The two, beating strictly together, are 'isochronous.' There are usually only two parts – melody and bass. When there happen to be three, the third part duplicates one of the two in the octave.[5]

Wherever, in or outside Polynesia, the two parts keep the same distance throughout, we speak of parallel singing – whether it is intentional or else unintentional and hence not meant to be polyphonic.

A PARALLEL, as this section defines it, is the simultaneous singing of a melody on two or three noticeable different pitches. The voice parts proceed at a certain interval and keep it mostly unchanged throughout a piece or only for a shorter stretch.

In the simplest case, the interval amounts to an octave and results in the East as in the West from the natural distances of men's, women's, and children's voices. Fifth and fourth parallels are almost as frequent as octaves. The West knows them from the older form of the *organum* in medieval holy day liturgies of the Roman Church. But we also hear them in folk-singing instead of the unison that the singers intend and believe to render.

Examples from extra-European fifth and fourth parallels are too numerous to encourage cataloguing. As two hardly known evidences I would like to mention the solemn fourths in the chant of Japanese Buddha priests:

Ex. 71*

* *EFw* FE 4449 (P 449) (Transcr. C. S.).

[5] E. G. Burrows, *Songs of Uvea and Futuna,* in *Bernice P. Bishop Museum Bulletin* 183, Honolulu, 1945.

and those of the archaic Takasago in the inner, 'inaccessible'
mountains of Formosa. The most ancient among the Takasago
clans, according to a Japanese source, sing "in chorus, using the
most beautiful chords." [6] When I mentioned this mystic polyphony to Jaap Kunst, he produced on the spot a dubbed recording of this enigmatic music which he happened to have in
his luggage.[7] It was a rare treat to listen to the "most beautiful
chords" sung by a men's chorus in an organ-like hum without
text. Actually, they were long drawn-out notes in a slowly
rising chain from an awe-inspiring low $D\flat$ to d, at first in micro-
tones and later in widening steps, with the accompaniment of a
second voice part, climbing, too, but lagging behind and almost
independent, so that the listener percieves ever different intervals,
of a second and a third, a fourth, a fifth, and a sixth, now in
painful friction, now in blissful consonance. One can hardly
imagine a truer musical rendition of the seeds which germinate
in the dark of the soil, laboriously grope to the light, and then,
in the open, are free to thrive. For this is exactly what the eerie
chorus means: a charm to help the growth of the millet.

We know or can infer that fifth and fourth parallels are
sometimes retrogressive traces of richer choral forms. The
Chinese mouth organ, today reduced to simple parallels, once
played pentatonic chords or clusters [8] as it still does in the
venerable *gagaku* music of the Japanese court; and the *organum*
of the medieval Church, far from being an awkward beginning,
is likely to be an offshoot of ancient chordal practice, possibly
passed on by the *paraphonistae* or 'fifth-singers' of the papal
schola cantorum in Rome.[9]

Third parallels, known in the history of European music from
the medieval *gymel* = *cantus gemellus* or 'twin song' of England,
are in folksongs actually used all over Europe.

Small wonder that European explorers, finding all the way
through Bantu Africa the same kind of parallel thirds, partly

[6] Takatomo Kurosawa, *The musical bow of the Bunun tribe in Formosa*, in *Toyô
ongaku kenkyû*, Dec. 1952, p. 2.

[7] Afterwards published by Constantin Brailoiu in the *World collection of recorded
folk music*, vol. V rec. no. 1.

[8] Curt Sachs, *The rise of music, l.c.*, p. 146.

[9] Otto Kinkeldey, in a paper read before the Annual Meeting of the American
Musicological Society at Princeton, December 1955, tried to identify them as drone-
singers.

major partly minor, thought of European influence via the Mediterranian or colonial settlements. It was perplexing to find harmony where harmony had no rightful place. Unfortunately, we are always prone to give chronological and causal priority to things learned first. We wronged the Bantu, however. There is not the slightest doubt that the third parallels are just as African as they are European. Negro melody, as we saw, is greatly built on tertial structures, and some of their pre-European instruments, such as the Madagascan tube-zither of bamboo, are tuned in consecutive thirds.[10]

An even more conclusive argument is the fact that parallel thirds occur on essentially lower, pre-Bantu levels. We meet them for instance on the western Caroline Islands in Micronesia as a frequent feature of a very archaic musical style. [11]

Ex. 72

The Carolinian melody consists sometimes of only three notes a second apart from each other – music could hardly be more primitive. And despite such primitivity, the accompaniment seems to form alternately major and minor thirds like ours. It is true that in the case of consecutive thirds, we must question the printed transcriptions, no matter how excellent otherwise. For our ears are never more biased than where they are conditioned by western similarities.

Even if we hear them correctly, neither the Caroline nor the Bantu parallels are exactly harmony in the sense of western 'functional' chord writing. But there is little doubt that this go-together represents the seed of what in Europe grew to chordal concepts.

Concluding our survey, we meet with a startling kind of parallel, almost unbearable to our ear, in a wide stretch from Micronesia to South Africa and the southeastern quarter of Europe: in the Pacific, we record, from east to west, the western

---

[10] Curt Sachs, *Les instruments de musique de Madagascar*, in *Université de Paris, Travaux et Mémoires de l'Institut d'Ethnologie* 28, Paris, 1938, p. 53. – Cf. *EFw* FE 4451 (P 451) II 1, FE 4504 (P 504) I 1.

[11] George Herzog, *Die Musik der Karolinen-Inseln*, Hamburg, 1936, *passim*.

islands of Polynesia,[12] the Melanesian Admiralty Archipelago,
and the Micronesian West Carolines:

Ex. 73

in Indonesia, the Moluccas and Flores; [13] in Africa, the Babira
(Bantu), the Mambuti (pygmies), and the Zulu (Bantu again) in
the South. There in a constant grating friction, the one or two
steps of the melody are accompanied at the minimal distance
of an often nondescript second. Strangely enough, the second
parallels recur in Russia, in Istria at the northern tip of the
Adriatic Sea,[14] and in Bosnia.[15] They do however *not* occur in
modern Lombardy, as has been asserted, although, according
to Franchinus Gaffori, a contemporary, they were used in the
fifteenth century for mourning services at the Cathedral of
Milan.[16] The closest kinship between European and non-European folkmusic is once more apparent.

How innate and unconscious these seconds are, though incomprehensible to the western ear, can be gathered from the
already quoted letter that Dr. Walter Lurje kindly wrote to me
in 1949 from Puerto Rico. Having been a Chinese army doctor
from 1939 to 1946, he had witnessed time and again how recruits
from primitive tribes in inner China, a few hundred at a time,
were every morning on raising the flag compelled to sing the
(westernized) national anthem. "At first it was impossible to
find a trace of the melody in their singing or, better, howling.
But after a week or so, the howling had abated, and the men

[12] E. G. Burrows, *Songs of Uvea and Futuna*, in *Bernice P. Bishop Museum
Bulletin* 183, Honolulu, 1945.

[13] Jaap Kunst, *Music in Flores*, Leyden, 1942, p. 8.

[14] Ludwig Kuba, *Einiges über das istro-dalmatinische Lied*, in *Bericht d. III.
Kongress der Internationalen Musikgesellschaft*, 1909, pp. 271–276.

[15] *EFw* FE 4434 (P 434) II 5.

[16] Ernest T. Ferand, *The "howling in seconds" of the Lombards*, in *The Musical
Quarterly*, vol. 25 (1939), pp. 313–324. – Cf. also: Gustave Reese, *Music in the Renaissance*, New York, 1954, p. 179.

sang in parallel seconds. After a few more days, occasional fifths appeared, and about a week later they sang in perfect fifths throughout. After a while, some octaves cropped up, and ultimately they sang in octaves throughout. I never heard thirds, fourths, or sixths. This happened again whenever a new batch of rookies came, and always in the same sequence." [17]

Whether or not this interesting development is compulsory and universal cannot be stated without similar reports from other countries.

A warning is in place not to hold 'harmonic' thirds against 'non-harmonic' seconds. In primitive music, we must not speak of harmonic relations in our sense; besides, the two intervals are not as strictly segregated as on our pianos and often run into one another.

The case of second parallels must be dismissed from the realm of vertical hearing and dissonance. Otherwise we could not find in a country as musical as Lithuania actual folksong Canons [18] with consistent clashes of semitones and wholetones:

' Ex. 74

Attention, strictly horizontal and focused on the re-entry of the theme in another voice every four measures, completely ignores the constant frictions on our vertically trained ears.

DRONES OR SUSTAINED NOTES, above or below the melody, are sometimes described as pedal notes. But this term, borrowed from European music, must not be used; it is too close to the

[17] Walter Lurje's letter is translated in *Journal of the American Musicological Society*, vol. 3 (1950), pp. 292 ff.

[18] *EFw* FM 4009 (P 1009) I 1, with transcription by Jonas Balys in the accompanying notes on p. 4.

specific practice of holding a foot on one of the pedal keys of an organ and too remote from what it means in the primitive world. Besides, it easily suggests some note far below the melody and becomes incongruous when – as so often happens in primitive and oriental music – this note lies in the range of the melody or even above.

Sustension, highly important in Middle Eastern music and indispensable in India, has a comparatively small impact on primitive singing. When a Kubu woman in Sumatra sustains one shrill high note while a man sings a simple two-step melody, she is unlikely to consider a two-part coöperation.[19] This is more probable in the case of the Lifou women in the Loyalty Islands who throw the same discordant note into each of the endless repetitions of the short melodicle that the chorus incessantly sings.[20] The primitive drone that has impressed me most is held in a song of the Temiar in Malaya: it impersonates a priest whom the mountain spirits warn in his trance to beware of diseases that the white men might bring to his people. The narrow melody, on the step *f–g*, moves above an eerie, intermittent drone on *c*.[21] In another Temiar song, the static one-note drone becomes a quartal-step *ostinato* on *g–d*, while the melody alternates between *a* and *g:*

Ex. 75*

On the level of high civilization, the drone was given a focal, indispensable role in the Indian subcontinent; [22] and from there it reached the folk music of Southeast Europe: with the Turkish conquest of the Balkans, drones affected the Yugoslavs; a long-necked lute of Middle-Eastern provenience, the *tamburica*, often

---

* *EFw* FE 4460 (P 460) I 4 (Transcr. C. S).

[19] Erich M. von Hornbostel, *Die Musik der Kubu*, in B. Hagen, *Die Orang-Kubu auf Sumatra*, Frankfurt am Main, 1908, phonogram no. 25.

[20] Curt Sachs, *The rise of music in the ancient world*, New York, 1943, ex. 27, transcribed by the author from a recording in the *Musée de l'Homme*.

[21] *EFw* FE 4423 (P 423) I 6.

[22] Sachs, *The rise of music in the ancient World*, New York, 1943, p. 181.

accompanies their songs with a high-pitched, ever repeated note,[23] as do the instruments in India.

This is of course not the sustained drone which expands below the melody in an uninterrupted horizontal. In the Polynesian Pacific we even find what I would like to call a synchronous drone following the melody beat on an unchanging pitch [24] (cf. p. 177).

Drones are found everywhere in a westward belt across the Pacific, India, the Caucasus, the Muhammedan countries of the West, and the eastern parts both of Africa and of Europe. Additionally, they occur in Mediterranean Antiquity and wherever bagpipes, hurdy-gurdies, and the Mediterranean fiddle ('lira') are played. In the Orthodox Georgian Church, the drone changes its pitch from stretch to stretch,[25] as does the *vox principalis* of *organa* in the Roman Church of the twelfth century. The distribution of drones seems to coincide with that of quartal patterns.

At times, as we saw, the drone consists in two alternating notes, transforming the simple drone into an *ostinato* ground. A recorded example comes from the Kpelle in Liberia; [26] a three-note ostinato, played by a bard's accompanying fiddle in East Africa, has been published by Erich M. von Hornbostel:

Ex. 76*

The Naga tribes in Assam, Burma, establish their chordal drone as the ostinato repetition of a harmonic cadence formula, known to musicians as

* From *African Negro music*, in Africa, vol. 1 (1928), p. 20.
[23] *EFw* FE 4434 (P 434) II 2.
[24] Cf. E. G. Burrows, *Songs of Uvea and Futuna*, in *Bernice P. Bishop Museum Bulletin* 183, Honolulu, 1945.
[25] *EFw* FE 4504 (P 504) I 3.
[26] *EFw* FE 4465 (P 465) I 5.

while the soloist proceeds unconcernedly. Therewith we are very close to 'alternation.'

ALTERNATION AND CANON. Intermittent sustentions of a note are early steps on the way to the two world-wide devices of alternating performance: antiphony and response or respond (cf. pp. 127 ff.). Antiphony is the alternation of two choruses, with or without overlapping; and response, the alternation of a chorus and a soloist. Either form keeps the performers from exhaustion and the listeners from boredom; they satisfy the aesthetic sense of neat articulation and symmetry and add dramatic spice in connecting performers and audience.

Such alternation, in itself a matter of structure, has developed to polyphony in Asia and in Africa. On a Stone Age level, Jenissei Siberians in their responses of the shaman and his aides, the very primitive pygmies in the jungles of Malaya,[27] Samoans and Australians,[28] and the diminutive tribes in the swamps between the sources of the Nile and the Congo:

Ex. 77*

as well as Bushmen and Dama – they all developed overlapping responses into regular canon singing. After this initial shock, it was a lesser surprise to hear the women of the Nagé tribe in West Flores in Indonesia sing such canons over double drones on tonic and fifth that the men sustain.[29] The primitive canons of the Mafulu in Australian New Guinea [30] seem to be merely what

---

* After M. Kolinski.

[27] M. Kolinski, *Die Musik der Primitivstämme auf Malakka*, in *Anthropos*, vol. 25 (1930), pp. 588 ff.

[28] A. P. Elkin, *Arnhem Land music*, in *Oceania*, vol. 24 (1953), p. 97, reprinted in *Oceania Monograph* No. 9, Sydney, 1957.

[29] The beginning of such a canon, transcribed by Jaap Kunst, is reprinted in Curt Sachs, *The rise of music in the ancient world*, New York, 1943, p. 51. – See, for more Florinese canons with and without drones, Jaap Kunst, *Music in Flores*, Leyden, 1942, pp. 52, 77, 78, 81 and 86.

[30] Robert W. Williamson, *The Mafulu*, London, 1912, p. 217.

the Germans call *Stimmtausch* or alternate presentation of the leading theme and its accompaniment in either voice.

How spontaneous, unpremeditated, and nearly unconscious this kind of polyphony can be, is described in the continuation of Dr. Lurje's letter: "When the stage of the octave was reached (sometimes even before, in the stage of fifths) some soldiers failed to start in time and therewith produced canons in two or more voice parts at the distance of a half, two, or more measures." [31]

It is evident that the strict rules of consonance in western canon writing do not apply to unvoluntary canons. They do not even apply to intentional folk rounds on European soil, mentioned before in this section on describing the Lithuanian rounds. They do not apply, because the listener's attention, focused on succession instead of coincidence, is obviously interested in the regular re-entries of the theme, but not in the vertical *dux-comes* concords which our harmonic training makes so important.

Still, nothing could be a more impressive warning against the prejudice of a 'plausible' evolution from simple to complicated forms. Nothing shows more clearly how much the concepts of simplex and complex are biased and unreliable.

HETEROPHONY, derived from the Greek word *héteros*, different, is a vague and noncommittal expression. It covers, or should cover, all possible types of otherness in voice coöperation, between the opposite extremes of unison and of invertible counterpoint; it should designate the slightest deviation from a tolerably accurate unison as well as a Bachian quadruple fugue – they all are 'other-sounding.' From the beginning of this century, when Carl Stumpf revived the old Greek term (which the Greeks themselves had never clearly defined),[32] the word served basically to denote the simultaneous appearance of a theme in two or more voice parts with a freedom that the nature of the competing voices or instruments and the players' fancy might prompt. Taken in this sense, the customary octave parallelism

---

[31] Lurje, *l.c.*

[32] Carl Stumpf, *Geschichte des Konsonanzbegriffes* (1897), in *Abhandlungen der Kgl. Bayerischen Akademie der Wissenschaften, philosophisch-philologische Klasse*, vol. 21 (1901), p. 1. – Guido Adler, *Ueber Heterophonie*, in *Jahrbuch der Musikbibliothek Peters*, vol. 15 (1909), pp. 17 ff.

of 'celli and doublebasses in a modern score would be heterophonic when the heavier basses simplify some rapid passages
for reasons of technique.

This definition is however both too wide and too narrow.
The divergence of voice parts can obviously be either unconscious
or conscious, according to whether the performers are not aware
of creating heterophony, and conscious, when heterophony is
an intentional enrichment.

Unconscious heterophony is, psychologically speaking, a non-
polyphonic type of music. The performers as well as the listeners
accept it as homophonic; they ignore occurring consonances
and dissonances and even tolerate, as unimportant, careless
entries, retarded conclusions, and the haphazard lengthening
or shortening of notes. Any congregational participation in
modern church music provides examples, even when the organ
and a professional choir support the singers. Such anarchic
singing would be unbearable if intention and attention were
focused on satisfactory sense perception, meaning, on art.
Instead, we behold the performance as an idea, in the philosophical sense of the word – an idea in which perceptive elements
like rhythmic precision and pure intonation are repressed. Apt
to detract from the sacred words and the mood of devotion,
they seem irrelevant or even undesirable.

We might compare such unconscious heterophony with the
natural, leisurely walk of a group of people who move in the
same direction without keeping unchangeable abreast or caring
for equal steps. These they leave to the unnatural, rigorous
unison of marching paraders.

Where a single voice or instrument is being accompanied,
heterophony begins to be conscious. Good examples are found
in Europe, Asia, and Africa, where the old-time bards still chant
their ancient epical poetry and relate the immortal deeds of
national heros. Here as elsewhere the same melodic idea is all-
present in either element of the performance, the singer's voice
and the supporting fiddle or whatever stringed instrument is
used. But there is never a rigid unison. So much are the two
parts distinct individuals – even when the singer is his own
accompanyist – that strict coincidence would seem artificial,
empty, and dead. Free walking side by side is essentially more

natural than drill parading in a stiff-legged left-right left-right. The accompaniment is not only free to proceed or to rest. As a rule, the singing voice delivers its melody in a simple, almost sober form, while the accompanying instrument presents the same melody profusely embroidered and dissolved in florid coloraturas. This kind of heterophony is best characterized as 'simultaneous' or 'coincident variation.' It is irrelevant whether or not coincident variation leads to dissonances and grating frictions; vertical hearing must be discounted almost completely.

A normalization of such heterophonies – again in a purely horizontal sense – can be observed in Japan, where the accompanying instrument follows the singer in free variation at the respectful distance of an eightnote without disturbing or confusing the listener with its random con- and dissonances.

Curiously enough, Richard Wagner has paralleled this Japanese mannerism in the score of *Lohengrin* (Elsa in act I scene 3: "Mein Schirm") by forcing the soprano voice to follow the clarinet at the distance of an eight [33] – a passage that our performers in their vertical training rarely bring out satisfactorily.

If heterophony is the simultaneous variation of one theme in two or more parts, practically all non-European ensembles, including orchestras, are heterophonic. Certainly they are heterophonic not always in the purest sense. *Gagaku*, the classic Japanese court music, of which finally an excellent edition in full score has been published,[34] assigns to flutes and oboes heterophonic parts, and sometimes the lutes and kotos join them. But the gongs and drums seem independent, and the mouth organs, forming clusters in the highest range and perpetually driving the pitch upward, determine the general impression almost more than the heterophonic lines.

The most widely known Far Eastern type of orchestra is the gamelan of Indonesia, in which the essential, kernel-forming instruments, gong chimes and metallophones, are often built in three sizes each, an octave apart from one another, to play the same melodic idea at the same time in a fast, a moderate,

---

[33] Musical examples in Curt Sachs, *Rhythm and tempo*, New York, 1953, pp. 66, 67.

[34] *Score of Gagaku*, transcribed by Sukehiro Shiba, vol. 1 (Tokyo, 1956). Reviewed by Rose Brandel in *Journal of the American Musicological Society*, vol. 10 (1957), pp. 39-44.

and a slower realization, if not in what our western counter-point calls diminution and augmentation.

Rigid diminution and augmentation, on the other hand, occur as dialogues of two hand-beaten drums in the refined chamber music of India: among the many sophisticated types of duos, one consists in the simultaneous playing of some metrical pattern or *tāla* and, on the other drum, its augmentation in the ratio 2 : 1.[35]

Not everywhere does heterophony attain to devices so artful or even at symphonies as rich and colorful as we admire them in Java and Bali. Still – much as heterophony is neither harmonic nor quite polyphonic and seemingly anarchic – the wilful maladjustment of similar melodic lines has often a particular charm in its blissful impression of personal freedom against mechanistic bondage.

Vocal polyphony of an almost harmonic type occurs in the music of wandering minstrels in South Rhodesia [36] as well as in Southeast Europe. Croatian mixed choruses proceed in unison, octave, and third parallels, but finish the stanza with a full chord on the subtonium and resolve it into an empty octave.[37] Indeed, we find similar peasants' choruses in many parts of the Austrian Alps,[38] Slovakia,[39] the Caucasus, the Ukraine and Russia.

An analysis of these strange and enchanting improvisations yields, for all their differences, a few recurring traits. All principal cadences end in unison or in an octave, the latter rarely with an added fifth; and a leading note in the preceding chord remains unsharped. The number of participating voices goes seemingly up to five; but only two or three are actual parts, with *Stimm-tausch,* or alternation of singers, in one or two of them. At least one part is a drone, which however shifts by a tone upwards or downwards after an undefined number of measures. This shift is obviously connected with the changing parallels that the upper voices form – now fifths now fourths. Third parallels, too, can

[35] Curt Sachs, *The rise of music in the ancient world*, New York, 1943, p. 190.

[36] A. M. Jones, *African music*, Livingstone, 1949, p. 12, pl. I B.

[37] Cf. *EFw* FE 4434 (P 434) I 1.

[38] Viktor Korda, *Genuine folk polyphony in the Austrian Alps* (summary), in *Journal of the International Folk Music Council*, vol. 9 (1957), pp. 9 ff.

[39] František Poloczek, *Slovakian folk song*, in *Journal of the International Folk Music Council*, vol. 9 (1957), p. 13.

be observed, but they might belong to another stratum.[40] Altogether, every single element in this polyphony is archaic and even primitive; the drones, the thirdless cadences, and the parallel as the essential form of tonal coincidence. These elements are known from the Pacific in the East to the West coast of Africa and, across the Atlantic, in the older American settlements of Negros. Whatever the roots of this polyphony may be, it is quite definitely not a retrocessive adaptation of European polyphony.

We cannot be equally sure in the case of Russian polyphony; the Orient has no prototype for such artful devices as contrary motion (with the voice parts moving in opposite directions). Here, an influence from the (later) polyphonic settings of the Orthodox Church [41] is by no means impossible.

Whatever form it assumes, folksinging in parts must be due to a special gift and trend. The geographic distribution of part singing seems to confirm this conclusion.

Finally, we must turn to the most widely quoted and most controversial evidence in the field that we are discussing: the passage in Plato's *Laws* (7; 812 D–E), which defines the 'heterophony' of Greece as answering short by wider steps, high by lower pitches both in consonance and dissonance, and also as adding various adornments. The passage holds a key position in the weighty question as to whether or not the Greeks knew polyphony. Still, the meaning of Plato's explanation is not at all unambiguous. Unconscious heterophony is not even discussible since Plato describes the elements as an intentional enrichment of the bare melody; neither does he mention any melodic theme that the voice parts have in common. Quite to the contrary the passage does insist on wilful contrast throughout: on steps of different widths, on notes of different pitches, and upon dissonances and consonances, which remind much more of modern contrapuntal devices than of the random coincidences of heterophonic playing.

[40] M. Antonowytsch, *Die Mehrstimmigkeit in den ukrainischen Volksliedern*, in *Kongressbericht der Internationalen Gesellschaft für Musikwissenschaft*, Utrecht 1952 (1953), pp. 55 ff. – *EFw* FE 4505 (P 505) I 3. – E. Lineff, *Velikorusskiia piesni*, S. Petersburg, 1904. – *id.*, *Peasant songs of Great Russia as they are in the folk's harmonization*, II, Moscow, 1911. – Viktor Korda, *l.c.*

[41] About them cf. Gustave Reese, *Music in the Middle Ages*, New York, 1940, pp. 103 ff.

As a matter of course, this does not mean that the Greeks had anything in the way of late-western counterpoint or harmony, with all the rules of part-writing, resolution of dissonances, and interdiction of parallels. But it might be appropriate to quote at least two evidences: Athenaios in the Sophists at Dinner 14: 618 (c. 200 A.D.), who warns a piper to keep the voice parts distinct without *problémata* when playing with "this girl"; and pseudo-Longinus (probably in the first century A.D.), who asserts that the melody is "usually sweetened" by the accompaniment of either a fifth or a fourth. Speaking repeatedly of the pleasant character of consonances – and this in a strict gradation from absolute to lesser perfection – the Greeks as well as the Romans were to a certain degree prepared for vertical hearing. But the current concept of heterophony collapses when and where its freedom and naivety are subjected to the critical control of vertical awareness.

In considering this, we realize that the use of the term heterophony should be more precisely defined than it has been done in the past. Terminology seems to have the choice of quite a number of possibilities: (1) heterophony is in every composition in which 'other notes' are heard at the same time, including a simple drone with a melody, but also including modern polyphony and harmony; (2) all forms of 'otherness' except the lawful polyphony and harmony of the West, but including almost all part-performing of the western Middle Ages; (3) simultaneous variation – a choice that would of necessity assign the more complicated forms of the Orient to polyphony proper.

We look over the numberless evidences extant from Polynesian canons to the ubiquitous drones; from the archaic court music of the Japanese emperor to the 'Andalusian' orchestra of the Moroccan sultan; from the formal, regular part-writing of the Later Ages forward to the contradictory forms of the twentieth century and back to the medieval types in church and folksong. Is it not impractical and against our common sense to cut off the orthodox part-writing of a few centuries in the official music of Europe from all the part singing and part playing in the overwhelming majority of countries and ages – unless we put emphasis on the word writing?

This is a highly important, indeed the most important criterion:

only European polyphony of the second millennium A.D., and actually only a certain part of it, has been written down instead of being improvised. If we realize that this polyphony owes its forms and its very existence to notation and elaboration at the desk, we see a fourth choice of terminology: heterophony is every type of part-performance left to tradition and improvisation – *contrapunto alla mente* as against *res facta*.

Possibilities (1) and (2) should be eliminated as unsuitable; (3) is covered by the title 'simultaneous variation,' a term much less ambiguous and therefore a better choice than 'heterophony.' Thus possibility (4) appears to be most commendable from the viewpoints of music history and of easy, unmistakable definition.

In establishing this definition, we must not allow ourselves to be lured into pedantry. Some 'scriptless' heterophonies – Japanese court music for example – were actually, although not flawlessly, notated; and, inversely, Bach was able to improvise fugues. But the beginnings of the Mikado's *gagaku* – a thousand or more years ago – were not contrived with a writing brush in the hand: Japanese notation, as all the musical scripts of the Orient, followed as a mere memorial help whenever a preceding oral tradition was in danger of oblivion; and improvising fugues is an organist's *tour de force*, impossible without a thorough training in written counterpoint. On the other hand we see in Europe notated music appropriating improvised forms: the sixth chords of the so-called English discant and the subsequent *fauxbourdon*, or the popular fifth parallels of the sixteenth century, especially in the Italian *villanella*, not to forget our modern swings and their scores.

Notated or not, such forms are heterophonic as long as they derive from improvisation and preserve its unmistakable spirit.[42]

---

[42] Essential parts of these paragraphs on heterophony are published in German language in *Musik in Geschichte und Gegenwart*, vol. 6 (1956), col. 327–330.

EIGHT

CROSS- OR POLYRHYTHM

Once upon a time I was sitting in the garden. The lilacs and the lilies of the valley united their sweet aromas to a smiling fragrance of spring. A friend came, remarked on the beautiful scent and unconcernedly lit a cigarette. This time, the odors did not merge to form a consonance; here were the flowers, there was the poignant tobacco smoke, foreign to one another and almost hostile. Yet I took them in, each in its own right; I focused my attention now on the blooms, now on the cigarette, without attempting at a fusion and without needing one. It was a pleasant coexistence, not an integration, of different olfactory perceptions.

After a while we left the garden. On our walk we passed in front of two churches, one, its door open, letting us hear the organ and the choir, the other, sending down the solemn clang of its bells. The bells did not agree with the choir and the organ, either in tempo or in harmony or even in pitch. Nevertheless, the coincidence was deeply moving and beautiful. Half consciously we felt that any adjustment in tempo, pitch, and harmony would weaken the three-dimensional power of unresolved discordance.

Some other day, a parade passed through a near-by street. The marchers kept time with the music; but the lookers-on strolled leisurely about, and a few children raced prestissimo to overtake the silent paraders and get at the band. There was a steady, organized tempo on the drive and a wholly unorganized, careless stir on the sidewalks. Yet it was one picture, one gay ado, one colorful, festive impression.

Just as unproblematic, natural, and attractive as the free combinations in the garden, church, and marching episodes can the rhythmical, para-rhythmical merger be in primitive and often in oriental music. Indeed, our generic term music is misleading. For it implies an all-embracing concept of the various elements that reach our ears and therewith a common rule for each of them. Such a concept is often absent in early civilizations; singing might obey one rule, and striking, another law – even when neither activity exists without the other. The simultaneous perceptions and acts of singing, playing, and dancing are often kept apart as being different, unrelated sensations, which do not call for fusion or mutual adaptation. As I earlier wrote: "The bliss that the rhythmic organization of clappers or drums conveys can be felt without in the least encroaching upon the coincident song." [1] The drummer might be slower, or else he might be faster. Frances Densmore, studying the music of Yuman and Yaquí Indians, found that the drummer was in 49 percent of all the songs slower or faster than the singer.[2] Such incongruities occur elsewhere, too; the voice and the drum have each a tempo and a rhythm of their own [3] (which does not exclude an occasional speeding up or a slowing down); or, in other cases, the drummer is strict, and the singer is not. In North Australia, too, the clicking tap-sticks are at times kept at a tempo different from that of the song.[4]

A similar independence can still be found on the level of high civilization. In the classical mask drama of Japan, the *no* play, a strange instrumental group is seated on the stage (like in Stravinsky's *Histoire du Soldat*). It is made up of one transverse flute and two or three drums – one stick-beaten (often absent) and two hand-beaten. "As a rule, the drummers strike an even rhythm though the voice is free. Now and then the flute joins in and soars above the voice; but its melody is neither coördinated nor even correlated to the song: the two parts are not supposed to be heard together, but to coëxist, in a magical, not in an aesthetic, sense." [5]

One might advance that, like any recurring motion of the

---

[1] Curt Sachs, *Rhythm and tempo*, New York, 1953, p. 43.

[2] Frances Densmore, *Yuman and Yaqui music*, in *Bulletin of the Bureau of American Ethnology*, no. 110 (1932).

[3] Zygmunt Estreicher, *La musique des Esquimaux-Caribous*, in *Bulletin de la Société Neuchâteloise de Géographie*, vol. 54 (1948), p. 4. – Cf. *EFw* FE 4444 (P 444) I 1, FE 4445 (P 445) II 7.

[4] A. P. Elkin, *Arnhem Land music, l.c.*, p. 99.

[5] Curt Sachs, *The rise of music in the ancient world*, New York, 1943, p. 137.

body, percussion invites a regular time, but that singing has no such urge: *rhythmus in corporis motu est.*[6] And as rhythm is indeed essential in the body's movement, and not in music, such rhythmic independence can here and there even separate a dance from its accompanying song. Loango Negros, so we are told, keep the two activities at different speeds, and eyewitnesses who saw the traditional *tratta* of Hellenic women on Easter Monday at Megara make a similar statement.[7] The two examples are quoted with due reserve.

ACTUAL POLYRHYTHM is of an entirely different nature. In using this term, I realize its ambiguity. While most competent authors in the field give it to part music in which the parts proceed in different rhythm (just as in polyphony they move in different melody lines), we find it here and there intended to cover successive changes of rhythm in the same melodic line. This is a doubtful terminology. When a composer writes a five-beat melody in equal measures of five beats, his work is mono-rhythmic; when he prefers to notate exactly the same melody in alternating two-beat and three-beat measures, it becomes polyrhythmic. This makes no sense. The reader might feel safer with the unmistakable word cross rhythm for simultaneous differences in several parts.

Cross-rhythm, in contrast with successive differences within one voice part, represents, as happens so often in the visual arts as well, a conscious, purposeful enrichment created by the joint, not segregated, perception of contradictory rhythmical patterns. Within primitive, oriental, and ancient-European civilizations, polyrhythm or cross-rhythm belongs exclusively to instrumental music, even in the highly sophisticated music of Greek Antiquity. Voices act collectively, very probably under the binding force of common texts; they sing in unison or, when the sexes and the ages coöperate, in parallels. Instruments, free from textual ties, preserve a remarkable independence, both against the voices and among themselves. They coördinate disparity and similarity, law and freedom; and in the fusion of contrasting and even disagreeing elements, they make *e pluribus unum.*

[6] Marcus Fabius Quintilianus, *Institutionum oratoriarum libri duodecim,* 9 : 4.
[7] Curt Sachs, *World history of the dance,* New York, 1937, pp. 176, 241.

HEMIOLA, or 'one and a half,' is the simplest form of hetero-rhythm, both as a change from measure to measure and as a cross-rhythm. Well known in western art music too, it derives from the ambiguous character of six time units as 2 × 3 and 3 × 2: the same series of notes might yield now a 6/8 now a 3/4 time. This ambigu¹ty is of course facilitated and normalized in styles where the accents are less pronounced than they are in the modern West. As a cross-rhythm, the hemiola pattern would be:

$$
3/4: x \cdot x \cdot x \cdot x \cdot x \cdot x \cdot x
$$
$$
 | \qquad\quad | \qquad\quad |
$$
$$
6/8: x \cdot \cdot x \cdot \cdot x \cdot \cdot x \cdot \cdot x
$$

If, as before, we accept the dance movements as one of the voice parts and their music as the other part, Yugoslav folk dances give a rich illustration of such crossing. The steps coincide with the time units of the melody but often devolve in periods so different that the accents do not necessarily agree. It is not yet polyrhythmic when 24 steps of dancing match 2 × 12 beats of melody; the latter is merely repeated for the second part of the dance. But cross-rhythm arises when the dance has four triple measures against three quadruple measures of the melody; or, in more interesting cases, 6 × 5 steps of dancing against 5 × 6 beats of melody; or 3 × 4 steps against 2 × 6 beats; or 2 × 12 against 3 × 8. Sometimes the dance and the melody reach a common ending only after many repetitions of either one; the maximum observed so far is a dance of five steps against a melody of sixty-four time units: they meet for the first time after 320 beats.[8]

The paradise of polyrhythmic music is Bantu Africa. "Whatever be the devices used to produce [polyrhythms]," says one of its noted experts, "in African music there is practically always a clash of rhythms: this is a cardinal principle. Even a song which appears to be mono-rhythmic will on investigation turn out to be constructed of two independent but strictly related rhythmic patterns, one inherent in the melody and one belonging to the accompaniment ... but it must always be remembered that the African normally makes no noticeable physical stress on any

[8] Danica S. and Ljubica S. Janković, *Pravilno u nepravilnome*, in *Zvuk*, 1955, pp. 65–79.

note and sings all the notes in a steady outpouring of even tones in a legato style." [9]

Western-trained musicians feel too easily tempted to speak of syncopation in this ravel of accents and voice parts. Syncopes, as we use this term, deviate from the regular beat and therewith heighten its power, as they are exceptions confirming the rule. In African cross rhythms, on drums as well as on xylophones, the allegedly syncopating voice part does not contradict or enhance the regular, normal pattern. Just as it would do in Japanese heterophony, it rather adds to the whole a second main beat of its own, independent from that of the neighboring part. And with the main beat, the whole rhythmical flow is shifted in the narrowest *stretto* – as a rule by half a time unit. There are then actually two (or more) rhythms with equal rights.

To think of an analogy in the visual arts is more than a mere simile: while the Later Ages of Europe, from the Renaissance on, have a strictly unified space illusion within a painting or a relief, with one common vanishing point in perspective, this unification, so self-evident to modern man, is absent from many, indeed, from almost every work of the Orient and Europe's own Middle Ages. Here, the eye must often roam and refocus from episode to episode and from object to object.

Individually, African rhythms are very simple and become confusingly involved only in their concurrence – especially when ternary and binary groupings clash – in such extraordinary ensembles as the seventeen xylophones that the younger Junod describes.[10] And in all this seeming confusion we will not forget how rightly Von Hornbostel once characterized the essential contrast between the rhythmic conception of the Negros and that of the West: "We proceed from hearing, the Negros from motion." [11] Hence, it may happen that, in reversal of our downbeats and upbeats, their stress is a powerful tension, which shows in a sudden lift of the body and the striking arm, while the

[9] A. M. Jones, *African rhythm*, in *Africa*, vol. 24 (1954), pp. 27, 28.

[10] Henri-Philippe Junod, *The mbila*, in *Bantu Studies*, vol. 3 (1927–1929), pp. 275–285.

[11] E. M. von Hornbostel, *African Negro music*, in *Africa*, vol. 1, 1928, p. 26. – John Blacking, *Some notes on a theory of African rhythm advanced by Erich von Hornbostel*, in *African Music*, vol. 1 (1955), no. 2, pp. 12–20.

resulting drop and sound comes only after the 'beat' as a relax-ation. This also occurs in Indian America.[12] We ourselves could often witness such shift when groups of 'Belgian' pavers rammed the stones in a rhythmic sequence.

Incidentally: German versification calls the poetical (down-beat) accent *Hebung* or 'lift'; and in full agreement, although as the result of a Roman mistake and against the original meaning in Greece, the modern accent or downbeat is generally called an *arsis*, which means a lift once more.[13]

This being as it is, our ears do not easily register what Negro motion dictates. Since unraveling such polyrhythms from phonographic recordings is next to impossible. A. M. Jones devised an electrograph in which the fingers of performing drummers and clapperers were connected with pencils marking individually everybody's contribution on a rotating band of paper.[14]

One more attempt of individualization has been made in the phonographic field: on a fine recording for *Ethnic Folkways*, entitled *Drums of the Yoruba of Nigeria*, William Bascom separately recorded the five parts of a drum set.[15] This is an-other possibility of transcribing correctly. But the objection is that the recording fails to indicate whether the five drummers enter on the same beat or, which is more probable, at certain distances.

The western hemisphere has inherited an essential part of this drum polyphony, if only in a limited area. With the Sudanese Yoruba slaves, trios of rhythmically different African drums entered Cuba and are to this day the backbone of indigenous music in that island, often complicated and enriched by the coöperation of a small bell (*cencerro*), a gourd rattle (*maraca*), and a scraped calabash (*guiro*), in six independent parts.[16]

Looking from African drums to those of India, we find in

[12] Carl Stumpf, *Lieder der Bellakula-Indianer*, in *Vierteljahrsschrift für Musik-wissenschaft*, vol. 2 (1886), p. 409, and in *Sammelbände für Vergleichende Musikwissen-schaft*, vol. 1 (1922), p. 92.

[13] Curt Sachs, *Rhythm and tempo*, New York, 1953, pp. 128 ff.

[14] A. M. Jones, *African music*, Livingstone, 1949, pp. 63–77.

[15] *EFw* FE 4441 (P 441) II 2.

[16] *EFw* FE 4403, 4407, 4410, 4435, 4440, 4461, 4500, 4502 (P 403, 407, 410, 435, 440, 461, 500, 502). – Cf. also: Fernando Ortiz, *Los instrumentos de la música afro-cubana*, 5 vols., La Habana, 1952–55.

either country the same importance given to single and to multiple drums and the same fondness of rhythmical patterns and cross rhythms. We also find the characteristic delight in improvised variations.

The most striking Afro-Indian concordance is almost conclusive: Uganda's kings possessed a quasi Indian or Burmese chime of twelve independent drums, tuned in the native scale of five equal steps per octave and spanning altogether two octaves and a ample wholetone.[17]

But there are differences as well. The first is that the Hindu tune their drum-skins carefully in octaves, fifths, or fourths against one another and strike them in different spots in order to distinguish dry and mellow sounds. The Negros, possibly afraid of diverting attention from rhythmic sensation, are often satisfied with a vaguer tuning in high and low and middle pitch (which however admits exceptions, such as Uganda's set of twelve or the unmistakable *G D* of the Yoruba drums in Cuba).[18] The second difference (even though the longs cannot well be sustained on a drum) is India's strict adherence to additive metrical patterns, such as long – short – short (3+2+2) or short – long – short (2+3+2). These are traditional and inviolable, unless the drummer tries to vary the pattern in artful, acrobatic circumscriptions. Contrariwise, Africa has rhythm by stress, and the unstressed beats between the accents are metrically indifferent. Cross rhythms emerge in India by combining one traditional pattern or *tāla* with its own 'augmentation' to double note values or with some other pattern (which might, in an almost African way, cause non-coincident 'bars'). But the first stresses of either one pattern coincide, while the Negros are particularly fond of shifting the entries in one or several parts. In India, the drum pattern follows in principle that of the voice; in Africa, it is completely independent – if it accompanies at all: the Negros have drum ensembles in their own right.

The result of this brief comparison is: the Indian drum is almost melodic and much less 'percussive' than that of Africa. It follows 'additive' meter, while the African drummer rather obeys 'divisive' rhythm by stress.

[17] J. Kyagambiddwa, *African music from the Source of the Nile, l.c.*, pp. 114 ff. – A beautiful recording on English Decca LF 1120 (rec. by Hugh T. Tracey) I 1.

[18] *EFw* FE 4502 (P 502) III 15 and FE 4410 (P 410).

These differences would hardly allow to relate the drums of either region directly, although they leave the door ajar for tracing a common origin somewhere in the middle between their habitats. Pages 77 and 78 of my *History of Musical Instruments* refer to a parallel between the extraordinary shape of an ancient Babylonian foot drum and one of modern East Africa and to the similarity of religious rituals devoted to the sacred drums of either civilization. At the end of that passage, mention is made of archaeological finds in Mesopotamia and ethnological facts in modern Africa. With all due reserve, the possibility of a fork relation radiating from an ancient Babylonian (not Sumerian) center may be suggested.[19]

---

[19] See, in this connection, also Jaap Kunst, *The origin of the kemanak*, in *Bijdragen tot de Taal-, Land- en Volkenkunde*, Deel 116 (1960) p. 263-269.

NINE

PROFESSIONAL MUSIC AND MUSICAL SYSTEMS

The high artistic development of African drum and xylophone music draws our attention to the beginnings of musical professionalism.

The neat separation of amateurs and professionals, a pillar of modern musical life, presents a concept not applicable in truly primitive culture. Here, the professional cannot exist because he depends on specializing forms that his society has not yet acquired. And by the same token his antipode, the dilettante in our sense cannot find a place either. In the village, more or less every member of a tribe participates in performing or even composing songs as an essential function of tribal life. He is not an amateur or self-complacent imitator of professionals, but a full-fledged and exclusive carrier of all the music in his community.

A specialist, although at best a semi-professional, is the song-man of an Australian tribe, who leads the tribal songs and dances, acts as the soloist in response forms, and often is the licensed owner of the tribal repertory. The medicine man in shamanistic societies is, to be sure, a professional – perhaps the first and only professional in his group – and singing and drumming are essential elements of his services. He is a singing professional, but not a professional singer; his magic incantations require no special musical training.

The professionals that we find in more complex, albeit still scriptless societies are the by-product of an economic merger.

In the older of the two basic layers, all mankind lives on nature in a way of simple appropriation: men hunt, and women gather food, collecting the fruit of trees or smaller animals that the beach or the woods provide without resistance. In the later layer, mankind takes care of nature with an intention to improve and increase what it provides; men, as a rule, convert their random hunting into a well planned breeding of herds, and women proceed from haphazard picking to sowing seeds and reaping the crops. Needless to say that breeding does not exclude the older hunt, nor agriculture the pristine food collecting.

There has been a trend to unite the two higher forms of economy by an interpenetration of herdsman tribes and of planters, in which the cattle drivers, alert, predaceous, bellicose, and experienced in fighting both cattle thieves and beasts of prey, contributed defense and security, while the working peasants provided a richer variety of food and sundry handicrafts. This symbiosis led forcibly to the formation of hereditary classes and castes as well as to a strict division of labor. Only in this kind of social atmosphere was an actual profession of musicians possible. But also music itself, its contents and techniques, indeed its very scope did profit from the new form of society. Economical strata created very different forms of religions, of world outlook, of social ideas, indeed of emotions. In short, mentality and, hence, the urge and content of self-expression through art became essentially different from what it had been in a tribal world, and in this difference it grew complex and centrifugal.

THE PROFESSIONALS in these complex societies must be carefully classified; they work in two fields with little common ground.

The first of the two groups connects directly with the preceding section on cross-rhythm. A growing sophistication of instrumental music in Asia and Africa acted of necessity as a dividing factor; persons with a gift for music gave time and energy to study and performance at the cost of other work, and men of lesser talent stepped back. Participants in African cross-rhythms are more often than not at least semi-professionals, unless they enter a king's or chieftain's band and acquire the status of full professionals. Carefully selected from a particular clan [1] for skill and reliability, they are conscientiously trained by reputed masters or by their own fathers, whom they often succeed in their positions.

[1] In Uganda the Hippopotamos Clan (Ralph Linton, *The tree of culture*, New York 1955, pp. 450–451).

African trumpeters are in a similar situation; and, just as their *confrères* in Europe up to the eighteenth century, they were only in special cases allowed to play with other, 'inferior' musicians,[2] – a likeness suggesting common origin in the Middle East.

The xylophones in Africa, too, were entrusted to professionals, since their tremendous requirements of technique exclude amateurish trifling.[3] As the performers toil in two shifts, the music goes on relentlessly till dawn while men and women keep dancing around the triangle that the usual three instruments form in the middle of the village square.[4]

THE SINGERS OR BARDS are connected with such players by the mastery of some artful instrument; otherwise they are completely set apart. Though often applauded for their skill in accompanying themselves on the fiddle, harp, or lyre, they have their center of gravity in being the sounding memories of their peoples and in bringing to life their genealogies, myths, and histories. We are reminded of the divine *aoidós* in Homer, of Demodokos, "the sacred master of celestical song dear to the Muse, who gave his days to flow with mighty blessings, mix'd with mighty woe, with clouds of darkness quench'd his visual ray, but gave him skill to raise the lofty lay." [5]

What we read in the immortal dactyls of ancient Greece applies to almost all of modern Eurasia and to parts of Africa, to the *laoutars* of Rumania and the *regös* of Hungary, to those who recite the Finnish *kalevala* and the *guslari* of Yugoslavia.[6] They all are painstakingly prepared for this art: in ancient Ireland, the bards or reciting poets (who, according to Irish tradition, had come from the Orient in times B.C.) [7] needed at least twelve years of study before becoming full-fledged *ollamhs*.[8]

---

[2] (Margaret Trowell and) K. P. Wachsmann, *Tribal crafts of Uganda*, London, 1953, p. 356.

[3] Evidenced as early as the sixteenth century by Fr. João dos Santos (1586), as quoted in Percival R. Kirby, *The musical instruments of the native races of South Africa*, Johannesburg, 1953, p. 47.

[4] *EFw* FE 4402 (P 402) I 8.

[5] *Odyssey*, book 8, transl. Alexander Pope.

[6] *EFw* FE 4506 (P 506) III 46.

[7] Michael Conran, *The national music of Ireland*, 2nd ed., London, 1850, p. 19.

[8] William H. Grattan Flood, *A history of Irish music*, Dublin, 1905, p. 2.

Thinking of bards evokes the picture of empty, sightless eyes, "quench'd with clouds of darkness." The singer's blindness has often been pointed out but never explained, except by associating blindness, introversion, clairvoyance, wisdom, and age.[9] Sociologically, the bard, as reciter of myth, history, and genealogy, belongs predominantly in herdsmen cultures: "there seems to be some intimate connection between a preponderant cattle economy and epic poetry." [10] Both bards and instrumentalists are respected members of the society, especially where, at least in principle, they work without pay.[11] "The status of a harp-player [bard] in Ganda [Uganda] is very exalted." K. P. Wachsmann tells us that most of them are officials "of the royal household, but chiefs of sufficient wealth and importance may keep a harpist without incurring the King's displeasure. There are very few of these men and the manual skill required in Ganda is considered beyond the reach of the ordinary person." [12] In Central Asia, as well, the singer is "everywhere received with reverence." [13]

It is in this spirit that in ancient Egypt the pharao invited the court musicians to build their tombs in the royal cemetery [14] – even though I suspect that this benevolence was more than probably due to the typically pharaonic desire to have his musicians at hand in the life to come.

Like the instrumentalists, the bards as well are preceded by a semi-professional stratum. Ernst Emsheimer, discussing the nomadic cattle-driver civilizations of Central Asia, tells us of such harp-playing bards, but warns it might not be quite accurate "to refer to them as 'professional singers,' as it is only very rarely that they can earn their living exclusively by singing. They do not form a separate group, but make an appearance only

---

[9] Cf. Hans Hickmann. *Le métier de musicien au temps des Pharaons*, in *Cahiers d'Histoire Egyptienne*, Le Caire, 2/1954, pp. 299 ff.

[10] Ralph Linton, *The tree of culture*, New York, 1955, p. 259.

[11] Cf., e.g., J. H. Nketia, *The role of the drummers in Akan society*, in *African Music*, vol. 1 (1954), pp. 34–43.

[12] K. P. Wachsmann, *Harp songs from Uganda*, in *Journal of the International Folk Music Council*, vol. 8 (1956), p. 24.

[13] E. Emsheimer, *Singing contests in Central Asia*, in *Journal of the International Folk Music Council*, vol. 8 (1956), p. 27.

[14] H. Hickmann, *l.c.*, p. 257.

in connection with certain festivals, after which they resume their usual way of life as pastoral nomads." [15]

THE DEGENERATED FORM OF BARDISM is minstrelsy. There is good reason to suppose that minstrelsy, like many other traits in African culture, has come to the Negros from the Mediterranean coast. Ethiopian minstrels accompany themselves on Arabian fiddles; minstrels of the Cameroons illustrate recitals in a way reminiscent of the Bedouins in Tunesia. Robert Lachmann gives us a detail description how in Tunesia one of them, playing a programmatic piece on the flute, enacted from his squatting position a horse shying from a lion or a girl arranging her hairdo and sash or grinding barley in the circle of her friends.[16]

In the Cameroons, "the travelling minstrel occupies a place of favor ... The old traditions are passing, but the minstrel remains as popular as ever. When he appears in a community, crowds gather to hear him. His traditional garb consists of a bark-fiber breech cloth, a kind of skirt made of monkey tails or strips of antelope skin, and leg rattles ... On his arms are fastened raffia cuffs and more monkey tails. His head-dress is prepared with feathers ... The minstrel is not only a story teller and a musician, he is a carrier of news from distant places ... In all of the minstrel's 'news' and stories, singing plays a major part. ... In the narration of a long tale he may talk for two or three minutes, then break in with the appropriate song, and again revert to the story. Sometimes, when the story calls for dramatic action, the minstrel will give his instrument to an assistant and, while the music continues, act out the drama with gestures and dance steps. He is at his best with a group of supporters to act as his chorus. Sometimes he brings his own with him. Other times he gets impromptu assistance from the villagers whom he is visiting ... men to sing, women to help with hand-clapping, stick clapping and the shaking of rattles." [17]

But welcome and respect are not necessarily one.

Henri Labouret has given us a vivid picture of professional performers in the western French Sudan, of their social position

---

[15] *l.c.*, p. 26.
[16] Robert Lachmann, *Die Weise vom Löwen und der pythische Nomos*, in *Festschrift für Johannes Wolf*, Berlin, 1929, pp. 97–101.
[17] Edwin Cozzens introducing *EFw* FE 4451 (P 451) (in free re-arrangement).

and of their duties. They are not artists but artisans; and as such they are not independent in our sense but caught in the meshes of a rigid system of despised castes. If they hold the rank of real 'musicians' and fiddlers, they belong to the higher crafts, together with weavers, leather workers, smiths, and founders of precious metals, and are allowed to intermarry with them. But the lower class of entertainers form the bottom caste of society and are not permitted to marry outside their class. These *griots*, as the French call them, importune the rich with either glorifications or insults, depending on whether their victims are open-handed or stingy. They often roam from village to village in gangs of about a dozen under a chief who is at the same time a seasoned historian and genealogist and knows to their last details the alliances, hostilities and conflicts that unite or oppose the families and the villages of the country. With this knowledge, they sing long, high-flown praises of the leading persons in the village and often achieve to reconcile, and probably just as often, to spur intertribal strife.[18]

From other sources we learn that the Wolof in the French Sudan, divided into a hierarchy of caste-like classes very much like those in medieval Europe, give their musicians, minstrels, praisers, and jesters the lowest status. They all are stereotyped as lazy beggars and buffoons who lack pride and modesty.[19] Indeed, they are regarded in some ways as untouchables: they are not allowed to eat out of the same dishes with members of other classes and must not be buried in the village graveyard. In earlier times it was not even sufficient contempt to deny them burial in a graveyard: a British source of 1745 reports disgustingly that the corpses of African minstrels, instead of being buried, were placed upright on their feet in hollow tree trunks for slow putrefaction.[20]

Although the latter treatment is unmatched, all these descriptions evoke familiar pictures. In ancient Greece as well,

---

[18] Henri Labouret, *Paysans d'Afrique occidentale*, Paris, 1941, p. 134. – Samples on *EFw* FE 4451 (P 451) I 3, 4, II 1 and FE 4462 (P 462) I 1, 3, 4, 5, II 1, 2, 5. – David Ames, introducing *EFw* FE 4462 (P 462). – Cf. also Jaap Kunst, *Ethnomusicology*, 3rd ed. The Hague, 1959, p. 238 s.v. *griots*.

[19] Ames, *l.c.*

[20] Thomas Astley, *A new general collection of voyages and travels*, London, 1745, vol. 2, pp. 277–9, quoted from Richard Wallaschek, *Primitive music*, London, 1893, p. 66, and *Anfänge der Tonkunst*, Leipzig, 1903, p. 69.

Homer's godly rhapsode yielded in post-Homeric times to a minstrel who more and more "came to be unfavourably regarded." [21] And alongside with the minstrel, instrumental players took the stage. At the Pythian games of 586 B.C., the piper Sakadas played a program piece on the famous fight of Apollo and the dragon – in its content and structure not unlike the tune of the lion mentioned on page 204.

Rhapsodes as well as pipers and lyrists degenerated to boastful, inflated virtuosos, applauded by ten thousands with thunderous cheers and pampered by hysterical ladies. [22]

We can draw a parallel less remote than ancient Greece between the misery of the African minstrel and the *Spielmann* and juggler in Europe, a misery that with excessive contempt, segregation, and outlawry lasted one thousand years. [23]

To be complete beyond the interests of the present book, we should include the professional wailers – mostly women – whom we find from the Middle East along the Mediterranean via Corsica and up to Ireland: "Did ever a wail make man's marrow quiver and fill his nostrils with the breath of the grave, like the *ululu* of the North or the *wirrasthrue* of Munster?" [24] A beautiful sample from Rumania, a *bocet*, has been recorded by Béla Bartók and is accessible in a Folkways record: [25]

Ex. 78*

Nor should we forget that upon entering the house of Jairus, Jesus "saw the minstrels" (St. Matthew 9 : 23) and "them that wailed greatly" (St. Mark 5 : 38).

A MUSICAL VOCABULARY, though modest in size and scope, is the inevitable tool and companion of professional music. Learning

* *EFw* FE 4419 (P419) II 9.
[21] *The Oxford classical dictionary*, Oxford, 1949–53, p. 765.
[22] Curt Sachs, *The rise of music in the ancient world*, New York, 1943, p. 271.
[23] Curt Sachs, *Our musical heritage*, 2nd ed., New York, 1955, pp. 74 ff.
[24] Thomas Davis, after Grattan Flood, *l.c.*, p. 1.
[25] The Greek distinguished between the *epikedeion*, over the dead body and the *thrènos* in memory of the dead. Cf. E. Reiner, *Die rituelle Totenklage der Griechen*, 1938.

and teaching the craft, much as it might be imitation of the teachers and, in return, the master's correction, is unthinkable without at least the rudiments of a terminology as a means of communication. And terminology in itself includes the opposite concepts of distinctiveness and affinity, of seeing differences and similarities; and therewith classification and system are born.

Examples are frequent in Africa. The Baganda in the East, despite their scriptless culture, used a rather involved terminology, and the South African peoples have names for every note. These words are actually names of notes, since they appear in the vocabulary of the xylophone as well as in that of the flute; [26] but there is little doubt that originally, before becoming abstract, they had been the distinctive names of sound-producing agents like the individual slabs of xylophones. This is particularly evident in Madagascar.[27] But then, the ancient Greeks adopted six of their seven note-names from the strings of the lyre, as the high, the next-to-high, the middle, the next-to-middle, the low, the next-to-low; and a seventh note they called *lichanós* or index finger. Indeed, they covered with the same word *chordē* both a string and a note.

Besides the names of notes, some African peoples have distinct scale theories. The instrumental scale of the Gwere in Uganda has four, in principle equal steps in the octave, and that of the Ganda had five intentionally equal steps in the octave,[28] in other words: an Indonesian *saléndro* gender.

A second surprise: the scale can be 'high' and 'low,' [29] an indication which, in connection with the arrangement of the note names in either one, leaves little .doubt that the Lower Scale was 'authentic' and the Higher Scale 'plagal,' one starting, say, from *C*, and the other one from *G*. The coupling of authentic and plagal modes occurs from Indonesia in the east to the Mediterranean in the west, including ancient Greece, the Gregorian chant, and Byzantine cantillation. If such dualism bewilders in the case of isotonic scales, where it is seemingly a case of mere transposition or change of gravitation and not of a

[26] Percival R. Kirby, *l.c.*, *passim*.

[27] Curt Sachs, *Les instruments de musique de Madagascar*, Paris, 1938, p. 63.

[28] K. P. Wachsmann, *l.c.*, pp. 23, 24.

[29] Joseph Kyagambiddwa, *African music from the sources of the Nile*, New York, 1955, pp. 19 ff.

different function as in the case of scales with steps of different sizes, the Uganda pattern is obviously paralleled in certain respects in the likewise Javanese and Balinese *saléndro* scales and their *paṭet*.[30]

As to the terminology of rhythm: in many parts of Africa, rhythmic formulas for drums have individual names, somewhat like the various Indian *tālas*. Similarly, the language of the Nootka in the Northwest (Vancouver Island) has at least twenty verbs expressing the various ways of drumming, such as 'beat-beat-rest,' or 'beat-beat-beat-rest,' or 'with a steady, even beat'; also 'sounding split' for part singing.[31]

Polynesian singers use different terms for each of the two or three voice parts in their polyphony.[32] And special names for the individual instruments of an ensemble are common in Africa.[33]

As a by-way, Bantu Africa has devised pitch syllables to replace the particular text of a piece – a terminology close to both the vocal solmisation of the West and to the distinctive syllables that Arabian drummers give the timbres of their beats: *dum*, muffled, *dim*, less muffled, *tik*, less clear, *tak*, clear.[34] The Lokele, near Stanleyville in the Belgian Congo, when shouting messages across a larger body of water in substitution of a slitdrum, replace the various syllables of the texts by a *ke* or *le* for the lower pitch and a *ki* or *li* for the higher pitch: the words *tokolokolo twatoala*, or 'little sticks of firewood,' are shouted as *Kekelekeke kikelike*. The Duala in the Cameroons substitute *to* for *ke*.[35]

Similarly, the drummers of India have a special syllable for every pitch and timbre of their instrument and learn their craft by memorizing the syllables of the various patterns and to recite

[30] Cf. Mantle Hood, *The nuclear theme as a determinant of paṭet in Javanese music*, Groningen, 1954.

[31] Helen H. Roberts and Morris Swadesh, *Songs of the Nootka Indians of western Vancouver Island*, in *Transactions of the American Philosophical Society*, N.S. vol. 45, part 1 (1955), p. 326.

[32] E. G. Burrows, *Songs of Uvea and Futuna*, in *Bernice P. Bishop Museum Bulletin* 183, Honolulu, 1945, p. 81.

[33] J. F. Carrington, *Individual names given to talking-gongs in the Yalemba area of Belgian Congo*, in *African Music*, vol. 1 no. 3 (1956), pp. 10–17.

[34] Cf. for a Central Javanese parallel: Jaap Kunst, *Music in Java*, The Hague, 1949, vol. 1, pp. 204 ff.

[35] John F. Carrington, *A comparative study of some Central African gong-languages* Ph D. dissertation, University of London, Brussels, 1949, p. 40.

them in a neck-breaking tempo before attacking their drums.[36]

It seems to be a bewildering practice when, evidently to facilitate learning, the apprentice must master two crafts instead of one (for memorizing a series of syllables and reproducing them at highest speed is indeed a craft in its own right). But such methods occur rather often, in the West as much as in the preliterate world. In Uganda, every Lango has a personal whistle motif ... which may be memorized by a few words, a catch or a phrase of a private song.[37] Indeed, did not centuries of European music impose the Guidonian hand on tyros? A similar hand had been used in India for the same purpose of locating the pitches of melodies, and in China, for marking the inflections of speech.

Did they not add to this tactile bridge the vocal bridge of solmisation up to the modern 'tonica do' method in order to read and remember melodies? And do we not ourselves substitute adequate texts for military bugle calls and symphonic themes to assist the memory of soldiers and appreciation adepts? Who, in the U.S.A., does not know the cello theme from the B minor symphony under its verbal counterpart "This is the symphony that Schubert wrote and never finished"?

A text is more readily learned when sung to a melody, and, inversely, a melody can be better fixed in our memories when it follows a text. This daily experience proves the advantage of what I might be allowed to call the concomittant method of learning.

---

[36] I am indebted to Rosette Renshaw of Montreal for providing me with an original tape on which the current patterns of Indian drum rhythms are spoken as well as struck.

[37] Driberg, *The Lango*, London, p. 124.

TEN

'PROGRESS'?

The picture this book has endeavored to draw is strange enough. All over the world, from the Eskimo to the Fuegians, from the Lapps to the Bushmen, people sing and shout and bleat with voices wild or monotonous; they scream and mumble, nasalize and yodel; they squeak and howl; they rattle, clapper, and drum. Their tonal range is limited, their intervals are foreign, their forms short-winded, their inventive capacaties, it seems, rather deficient, their traditional shackles all powerful. Is it permissible to call these noises music, if the word denotes the sacred art of Bach and of Mozart?

And if it is music – how many steps were needed to lead from the humble, anonymous inventor of palaeolithic songs through untold thousands of years to the divinized genius of the Later Ages with his boundless imagination and master technique, how many steps to climb from an ever repeated, unassuming scrap of melody to modern music dramas and symphonies?

Beholding these steps, these numberless changes in style, ideas, craftmanship, and social connotations, the reader must have had the dangerous slogan 'progress' in mind.

But was it actually progress that marked the long peregrination through ages and cultures?

Not long ago, the answer would have been a wholehearted Yes.

"The dominant theory of ethnology at the time Boas entered anthropology was that culture – or society, as it was variously phrased – had evolved, and was evolving from simple to complex forms, from lower to higher modes of life. It was, like all theories, a product of its times. It is commonly assumed to have been an offshoot of the Darwinian hypothesis ..." [1]

[1] Melville J. Herskovits, *Franz Boas*, New York, 1953, p. 51.

We no longer believe in a neat evolution from low to high, a constant development from unassuming simplicity towards an ever growing complication, from infancy through boyhood and maturity to a doting old age – and to what next?

Those were the days when ancient Egyptian art was disdain-fully judged as a not yet matured precursor of Greek and Roman classicism, and Romanesque architecture as a somewhat lowly preparatory step towards the dizzying Gothic cathedrals, which in due time led the way to the noble perfection of Renaissance building.

There occurred a few mishaps, however: evolution from poor to better had a number of disturbing flaws. In the official, classicistic mentality of the nineteenth century, the arts of Greece and the High Renaissance were 'perfect.' The Romans ranked not quite as high; the Middle Ages acquired in Italy the disreputable name of Gothic or barbarian; and the Baroque was repellent to classicistically refined tastes. Neither did Frank Lloyd Wright evolve from Phidias, or Picasso from Zeuxis. There were connections and disconnections, attractions and repulsions; in short, there were fluctuations but no evolution to an ever greater perfection. The evolutionists found themselves on an artificial flight of stairs, on which they climbed up from step to step while the landing of highest perfection should be at the upper end but actually was, according to their own aesthetics, two thousand five hundred years behind and below the step on which they were climbing.

When we exclude the science concept of evolution from the humanities, we do by no means believe in a standstill in the arts. On the contrary, we are aware of unending change. I quote Malinowski: "In the widest sense of the term, culture change is a permanent factor of human civilization; it goes on everywhere and in all times. It may be induced by factors and forces spon-taneously arising within the community, or it may take place through the contact of different cultures." Indeed, all elements of culture, art included, must change, under the impact of tribal interpenetration, of talent, or of the kind of spontaneous variation that biologists call a mutation.

Before examining such alterations, we must realize that they appear in three fundamental forms: culture graft, progress, and simple change.

INORGANIC GRAFT is well documented in the musical culture of the utterly primitive Orang Kubu in Sumatra. Their instruments – carefully manufactured drums and whistle flutes with fingerholes, both of unmistakably Malay provenance – are inorganically pasted upon a merely vocal, pre-instrumental culture. They are like an attic without stories built on a basement. And so is the musical contribution of these instruments: songs of a ripe pentatonic structure and complicated rhythms independent from the tunes they accompany. After removing the Malay veneer, we find, as expected, characteristics of oldest age: a horizontal alternation of two notes a second apart or else a passionate strain tumbling down from a fortissimo peak, at times united in duets of either sex, with the women's strain cascading down and the men's cantillation steadily shuttling between two notes.[2]

THE WORD PROGRESS, all too often indiscriminately used or misused and oftener misunderstood, is semantically so rich that Webster's *New International Dictionary* (2nd edition, 1950) gives it no less than seven definitions. The first three and the last three do not apply to our case. The fourth one does; and it is excellent: progress means "advance to an objective, a going or getting ahead."

The salient point is: progress implies advance to an objective or final aim.

Franz Boas – and many others with him – recognized accordingly "progress in a definite direction in the development of invention and knowledge. If we should value a society entirely on the basis of its technical and scientific achievements it would be easy to establish a line of progress which, although not uniform, leads from simplicity to complexity. Other aspects of cultural life are not with equal ease brought into a progressive sequence." [3]

Of "technical and scientific achievements," closest to our lives and concerns is medicine with its incontestable possibility and record of progress. Its definite objective being the relentless

[2] Erich M. von Hornbostel, *Ueber die Musik der Kubu*, in B. Hagen, *Die Orang-Kubu auf Sumatra*, Frankfurt a/M., 1908, pp. 245–257.

[3] Franz Boas, *Anthropology and modern life*, quoted from Melville J. Herskovits, *Franz Boas*, New York, 1953, p. 99.

fight against sickness and death, every new insight, technique, discovery in diagnosis and treatment is a step towards this goal. To switch to the contrary: hunt and war have the definite objective of killing, and, seen from this viewpoint, atomic bombs and radar-fired guns are doubtless progressive when compared with David's slingshot and the crossbows of Agincourt.

In a book on ethnomusicology, we cannot avoid adding the example of our principal tool: the phonograph. Its objectives are a faithful reproduction of sound, undisturbed by distortions and improper noises; avoidance of interruption in the midst of a piece in both recording and backplaying; mechanical reliability; and as little peril of damage as possible. Unbreakable, long-playing micro-groove disks and magnetic tape-recording represent a remarkable progress when compared with Edison's fragile cylinders and his annoying crank action.

But already in a field like language, not technical and not scientific and yet belonging to usefulness, matters are less obvious. Its objective is indubitable: speech is the exhaustive communication of facts, emotions, and thoughts within a certain group of men. Much actual progress had to be made before the dawn of history, before vowels, consonants, and other sounds formed syllables, words, and sentences. What an advance from the inarticulated grunt in the world of anthropoid primates to the highly developed and differentiated languages even of our most archaic, primitive contemporaries! But once the objective of perfect communication and understanding is reached, the only further objective left is a continuous adaptation to the ever changing needs of those who speak it. In this adjustment there is no trace of the once so cherished trend from simplicity to complexity. Finnish has no less than fifteen cases in its declensions, and archaic languages of the Indo-European family, like Sanskrit, Lithuanian, or Russian, have still eight, with vocative, ablative, locative, and instrumental; English, one of the most recent languages, needs more or less but one.

It is no different with vocables. "Eskimo has twenty or more precise words for conditions of snow; and the Tokelau islanders in northwestern Polynesia have nine names for distinct stages of ripeness in a coconut, their main food." [4] In our languages,

4 William Howells, *Back of history*, Garden City, 1954, p. 68.

family relationship terms, such as cousin or brother-in law, are rather poor and vague when compared with those of primitive societies, where family ties and marriage taboos play a complicated legal and social role unknown in the West: the Baiga in North India have no less than ninety-eight terms of this kind.[5]

Such constant adaptation to specific trends and conditions of culture has little bearing on 'perfection.' The Authorized King James version is neither more nor less perfect than Shakespeare or Shelly. The British language has changed and will continue doing so with English-speaking men, their ways of life, and their scope of thought.

In art, the concept of an objective is even more limited. No absolute goal hovers in some immeasurably distant future and seems to draw nearer with every step we take. If at all we may speak of a goal, it can only mean a sublimation, the purest fulfilment of an urge to express ourselves – an urge that changes its character almost perpetually and differs in every area of culture, not only between the West and the East, but even between Milan and Venice, between the *nord* of France and its *midi*, and between the Germanies to the north and to the south of the Main.

As a consequence, there cannot be a steady, straight evolution from childish beginnings to an ever more perfect art, as evolutionists once dreamed. There is rather a bewildering sequence of sudden changes by leaps and bounds, indeed, a constant reversal to older, new, and foreign ideals. Everyone of these changes leads to perfection in its own right – perfections that we cannot compare because they are based on incomparable changes.

'Functional' architecture in our time is so infinitely simpler than the often overdecorated, redundant palaces of the Baroque or, half a millennium earlier, the Gothic cathedrals whose walls dissolve in a dizzying polyphony of ogives, columns, buttresses, roses, statues, and tracery. But the Renaissance, which bridged the gap between the Gothic age and the Baroque, was in its sober simplicity almost as bald as our modern architecture. Or, to recall something different, yet related: compare the unassuming hairdo of ladies of our day with the incredible complication of the *coiffures* in which Italian society delighted at the end of the

[5] Verrier Elwin, *The Baiga*, London, 1939, pp. 527 ff.

fifteenth century; look at the sudden about-face around 1500 that led to the sleek and sober parting of Mona Lisa's hair; and hold this against the sophisticated hairdress of the following generation. What a curious way of progress!

Music history offers striking parallels with the quite unprogressive alternation of complex and simplex. How sudden was the turn from the almost unbelievable crossrhythms of the French generation around 1400 [6] to the simplicity of the subsequent masters of Burgundy in the age of Binchois and Dufay; or the sober clarity of Peri's and Monteverdi's monodic *recitativo* style about 1600 after the contrapuntal excesses of Italo-Flemish polyphony; or the trickle of the *style galant* after the grandiose flow of Bach's and Handel's fugues.

There is no steady evolution from simplicity to complication; nor is there a reverse development. The sequence of styles seems to be confused, capricious, arbitrary – until we begin to see the iron law behind the happenings. The interested reader may find in my Commonwealth of Art (New York, 1946) a tentative answer. First: subsequent generations set against one another in their tastes; and second: in supragenerational cycles (like the ones that we call Hellenistic, Romanesque, Gothic, Romantic) the beginnings are of necessity simple and strict, and the endings complex, profuse, naturalistic – only to yield in a rapid reversal to new simplicity and strictness at the entry of another cycle. All this is inherent; it cannot be called progress.

The word progress has indeed little meaning in this eternal zigzag. There was change, not progress, from Raphael to Velasquez and Rembrandt, from Bach to Mozart or Beethoven, from the Gothic masters to Lorenzo Bernini and Christopher Wren. And yet they all are woven in the untearable fabric of history, as each of the masters reflects and expresses the endless renewal to which we have given this name.

A rather recent reversal assailing the concept of 'history' altogether and accusing it of misrepresentation [7] is already obsolete: "historical perspective is again coming into the fore-

---

[6] Cf. Willi Apel, *French secular music of the late fourteenth century*, Cambridge (Mass.), 1950.

[7] Cf. e.g. Fritz Bose, *Musikalische Völkerkunde*, Freiburg, 1953 [or do I misread him?].

ground of comparative musicology." [8] Unless one confuses history and evolution, history, the Greater Memory of mankind and our only account of lapsing time and of change, is an eternal function of the mind, whether it appears in nebulous sagas of yore or in the modern search for provable facts and convincing interpretation. Much as we know that there has not been a neat evolution of the arts from infancy to maturity and old age; that the Gothic cathedrals did not sire the *palazzi* and *duomi* of the Renaissance; and that Palestrina did not lead the way to Wagner, Schoenberg, and Stravinsky – still the history of the arts is an eloquent document of mankind's changing urge and behavior, in other words, of our ever changing taste.

Let us not reject the good with the bad and not mistake historical facts and connections for progressive evolution.

Progress, without doubt, is never completely absent from art. Although there cannot be an all-time goal, every period, in its characteristic, novel mentality, has an urge of specific self-expression, setting for art a temporary goal of its own. Such new ideal imposes on artists an arduous fight for perfection or progress in one direction. A new technique towards a new expression must be learned in steady, laborious efforts, by generations as well as by individuals, who in toilsome years improve their senses and hands before they master the craft. The artists of the early Renaissance, still steeped in the irrealistic, anti-realistic ideals of the Middle Ages but almost suddenly confronted with the new ideal of three-dimensional realism and unified space as a definite objective, had to make progress in that special field before they were able to reproduce with convincing power what they saw with their eyes. The gigantic strife for mastering the laws of perspective in the fifteenth century was 'progress.' In a similar way, the evolution from Peri's often so dry and wooden recitatives to the subtle flow and expressive intenseness of Monteverdi's *stile rappresentativo* was progress too.

But the Renaissance itself, as an attitude and a style, was not an advance or a progress against the preceding Gothic mentality; nor was the austere monodic style of the 1590es a progress from the luscious, mellow polyphony of Palestrina, Lassus, or Byrd.

[8] Bruno Nettl, *Change in folk ond primitive music*, in *Journal of the American Musicological Society*, vol. 8 (1955), p. 109.

Whatever you prefer according to your personal taste, these styles are so different that any unbiased comparison of values is impossible. Progress exists at best within a limited span; as to the total of art, there is no progress, no regress, but simply otherness.

My readers might accept these judgments as sound and to the point and yet be reluctant to delete the handy word progress from comparing an Eskimo melody and a symphony of Beethoven or whatever to them represents the all-time peak of musical creation.

There is no doubt: songs of the primitive are in many respects more limited than the 'great' music of the modern West to a degree of excluding comparison. They have nowhere the breath and breadth of our symphonies; they lack in the third dimension that the vertical expanse of harmony adds to the horizontal stretch of melody; they are monotonous and almost drab against the glittering orchestration of the romantic age; and they are narrow in scope when we think of the wealth of emotions, thoughts, and images that the West conveys in its manifold forms, in the intimacy of quartets and trios and the overwhelming mass effects of orchestral music, in the playful charm of dances and the profundity of adagios, in the pleasantness of catchy melodies and the 'learned' sophistication of triple and quadruple fugues.

Our music has become wider, no doubt. It has become wider, as man, its creator, has widened the scope of his life. His God rules a boundless world, not just a few huts around an almost timeless village square; the earth is open to his railroads, planes, and liners; and hundreds of trades and vocations shape his mind in hundreds of molds. And with the world we rule, our problems have grown. We are sceptical; we are in doubt about ourselves and our progress. Somehow we are lost and lorn in the universe whose dimensions we can no longer express in miles but at best in sideral years; lost in a wealth of knowledge that yields more questions than answers; lost in our individualism, which is strong enough to uproot us and estrange ourselves from our fellow men and yet too weak to prevent incredible, bloody mass psychoses.

The age of Rousseau longed for the bliss of living outside the pernicious web of western civilization. The paradise that Rousseau saw in the world of close-to-nature man was certainly a dream with little reality. Still, his anguish was justified and would have been deeper had he anticipated the next two hundred years of western destiny.

We have lost our paradise; and, with it, we have lost music as an unseverable part of life itself. Rarely do we realize our loss and its magnitude. We are too hopelessly blinded and deafened by our assumed progress towards enormous symphony orchestras, giant concert halls, ticket offices, managers, and publicity, and we take for granted that there must be dilettantes and professionals, insatiable fans as well as indifferent and outright unmusical persons, music lovers and music haters – and we do not see that this is not progress but simply change in aims and values.

IT IS THE OTHER MAN who knows and understands: the Oriental and even the Primitive. And once in a while he speaks out and opens the eyes of those who want to see.

When one day an arctic traveler played a recorded song by one of the most famous European composers (*sic!*) to an Eskimo singer, the man smiled somewhat haughtily and stated: "Many many notes, but no better music." [9]

Yury Arbatsky told me in 1953 a related story: in Belgrade he once had taken an excellent Albanian folk musician to Beethoven's Ninth Symphony. Asked how he had liked it, the man hesitated and at last, after a couple of brandies, gave the astonishing answer: "Fine – but very, very plain (lepo ali preprosto)."

The Albanian was neither arrogant nor incompetent. He just had a different standard. The unified, oversimplified, divisive rhythm could not possibly satisfy his eastern ears – exactly as "to an illiterate African the regular crotchets and quavers in a piece of music would appear rather dull." [10] The man must have felt frustrated by the total absence of all the enlivening, sensitive spices of 'additive' rhythm, where measures of, say, nine beats would appear as picturesque sums of $2 + 2 + 2 + 3$ units, or groups of ten as sums of $7 + 1 + 2$ – not even to mention the delicate, complex, ever-varying, and oddly stirring accompani-

[9] Christian Leden, *Ueber die Musik der Smith Sund Eskimos*, Copenhagen, 1952.
[10] Phillip Gbeho, *Music of the Gold Coast*, in *African Music*, vol. 1, no. 1 (1954), p. 63.

ment of hand-beaten drums. Instead of such refinement, he was presented with western 'divisive' rhythm, where quite mechanically a stress preceded every two or three unstressed units of equal duration, as *one*-two-three, *one*-two-three – an impoverishment of European music owed to the growing impact of chordal harmony.

The delicate art of connecting meaningful chords in a harmonic sequence of dissonant tension and relaxation, vital and expressive even to western ears for hardly four hundred years, left the oriental man utterly unmoved. The constant change of orchestral color and intensity up to nerve-wrecking fortissimi must have been little significant and starkly confusing if not repulsive to a man whose native music was intended for a small and intimate audience only and not for often gigantic concert halls.

The little episode illustrates in a striking way the urgent problem at the bottom of this book. Music is not the universal language. Even the Westerner has to learn his own musical idiom as if it were a foreign tongue. Otherwise we would not need Music Appreciation in high schools and colleges, nor would so alarming a number of Introductions to Music and Listening Guides flood our book market. White man is convinced he stands on the peak of the world – including our music, of which we are so rightfully proud. He should learn to realize that, once more including music, we can be as primitive in other peoples' eyes as they appear in ours. "There are many European traits that seem uncouth, impolite, incomprehensible or downright 'primitive' to a sophisticated 'native'." [11]

THE BELGRADE STORY is one of many. When I discussed its implications with Eric Werner, he volunteered a similar experience: a highly educated Chinese lady whom he had introduced to Mozart's Requiem politely acknowledged its beauty and craftsmanship but thought little of its . . . . . . "superficiality."

The verdict superficial passed on Mozart is somehow disarming. Yet, it might be wise to take the lady's judgment seriously and, instead of delivering riposte from our own position, conjure up the Chinese magi of the past.

In the words of Confucius (551–478 B.C.), "a vulgar-minded

[11] J. Manchip White, *Anthropology*, New York, 1955, p. 119.

man's performance is loud and fast, and again fading and dim, a picture of violent death-agony. His heart is not harmonically balanced; mildness and graceful movements are foreign to him ...," and again: "The noble-minded man's music is mild and delicate, keeps a uniform mood, enlivens and moves. Such a man does not harbor pain or mourn in his heart; violent and daring movements are foreign to him." Lü Pu-we, the poet, "was able to speak of music only with a man who has grasped the meaning of the world." Confucius himself knew how to play such a music. As he once struck "the ch'ing, a man who passed his house exclaimed: 'this heart is full that so beats the sounding stone.' " And there is the story of Cheng, who after three years of endeavor laid his zither down, sighed, and said: "It is not that I cannot bring the melody about. What I have in my mind does not concern strings; what I aim at is not tones. Not until I have reached it in my heart can I express it on the instrument." [12]

This is truly Chinese; but not Chinese alone. Far away in South Africa, a Baronga-boy once played his pristine, one-stringed musical bow with the slender stick while the missionary was listening. Suddenly he began to suck the wooden bow with a pensive air. "Why are you doing this?" inquired the missionary. And the boy: "To allow that which I say in my heart to glide into the instrument." [13]

Neither are, what we hear from China, just legends of olden: the present time has still preserved a certain awareness of the sacred music of the ancient. Frau Marie du Bois Reymond, in a musical diary kept during her stay in China from 1909 to 1911 and now my treasured possession, writes about the *ch'in* or *koto*-like zither, which to this day is never played without reverent solemnity. Before sitting down, she relates, the performer washed his hands and burned a few incense candles, because, to the educated Chinese, playing the *ch'in* is not only art in our sense but rather a mystic, sacred act through which he might summon a supernatural being. "There are ideas and emotions in his performance that are hidden from us Westerners," adds Frau Du Bois.

This modest sentence can and must be expanded: the ideas

---

[12] Curt Sachs, *The rise of music in the ancient world*, New York, 1943, p. 106.
[13] Henri-A. Junod, *Les chants et les contes des Ba-Ronga*, Lausanne, 1897, p. 22.

and emotions, the essence, the soul of all non-western music is indeed hidden from Westerners – just as the soul of our own so magnificently written scores is inaccessible to Easterners. And again it must be underlined that music is *not* the universal language.

In realizing this fact, we have found the answer to our initial question. The advance from the oldest one-step sing-song to our giant scores is a tremendous gain in scope. Is it also a gain in depth and significance? Depth is a matter of social and personal empathy and beyond the reach of musical science; significance depends on the various cultures and their emotional needs.[14]

This statement should exclude any misunderstanding. Neither do I praise the past, nor do I chide the present. I do not exalt the Primitive or despise the Westerner. I do not want to exchange what we possess for what we have lost; I do not trade the *B* minor Mass for an Eskimo melody; I am a denizen of this world and of this time as much as my most critical reader. I write without nostalgia, without mourning for the paradise lost that Rousseau's age beheld in the pristine purity ascribed to dawning culture. The phenomena I mention are facts, not dreams.

One of these facts is the infinitely wider scope of western art music; its wealth of artistic means from the inimitable single Stradivari to the giant orchestras and their saturated, ever-changing colors; the concept of a space-suggesting third dimension achieved through counterpoint and chordal harmony; the broader, breathtaking forms extending to symphonies of more than an hour duration and a dramatic development; and an area of expression that comprises all human emotions from a cool and almost unemotional courtly elegance to the unfathomable depth of humaneness and religious experience.

A second, sobering fact is the limited social significance of this venerable art. High civilization, in all its facets, drives of necessity to diversification, and diversification leads to estrangement – estrangement from person to person, from group to group, and hence from audience to audience. Statistically speaking, our art music, with all its concerts, recordings, and radios, reaches but a small, almost insignificant layer of mankind, and

[14] The subject has received extensive attention in Leonard B. Meyer, *Emotion and meaning in music*, Chicago, 1956.

even within this limited stratum its impact is very uneven. Side by side with art music, and numerically to an essentially higher degree, we are daily exposed to all shades of popular and non-descript sheet music for shallow entertainment; and the total suppression of these characteristic products is probably a pious fraud. An annex in our accounts of modern music also should indicate the enormous percentage of persons unmusical or indifferent who have no part in the delight and edification that 'high-brow' music gives its devotees. Our music is, alas, a marginal phenomenon.

To this sketch of music in western society we have opposed the picture of primitive music – a picture certainly poorer when drawn from the viewpoint of art, but always meaningful, dignified, and hence never vulgar. Primitive music is not compelled to fight the indifferent and the unmusical with 'appreciation' or to appease critics, board members, and managers with tame and carefully balanced programs. Everyone in a tribe is part of this music; everyone sings, and many enrich the inherited stock by creations of their own. No rite in religious services, no secular act can be performed without the appropriate songs; and as a vital part of social existence music is firmly integrated in primitive life and an indispensable part of it.

The awareness of this deep-rooted contrast will not change our destined ways. We cannot escape from the culture that we ourselves have made. But seeing and weighing the differences between the two musical worlds might help us in realizing that our gain is our loss, that our growth is our wane. It might help to understand that we have not progressed, but simply changed. And, when seen from a cultural viewpoint, we have not always changed to the better.

A NOTE ON BIBLIOGRAPHY

Although many readers are less interested in an author's thought and text than in the titles that he might compile in a bibliographical appendix, I felt I should not unduly increase the size, the weight, and the price of this volume with the dead ballast of lists.

A pertinent ethnomusicological bibliography can be found in Jaap Kunst's comprehensive *Ethnomusicology*, 3rd edition (The Hague, 1959, pp. 79–215, which, together with a Supplement (The Hague, 1960) contains over five thousand items. I also might refer the reader to Charles Haywood, *A bibliography of North American folklore and folksong* (New York, 1951), and to the *Bibliography of Asiatic musics*, published in *Notes*, vols. 5–8 (1947–51) under the leadership of William Lichtenwanger and Richard A. Waterman.

The non-musical literature I had to absorb – anthropology, travel diaries, sociology, culture history – can hardly be caught in a catalogue that pretends to be complete and meaningful. Ample footnote quotations will provide the reader with all the information he needs.

All the same, it seems to be indicated to refer to a few comprehensive surveys of the whole field:

Fritz Bose, *Musikalische Völkerkunde*, Freiburg i.Br., 1953;

Jaap Kunst, *Ethnomusicology*, The Hague, 2nd ed. 1955, 3rd ed. 1959; *Supplement*, The Hague, 1960.

Bruno Nettl, *Music in primitive culture*, Cambridge (Mass.), 1956.

INDEX OF NAMES